Angular 2 Cookbook

Discover over 70 recipes that provide the solutions you need to know to face every challenge in Angular 2 head on

Matt Frisbie

BIRMINGHAM - MUMBAI

Angular 2 Cookbook

First published: January 2017

Production reference: 1160117

Published by Packt Publishing Ltd.
Livery Place
35 Livery Street
Birmingham
B3 2PB, UK.
ISBN 978-1-78588-192-3

www.packtpub.com

Credits

Author

Matt Frisbie

Reviewer

Patrick Gillespie

Acquisition Editor

Vinay Argekar

Content Development Editor

Arun Nadar

Technical Editor

Vivek Arora

Copy Editor

Gladson Monteiro

Project Coordinator

Ritika Manoj

Proofreader

Safis Editing

Indexer

Francy Puthiry

Graphics

Kirk D'Penha

Production Coordinator

Deepika Naik

Cover Work

Deepika Naik

About the Author

Matt Frisbie is currently a software engineer at Google. He was the author of the Packt Publishing bestseller *AngularJS Web Application Development Cookbook* and also has published several video series through O'Reilly. He is active in the Angular community, giving presentations at meetups and doing webcasts.

Writing a book on Angular 2 while the framework itself was unfinished was an immensely challenging endeavor. Fragmented examples, incomplete documentation, and a nascent developer community were just a handful of the many roadblocks I encountered on the journey to finishing this title, and it was only because of a legion of supporters that this book was finished and was able to do justice to the framework.

This book would not have been possible without the tireless work of all the Packt staff involved. I'd specifically like to thank Arun Nadar, Vivek Arora, Merwyn D'Souza, and Vinay Argekar for their editorial oversight and expertise, as well as Patrick Gillespie for his work as content reviewer. I'd also like to thank Jordan, Zoey, Scott, and my family and friends for cheering me on.

About the Reviewer

Patrick Gillespie has been into software development since 1996. He has both a bachelor's and a master's degree in computer science. In his spare time, he enjoys photography, spending time with his family, and working on various side projects for his website (`http://patorjk.com/`).

www.PacktPub.com

For support files and downloads related to your book, please visit www.PacktPub.com.

Did you know that Packt offers eBook versions of every book published, with PDF and ePub files available? You can upgrade to the eBook version at www.PacktPub.com and as a print book customer, you are entitled to a discount on the eBook copy. Get in touch with us at service@packtpub.com for more details.

At www.PacktPub.com, you can also read a collection of free technical articles, sign up for a range of free newsletters and receive exclusive discounts and offers on Packt books and eBooks.

https://www.packtpub.com/mapt

Get the most in-demand software skills with Mapt. Mapt gives you full access to all Packt books and video courses, as well as industry-leading tools to help you plan your personal development and advance your career.

Why subscribe?

- Fully searchable across every book published by Packt
- Copy and paste, print, and bookmark content
- On demand and accessible via a web browser

Customer Feedback

Thank you for purchasing this Packt book. We take our commitment to improving our content and products to meet your needs seriously—that's why your feedback is so valuable. Whatever your feelings about your purchase, please consider leaving a review on this book's Amazon page. Not only will this help us, more importantly it will also help others in the community to make an informed decision about the resources that they invest in to learn.

You can also review for us on a regular basis by joining our reviewers' club. **If you're interested in joining, or would like to learn more about the benefits we offer, please contact us**: customerreviews@packtpub.com.

To my grandparents, Richard and Margery. Here's to upholding the family honor.

Table of Contents

Preface

"Everybody has a plan until they get punched in the mouth."
-Mike Tyson, undisputed heavyweight champion boxer

Soon after its creation in 2009, AngularJS grew into a widely popular foundational tool for building frontend applications. As years and releases went by, and the JavaScript community matured, the world of client-side programming broadened beyond what Angular was originally designed for. Its caretakers took stock and decided that a sweeping overhaul of the framework was in order.

AngularJS, now Angular 1, still exists and will be supported for the years to come, but in its wake lies Angular 2—a wholly different animal built for the future of client-side computing. Angular 2 abandons antipatterns by the fistful and, instead, is reshaped into a precise and elegant software instrument. It embraces the impending renaissance of web technologies, building atop ES6, web components, web workers, TypeScript, and reactive programming, to name a few. It brings framework modularity to new heights, building itself around the concept that any modular piece of Angular 2 should be easily discarded or replaced. Best of all, Angular 2 offers a bountiful collection of configuration and tooling that will make your applications run at breakneck speed.

To many developers, Angular 2 is frightening because so much of it is new and unfamiliar. This book exists to offer you an approachable path to a full understanding of Angular 2, what it offers, and how best to use it. You will find both simple examples to set a foundational understanding, and complex demonstrations to hint at the framework's power. The book is organized into recipes that are independent of each other, so you are able to jump in at any point and immediately begin learning.

What this book covers

This book is up to date for the 2.4 release and is compatible through the 4.0 release as well, and it does not have any code based on the beta or release candidates.

Chapter 1, *Strategies for Upgrading to Angular 2*, is an overview of a number of ways to migrate an Angular 1 application to Angular 2. Although there is no one-size-fits-all upgrade strategy, you will find that these recipes demonstrate some ways that will allow you to preserve a large amount of your existing Angular 1 code base.

Chapter 2, *Conquering Components and Directives*, gives a broad and deep set of examples involving what Angular 2 components are and how to use them. Angular 2 applications are built entirely of components, and this chapter offers you a total rundown of their role.

Chapter 3, *Building Template-Driven and Reactive Forms*, covers the reworked Angular 2 form modules. Angular 2 offers you two primary styles of erecting form features, and this chapter covers both of them in depth.

Chapter 4, *Mastering Promises*, shows how the Promise object has a role in Angular 2. Although RxJS has subsumed some of the usefulness of Promises, they are still first-class citizens in ES6 and still play a crucial role.

Chapter 5, *ReactiveX Observables*, gives you a crash course in how Angular 2 has embraced reactive programming. It includes recipes that demonstrate the basics of Observables and Subjects, as well as advanced implementations that take RxJS to its limits.

Chapter 6, *The Component Router*, takes you through the totally reworked routing module in Angular 2. It covers both routing basics as well as an array of advanced routing concepts unique to Angular 2.

Chapter 7, *Services, Dependency Injection, and NgModule*, describes the new and improved dependency injection and module strategies of Angular 2. It gives you all the pieces you need to break your application into independent services and modules, as well as ideal strategies for connecting those pieces together.

Chapter 8, *Application Organization and Management*, is a broad overview of how you can manage your Angular 2 application inside and outside the client. Angular 2 introduces a number of layers of complexity that require advanced tooling, and this chapter will guide you through how to approach them.

Chapter 9, *Angular 2 Testing*, will guide you through both how to set up test suites for Angular 2 as well as how to write various types of tests for these suites. Many developers avoid testing when learning a framework anew, and this chapter gently guides you through Angular 2's excellent test infrastructure.

Chapter 10, *Performance and Advanced Concepts*, is a crash course on the dizzying array of complex concepts that Angular 2 comes with out of the box. This chapter covers program organization and architecture, framework features and tooling, as well as compile-time optimizations.

What you need for this book

Every recipe in this book is accompanied by a link to the book's companion site, `http://ngcookbook.herokuapp.com/`. Recipes that involve code examples will include a link to a live example on Plunker. This will allow you to inspect and test code in real time without having to worry about compilation, local servers, or anything of that ilk. It must be noted, however, that this setup is only appropriate for experimentation and should not be used for user-facing or production applications.

Angular 2 comes in both JavaScript and TypeScript flavors, but this book aims directly at the TypeScript edition, since it is syntactically superior (as you will soon realize). For proper production applications, TypeScript will be compiled into JavaScript before it is served to the browser. The way this book accomplishes this (and many other code preparation tasks) is inside a Node.js install on your local machine. Node.js includes the Node Package Manager (npm), which lets you install and run open source JavaScript software from the command line.

Some chapters in this book will require that you have Node.js installed before running commands and launching a local server or test suite. Furthermore, it is recommended (but not required) that you install the Node Version Manager on top of Node.js, which will make managing your installed packages much easier.

Who this book is for

The universe of Angular 2 learning materials is currently fragmented and gross. This book is for both beginner developers looking to sink their teeth into a new framework, as well as advanced developers interested in rounding out their knowledge of a framework that embraces the coming world of web tech.

For newer developers, ingesting all these new technologies at once may seem overwhelming. The organization and pace of this book is designed so that topics are gradually introduced, and design decisions and rationales are explained. Don't worry, this book is still for you.

Conventions

In this book, you will find a number of text styles that distinguish between different kinds of information. Here are some examples of these styles and an explanation of their meaning.

Code words in text, database table names, folder names, filenames, file extensions, pathnames, dummy URLs, user input, and Twitter handles are shown as follows: "Karma reads its configuration out of a `karma.conf.js` file."

A block of code is set as follows:

```
<p>{{date}}</p>
<h1>{{title}}</h1>
<h3>Written by: {{author}}</h3>
```

When we wish to draw your attention to a particular part of a code block, the relevant lines or items are set in bold:

```
@Component({
  selector: 'article',
  template: `
    <p>{{currentDate|date}}</p>
    <h1>{{title}}</h1>
    <h3>Written by: {{author}}</h3>
  `
})
```

Any command-line input or output is written as follows:

```
npm install karma jasmine-core karma-jasmine --save-dev
npm install karma-cli -g
```

New terms and **important words** are shown in bold.

Warnings or important notes appear in a box like this.

Tips and tricks appear like this.

Reader feedback

Feedback from our readers is always welcome. Let us know what you think about this book-what you liked or disliked. Reader feedback is important for us as it helps us develop titles that you will really get the most out of. To send us general feedback, simply e-mail feedback@packtpub.com, and mention the book's title in the subject of your message. If there is a topic that you have expertise in and you are interested in either writing or contributing to a book, see our author guide at www.packtpub.com/authors.

Customer support

Now that you are the proud owner of a Packt book, we have a number of things to help you to get the most from your purchase.

Downloading the example code

You can download the example code files for this book from your account at http://www.packtpub.com. If you purchased this book elsewhere, you can visit http://www.packtpub.com/supportand register to have the files e-mailed directly to you.

You can download the code files by following these steps:

1. Log in or register to our website using your e-mail address and password.
2. Hover the mouse pointer on the **SUPPORT** tab at the top.
3. Click on **Code Downloads & Errata**.
4. Enter the name of the book in the **Search** box.
5. Select the book for which you're looking to download the code files.
6. Choose from the drop-down menu where you purchased this book from.
7. Click on **Code Download**.

Once the file is downloaded, please make sure that you unzip or extract the folder using the latest version of:

- WinRAR / 7-Zip for Windows
- Zipeg / iZip / UnRarX for Mac
- 7-Zip / PeaZip for Linux

The code bundle for the book is also hosted on GitHub at https://github.com/PacktPublishing/Angular-2-Cookbook. We also have other code bundles from our rich catalog of books and videos available at https://github.com/PacktPublishing/. Check them out!

Errata

Although we have taken every care to ensure the accuracy of our content, mistakes do happen. If you find a mistake in one of our books-maybe a mistake in the text or the code-we would be grateful if you could report this to us. By doing so, you can save other readers from frustration and help us improve subsequent versions of this book. If you find any errata, please report them by visiting http://www.packtpub.com/submit-errata, selecting your book, clicking on the **Errata Submission Form** link, and entering the details of your errata. Once your errata are verified, your submission will be accepted and the errata will be uploaded to our website or added to any list of existing errata under the Errata section of that title.

To view the previously submitted errata, go to https://www.packtpub.com/books/content/support and enter the name of the book in the search field. The required information will appear under the **Errata** section.

Piracy

Piracy of copyrighted material on the Internet is an ongoing problem across all media. At Packt, we take the protection of our copyright and licenses very seriously. If you come across any illegal copies of our works in any form on the Internet, please provide us with the location address or website name immediately so that we can pursue a remedy.

Please contact us at copyright@packtpub.com with a link to the suspected pirated material.

We appreciate your help in protecting our authors and our ability to bring you valuable content.

Questions

If you have a problem with any aspect of this book, you can contact us at questions@packtpub.com, and we will do our best to address the problem.

1
Strategies for Upgrading to Angular 2

This chapter will cover the following recipes:

- Componentizing directives using the controllerAs encapsulation
- Migrating an application to component directives
- Implementing a basic component in AngularJS 1.5
- Normalizing service types
- Connecting Angular 1 and Angular 2 with UpgradeModule
- Downgrading Angular 2 components to Angular 1 directives with downgradeComponent
- Downgrading Angular 2 providers to Angular 1 services with downgradeInjectable

Introduction

The introduction of Angular 2 into the Angular ecosystem will surely be interpreted and handled differently for all developers. Some will stick to their existing Angular 1 codebases, some will start brand new Angular 2 codebases, and some will do a gradual or partial transition.

It is recommended that you become familiar with the behavior of Angular 2 components before you dive into these recipes. This will help you frame mental models as you adapt your existing applications to be more compliant with the Angular 2 style.

Componentizing directives using controllerAs encapsulation

One of the unusual conventions introduced in Angular 1 was the relationship between directives and the data they consumed. By default, directives used an inherited scope, which suited the needs of most developers just fine. While this was easy to use, it had the effect of introducing extra dependencies in the directives, and also the convention that directives often did not own the data they were consuming. Additionally, the data interpolated in the template was unclear in relation to where it was being assigned or owned.

Angular 2 utilizes components as the building blocks of the entire application. These components are class-based and are therefore in some ways at odds with the scope mechanisms of Angular 1. Transitioning to a controller-centric directive model is a large step towards compliance with the Angular 2 standards.

 The code, links, and a live example related to this recipe are available at `http://ngcookbook.herokuapp.com/8194.`

Getting ready

Suppose your application contains the following setup that involves the nested directives that share data using an isolate scope:

```
[index.html]

<div ng-app="articleApp">
  <article></article>
</div>
[app.js]

angular.module('articleApp', [])
.directive('article', function() {
  return {
```

```
  controller: function($scope) {
    $scope.articleData = {
      person: {firstName: 'Jake'},
      title: 'Lesotho Yacht Club Membership Booms'
    };
  },
    template: `
      <h1>{{articleData.title}}</h1>
      <attribution author="articleData.person.firstName">
      </attribution>
    `
  };
})
.directive('attribution', function() {
  return {
    scope: {author: '='},
    template: `<p>Written by: {{author}}</p>`
  };
});
```

How to do it...

The goal is to refactor this setup so that templates can be explicit about where the data is coming from and so that the directives have ownership of this data:

```
[app.js]

angular.module('articleApp', [])
.directive('article', function() {
  return {
  controller: function() {
    this.person = {firstName: 'Jake'};
    this.title = 'Lesotho Yacht Club Membership Booms';
  },
    controllerAs: 'articleCtrl',
    template: `
      <h1>{{articleCtrl.title}}</h1>
      <attribution></attribution>
    `
  };
})
.directive('attribution', function() {
  return {
    template: `<p>Written by: {{articleCtrl.author}}</p>`
  };
});
```

[9]

In this second implementation, anywhere you use the article data, you are certain of its origin. This is better, but the child directive is still referencing the parent controller, which isn't ideal since it is introducing an unneeded dependency. The attribution directive instance should be provided with the data, and it should instead interpolate from its own controller instance:

```
[app.js]

angular.module('articleApp', [])
.directive('article', function() {
  return {
    controller: function() {
      this.person = {firstName: 'Jake'};
      this.title = 'Lesotho Yacht Club Membership Booms';
    },
    controllerAs: 'articleCtrl',
    template: `
      <h1>{{articleCtrl.title}}</h1>
      <attribution author="articleCtrl.person.firstName">
      </attribution>
    `
  };
})
.directive('attribution', function() {
  return {
    controller: function() {},
    controllerAs: 'attributionCtrl',
    bindToController: {author: '='},
    template: `<p>Written by: {{attributionCtrl.author}}</p>`
  };
});
```

Much better! You provide the child directive with a stand-in controller and give it an alias in the `attributionCtrl` template. It is implicitly bound to the controller instance via `bindToController` in the same way you would accomplish a regular isolate scope; however, the binding is directly attributed to the controller object instead of the scope.

Now that you have introduced the notion of data ownership, suppose you want to modify your application data. What's more, you want different parts of your application to be able to modify it. A naïve implementation of this would be something as follows:

```
[app.js]

angular.module('articleApp', [])
.directive('attribution', function() {
  return {
    controller: function() {
```

```
      this.capitalize = function() {
        this.author = this.author.toUpperCase();
      }
    },
    controllerAs: 'attributionCtrl',
    bindToController: {author: '='},
    template: `
      <p ng-click="attributionCtrl.capitalize()">
        Written by: {{attributionCtrl.author}}
      </p>`
  };
});
```

The desired behavior is for you to click on the author, and it will become capitalized. However, in this implementation, the article controller's data is modified in the attribution controller, which does not own it. It is preferable for the controller that owns the data to perform the actual modification and instead supply an interface that an outside entity—here, the attribution directive—could use:

```
[app.js]

angular.module('articleApp', [])
.directive('article', function() {
  return {
    controller: function() {
      this.person = {firstName: 'Jake'};
      this.title = 'Lesotho Yacht Club Membership Booms';
      this.capitalize = function() {
        this.person.firstName =
          this.person.firstName.toUpperCase();
      };
    },
    controllerAs: 'articleCtrl',
    template: `
      <h1>{{articleCtrl.title}}</h1>
      <attribution author="articleCtrl.person.firstName"
                   upper-case-author="articleCtrl.capitalize()">
      </attribution>
    `
  };
})
.directive('attribution', function() {
  return {
    controller: function() {},
    controllerAs: 'attributionCtrl',
    bindToController: {
      author: '=',
```

```
        upperCaseAuthor: '&'
    },
     template: `
       <p ng-click="attributionCtrl.upperCaseAuthor()">
         Written by: {{attributionCtrl.author}}
       </p>`
 };
});
```

Vastly superior! You are still able to namespace within the click binding, but the owning directive controller is providing a method to outside entities instead of just giving them direct data access.

How it works...

When a controller is specified in the directive definition object, one will be explicitly instantiated for each directive instance that is created. Thus, it is natural for this controller object to encapsulate the data that it owns and for it to be delegated the responsibility of passing its data to the members that require it.

The final implementation accomplishes several things:

- **Improved template namespacing**: When you use the $scope properties that span multiple directives or nestings, you are creating a scenario where multiple entities can manipulate and read data without being able to concretely reason about where it is coming from or what is controlling it.
- **Improved testability**: If you look at each of the directives in the final implementation, you'll find they are not too difficult to test. The attribution directive has no dependencies other than what are explicitly passed to it.
- **Encapsulation**: Introducing the notion of data ownership in your application affords you a much more robust structure, better reusability, and additional insight and control involving pieces of your application interacting.
- **Angular 2 style**: Angular 2 uses the @Input and @Output annotations on component definitions. Mirroring this style will make the process of transitioning to an application easier.

There's more...

You will notice that `$scope` has been made totally irrelevant in these examples. This is good as there is no notion of `$scope` in Angular 2, which means you are heading towards having an upgradeable application. This is not to say that `$scope` does not still have utility in an Angular 1 application, and surely, there are scenarios where this is unavoidable, like with `$scope.$apply()`.

However, thinking about the application pieces in this component style will allow you to be more adequately prepared to adopt Angular 2 conventions.

See also

- *Migrating an application to component directives* demonstrates how to refactor Angular 1 to a component style
- *Implementing a basic component in AngularJS 1.5* details how to write an Angular 1 component
- *Normalizing service types* gives instruction on how to align your Angular 1 service types for Angular 2 compatibility

Migrating an application to component directives

In Angular 1, there are several built-in directives, including `ngController` and `ngInclude`, that developers tend to lean on when building applications. While not anti-patterns, using these features moves away from having a component-centric application.

All these directives are actually subsets of component functionality, and they can be entirely refactored out.

 The code, links, and a live example related to this recipe are available at `http://ngcookbook.herokuapp.com/1008/`.

Getting ready

Suppose your initial application is as follows:

```
[index.html]

<div ng-app="articleApp">
  <ng-include src="'/press_header.html'"></ng-include>
  <div ng-controller="articleCtrl as article">
    <h1>{{article.title}}</h1>
    <p>Written by: {{article.author}}</p>
  </div>
  <script type="text/ng-template"
          id="/press_header.html">
  <div ng-controller="headerCtrl as header">
    <strong>
      Angular Chronicle - {{header.currentDate | date}}
    </strong>
   <hr />
  </div>
  </script>
</div>
[app.js]

angular.module('articleApp', [])
.controller('articleCtrl', function() {
  this.title = 'Food Fight Erupts During Diplomatic Luncheon';
  this.author = 'Jake';
})
.controller('headerCtrl', function() {
   this.currentDate = new Date();
});
```

 Note that this example application contains a large number of very common Angular 1 patterns; you can see the ngController directives sprinkled throughout. Also, it uses an ngInclude directive to incorporate a header. Keep in mind that these directives are not inappropriate for a well-formed Angular 1 application. However, you can do better, and this involves refactoring to a component-driven design.

How to do it...

Component-driven patterns don't need to be frightening in appearance. In this example (and for essentially all Angular 1 applications), you can do a component refactor while leaving the existing template largely intact.

Begin with the `ngInclude` directive. Moving this to a component directive is simple—it becomes a directive with `templateUrl` set to the template path:

```
[index.html]

<div ng-app="articleApp">
  <header></header>
  <div ng-controller="articleCtrl as article">
    <h1>{{article.title}}</h1>
    <p>Written by: {{article.author}}</p>
  </div>
  <script type="text/ng-template"
          id="/press_header.html">
  <div ng-controller="headerCtrl as header">
   <strong>
      Angular Chronicle - {{header.currentDate | date}}
    </strong>
   <hr />
  </div>
  </script>
</div>
[app.js]

angular.module('articleApp', [])
.controller('articleCtrl', function() {
  this.title = 'Food Fight Erupts During Diplomatic Luncheon';
  this.author = 'Jake';
})
.controller('headerCtrl', function() {
   this.currentDate = new Date();
})
.directive('header', function() {
   return {
   templateUrl: '/press_header.html'
 };
});
```

Next, you can also refactor `ngController` everywhere it appears. In this example, you find two extremely common appearances of `ngController`. The first is at the head of the `press_header.html` template, acting as the top-level controller for that template. Often, this results in needing a superfluous wrapper element just to house the `ng-controller` attribute. The second is `ngController` nested inside your primary application template, controlling some arbitrary portion of the DOM. Both of these can be refactored to component directives by reassigning `ngController` to a directive controller:

```
[index.html]
```

```
<div ng-app="articleApp">
  <header></header>
  <article></article>
</div>
[app.js]

angular.module('articleApp', [])
.directive('header', function() {
  return {
    controller: function() {
      this.currentDate = new Date();
    },
    controllerAs: 'header',
    template: `
      <strong>
        Angular Chronicle - {{header.currentDate | date}}
      </strong>
      <hr />
    `
  };
})
.directive('article', function() {
  return {
    controller: function() {
      this.title = 'Food Fight Erupts During Diplomatic Luncheon';
      this.author = 'Jake';
    },
    controllerAs: 'article',
    template: `
      <h1>{{article.title}}</h1>
      <p>Written by: {{article.author}}</p>
    `
  };
});
```

 Note that templates here are included in the directive for visual congruity. For large applications, it is preferred that you use templateUrl and locate the template markup in its own file.

How it works...

Generally speaking, an application can be represented by a hierarchy of nested MVC components. ngInclude and ngController act as subsets of a component functionality, and so it makes sense that you are able to expand them into full component directives.

In the preceding example, the ultimate application structure is comprised of only components. Each component is delegated its own template, controller, and model (by virtue of the controller object itself). Sticklers will dispute whether or not Angular belongs to true MVC style, but in the context of component refactoring, this is irrelevant. Here, you have defined a structure that is completely modular, reusable, testable, abstractable, and easily maintainable. This is the style of Angular 2, and the value of this should be immediately apparent.

There's more...

An alert developer will notice that no attention is paid to scope inheritance. This is a difficult problem to approach, mostly because many of the patterns in Angular 1 are designed for a mishmash between a scope and `controllerAs`. Angular 2 is built around strict input and output between nested components; however, in Angular 1, scope is inherited by default, and nested directives, by default, have access to their encompassing controller objects.

Thus, to truly emulate an Angular 2 style, one must configure their application to explicitly pass data and methods to children, similar to the `controllerAs` encapsulation recipe. However, this does not preclude direct data access to ancestral component directive controllers; it merely wags a finger at it since it adds additional dependencies.

See also

- *Componentizing directives using controllerAs encapsulation* shows you a superior method of organizing Angular 1 directives
- *Implementing a basic component in AngularJS 1.5* details how to write an Angular 1 component
- *Normalizing service types* gives instruction on how to align your Angular 1 service types for Angular 2 compatibility

Implementing a basic component in AngularJS 1.5

The 1.5 release of AngularJS introduced a new tool: the component. While it isn't exactly similar to the concept of the Angular 2 component, it does allow you to build directive-style pieces in an explicitly componentized fashion.

 The code, links, and a live example related to this recipe are available at `http://ngcookbook.herokuapp.com/7756/`.

Getting ready

Suppose your application had a directive defined as follows:

```
[index.html]

<div ng-app="articleApp">
  <article></article>
</div>
[app.js]

angular.module('articleApp', [])
.directive('article', function() {
  return {
    controller: function() {
      this.person = {firstName: 'Jake'};
      this.title = 'Police Bust Illegal Snail Racing Ring';
      this.capitalize = function() {
        this.person.firstName =
          this.person.firstName.toUpperCase();
      };
    },
    controllerAs: 'articleCtrl',
    template: `
      <h1>{{articleCtrl.title}}</h1>
      <attribution author="articleCtrl.person.firstName"
                   upper-case-author="articleCtrl.capitalize()">
      </attribution>
    `
  };
};
```

```
})
.directive('attribution', function() {
  return {
    controller: function() {},
    controllerAs: 'attributionCtrl',
    bindToController: {
      author: '=',
      upperCaseAuthor: '&'
    },
    template: `
      <p ng-click="attributionCtrl.upperCaseAuthor()">
        Written by: {{attributionCtrl.author}}
      </p>`
  };
});
```

How to do it...

Since this application is already organized around the `controllerAs` encapsulation, you can migrate it to use the `component()` definition introduced in the Angular 1.5 release.

Components accept an object definition similar to a directive, but the object does not demand to be returned by a function—an object literal is all that is needed. Components utilize the bindings property in this object definition object in the same way that `bindToController` works for directives. With this, you can easily introduce components in this application instead of directives:

```
[index.html]

<div ng-app="articleApp">
  <article></article>
</div>
[app.js]

angular.module('articleApp', [])
.component('article', {
  controller: function() {
    this.person = {firstName: 'Jake'};
    this.title = ' Police Bust Illegal Snail Racing Ring ';
    this.capitalize = function() {
      this.person.firstName =
        this.person.firstName.toUpperCase();
    };
  },
  controllerAs: 'articleCtrl',
```

```
    template: `
      <h1>{{articleCtrl.title}}</h1>
      <attribution author="articleCtrl.person.firstName"
                   upper-case-author="articleCtrl.capitalize()">
      </attribution>`
  })
  .component('attribution', {
    controller: function() {},
    controllerAs: 'attributionCtrl',
    bindings: {
      author: '=',
      upperCaseAuthor: '&'
    },
    template: `
      <p ng-click="attributionCtrl.upperCaseAuthor()">
        Written by: {{attributionCtrl.author}}
      </p>
      `
  });
```

How it works...

Notice that since your controller-centric data organization matches what a component definition expects, no template modifications are necessary. Components, by default, will utilize an isolate scope. What's more, they will not have access to the alias of the surrounding controller objects, something that cannot be said for component-style directives. This encapsulation is an important offering of the new component feature, as it has direct parity to how components operate in Angular 2.

There's more...

Since you have now entirely isolated each individual component, there is only a single controller object to deal with in each template. Thus, Angular 1.5 automatically provides a convenient alias for the component's controller object, namely—`$ctrl`. This is provided whether or not a `controllerAs` alias is specified. Therefore, a further refactoring yields the following:

```
[index.html]

<div ng-app="articleApp">
  <article></article>
</div>
[app.js]
```

```
angular.module('articleApp', [])
.component('article', {
  controller: function() {
    this.person = {firstName: 'Jake'};
    this.title = 'Police Bust Illegal Snail Racing Ring';
    this.capitalize = function() {
      this.person.firstName =
        this.person.firstName.toUpperCase();
    };
  },
  template: `
    <h1>{{$ctrl.title}}</h1>
    <attribution author="$ctrl.person.firstName"
                 upper-case-author="$ctrl.capitalize()">
    </attribution>
  `
})
.component('attribution', {
  controller: function() {},
  bindings: {
    author: '=',
    upperCaseAuthor: '&'
  },
  template: `
    <p ng-click="$ctrl.upperCaseAuthor()">
      Written by: {{$ctrl.author}}
    </p>
  `
});
```

See also

- *Componentizing directives using controllerAs encapsulation* shows you a superior method of organizing Angular 1 directives
- *Migrating an application to component directives* demonstrates how to refactor Angular 1 to a component style
- *Normalizing service types* gives instruction on how to align your Angular 1 service types for Angular 2 compatibility

Normalizing service types

Angular 1 developers will be quite familiar with the factory/service/provider trifecta. In many ways, this has gone largely unaltered in Angular 2 conceptually. However, in the interest of upgrading an existing application, there is one thing that should be done to make the migration as easy as possible: eliminate factories and replace them with services.

 The code, links, and a live example related to this recipe are available at `http://ngcookbook.herokuapp.com/5637/`.

Getting ready

Suppose you had a simple application as follows:

```
[index.html]

<div ng-app="articleApp">
  <article></article>
</div>
[app.js]

angular.module('articleApp', [])
.factory('ArticleData', function() {
  var title = 'Incumbent Senator Ousted by Stalk of Broccoli';
  return {
    getTitle: function() {
      return title;
    },
    author: 'Jake'
  };
})
.component('article', {
  controller: function(ArticleData) {
    this.title = ArticleData.getTitle();
    this.author = ArticleData.author;
  },
  template: `
    <h1>{{$ctrl.title}}</h1>
    <p>Written by: {{$ctrl.author}}</p>
  `
});
```

How to do it...

Angular 2 is class-based, and it includes its service types as well. The example here does not have a service type that is compatible with a class structure. So it must be converted. Thankfully, this is quite easy to do:

```
[index.html]

<div ng-app="articleApp">
  <article></article>
</div>
[app.js]

angular.module('articleApp', [])
.service('ArticleData', function() {
    var title = 'Incumbent Senator Ousted by Stalk of Broccoli';
    this.getTitle = function() {
    return title;
 };
  this.author = 'Jake';
})
.component('article', {
  controller: function(ArticleData) {
    this.title = ArticleData.getTitle();
    this.author = ArticleData.author;
  },
  template: `
    <h1>{{$ctrl.title}}</h1>
    <p>Written by: {{$ctrl.author}}</p>
    `
});
```

How it works...

You still want to keep the notion of `title` private, but you also want to maintain the API that the injected service type is providing. Services are defined by a function that acts as a constructor, and an instance created from this constructor is what is ultimately injected. Here, you are simply moving `getTitle()` and `author` to be defined on the `this` keyword, which thereby makes it a property on all instances. Note that the use in the component and template does not change in any way, and it shouldn't.

There's more…

The simplest to implement service types, Angular 1 factories were often used first by many developers, including myself. Some developers might take offense at the following claim, but I don't think there was ever a good reason for both factories and services to exist. Both have a high degree of redundancy, and if you dig down into the Angular source code, you will see that they essentially converge to the same methods.

Why services over factories then? The new world of JavaScript, ES6, and TypeScript is being built around classes. They are a far more elegant way of expressing and organizing logic. Angular 1 services are an implementation of prototype-based classes, which when used correctly function in essentially the same way as formal ES6/TypeScript classes. If you stop here, you will have modified your services to be more extensible and comprehensible. If you intend to upgrade, you will find that Angular 1 services will cleanly upgrade to Angular 2 services.

See also

- *Componentizing directives using controllerAs encapsulation* shows you a superior method for organizing Angular 1 directives
- *Migrating an application to component directives* demonstrates how to refactor Angular 1 to a component style
- *Implementing a basic component in AngularJS 1.5* details how to write an Angular 1 component

Connecting Angular 1 and Angular 2 with UpgradeModule

Angular 2 comes with the ability to connect it to an existing Angular 1 application. This is obviously advantageous since this will allow you to utilize existing components and services in Angular 1 in tandem with Angular 2's components and services. UpgradeModule is the tool that is supported by Angular teams to accomplish such a feat.

 The code, links, and a live example in relation to this recipe are available at http://ngcookbook.herokuapp.com/4137/.

Getting ready

Suppose you had a very simple Angular 1 application as follows:

```
[index.html]

<!DOCTYPE html>
<html>
  <head>
    <!-- Angular 1 scripts -->
    <script src="angular.js"></script>
  </head>
  <body>
    <div ng-app="hybridApp"
         ng-init="val='Angular 1 bootstrapped successfully!'">
      {{val}}
    </div>
  </body>
</html>
```

This application interpolates a value set in an Angular expression so you can visually confirm that the application has bootstrapped and is working.

How to do it…

Begin by declaring the top-level angular module inside its own file. Instead of using a script tag to fetch the angular module, require Angular 1, import it, and create the root Angular 1 module:

```
[ng1.module.ts]

import 'angular'

export const Ng1AppModule = angular.module('Ng1AppModule', []);
```

Angular 2 ships with an upgrade module out of the box, which is provided inside `upgrade.js`. The two frameworks can be connected with `UpgradeModule`.

This recipe utilizes SystemJS and TypeScript, the specifications for which lie inside a very complicated config file. This is discussed in a later chapter, so don't worry about the specifics. For now, you are free to assume the following:

- SystemJS is configured to compile TypeScript (.ts) files on the fly
- SystemJS is able to resolve the import and export statements in TypeScript files
- SystemJS is able to resolve Angular 1 and 2 library imports

Angular 2 requires a top-level module definition as part of its base configuration:

```
[app/ng2.module.ts]

import {NgModule} from '@angular/core';
import {BrowserModule} from '@angular/platform-browser';
import {UpgradeModule} from '@angular/upgrade/static';
import {RootComponent} from './root.component';

@NgModule({
  imports: [
    BrowserModule,
    UpgradeModule,
  ],
  bootstrap: [
    RootComponent
  ],
  declarations: [
    RootComponent
  ]
})
export class Ng2AppModule {
  constructor(public upgrade: UpgradeModule){}
}
export class AppModule {}
```

The reason why this module definition exists this way isn't critical for understanding this recipe. Angular 2 modules are covered in Chapter 7, *Services, Dependency Injection, and NgModule*.

Create the root component of the Angular 2 application:

```
[app/root.component.ts]
import {Component} from '@angular/core';

@Component({
  selector: 'root',
  template: `
    <p>Angular 2 bootstrapped successfully!</p>
  `
})
export class RootComponent {}
```

Since Angular 2 will often bootstrap from a top-level file, create this file as `main.ts` and bootstrap the Angular 2 module:

```
[main.ts]
import {platformBrowserDynamic}
  from '@angular/platform-browser-dynamic';

import {Ng1AppModule} from './app/ng1.module';
import {Ng2AppModule} from './app/ng2.module';

platformBrowserDynamic()
  .bootstrapModule(Ng2AppModule);
```

Connecting Angular 1 to Angular 2

Don't use an ng-app to bootstrap the Angular 1 application; instead, do this after you bootstrap Angular 2:

```
[main.ts]

import {platformBrowserDynamic}
  from '@angular/platform-browser-dynamic';

import {Ng1AppModule} from './app/ng1.module';
import {Ng2AppModule} from './app/ng2.module';

platformBrowserDynamic()
  .bootstrapModule(Ng2AppModule)
  .then(ref => {
    ref.instance.upgrade
      .bootstrap(document.body, [Ng1AppModule.name]);
  });
```

With this, you'll be able to remove Angular 1's JS script, the `ng-app` directive, and add in the root element of the Angular 2 app:

```
[index.html]

<!DOCTYPE html>
<html>
  <head>
    <!-- Angular 2 scripts -->
    <script src="zone.js "></script>
    <script src="reflect-metadata.js"></script>
    <script src="system.js"></script>
    <script src="system-config.js"></script>
  </head>
  <body>
    <div ng-init="val='Angular 1 bootstrapped successfully!'">
      {{val}}
    </div>
    <root></root>
  </body>
</html>
```

 The new scripts listed here are dependencies of an Angular 2 application, but understanding what they're doing isn't critical for understanding this recipe. This is explained later in the book.

With all this, you should see your Angular 1 application template compile and the Angular 2 component render properly again. This means that you are successfully running Angular 1 and Angular 2 frameworks side by side.

How it works...

Make no mistake, when you use `UpgradeModule`, you create an Angular 1 and Angular 2 app on the same page and connect them together. This adapter instance will allow you to connect pieces from each framework and use them in harmony.

More specifically, this creates an Angular 1 application at the top level and allows you to uses pieces of an Angular 2 application inside it.

There's more...

While useful for experimentation and upgrading purposes, this should not be a solution that any application should rely on in a production context. You have effectively doubled the framework payload size and introduced additional complexity in an existing application. Although Angular 2 is a far more performant framework, do not expect to have the same pristine results with the `UpgradeModule` cross-pollination.

That said, as you will see in subsequent recipes, you can now use Angular 2 components in an Angular 1 application using the adapter translation methods.

See also

- *Downgrading Angular 2 components to Angular 1 directives with downgradeComponent* demonstrates how to use an Angular 2 component inside an Angular 1 application
- *Downgrade Angular 2 providers to Angular 1 services with downgradeInjectable*, which demonstrates how to use an Angular 2 service inside an Angular 1 application

Downgrading Angular 2 components to Angular 1 directives with downgradeComponent

If you have followed the steps in *Connecting Angular 1 and Angular 2 with UpgradeModule*, you should now have a hybrid application that is capable of sharing different elements with the opposing framework.

If you are unfamiliar with Angular 2 components, it is recommended that you go through the components chapter before you proceed.

This recipe will allow you to fully utilize Angular 2 components inside an Angular 1 template.

The code, links, and a live example in relation to this recipe are available at `http://ngcookbook.herokuapp.com/1499/`.

Getting ready

Suppose you had the following Angular 2 component that you wanted to use in an Angular 1 application:

```
[app/article.component.ts]

import {Component, Input} from '@angular/core';

@Component({
  selector: 'ng2-article',
  template: `
    <h1>{{title}}</h1>
    <p>Written by: {{author}}</p>
  `
})
export class ArticleComponent {
  @Input() author:string
  title:string = 'Unicycle Jousting Recognized as Olympic Sport';
}
```

Begin by completing the *Connecting Angular 1 and Angular 2 with UpgradeModule* recipe.

How to do it...

Angular 1 has no comprehension of how to utilize Angular 2 components. The existing Angular 2 framework will dutifully render it if given the opportunity, but the definition itself must be connected to the Angular 1 framework so that it may be requested when needed.

Begin by adding the component declarations to the module definition; this is used to link the two frameworks:

```
[app/app.module.ts]

import {NgModule} from '@angular/core';
import {BrowserModule} from '@angular/platform-browser';
import {UpgradeModule} from '@angular/upgrade/static';
```

```
import {RootComponent} from './root.component';
import {ArticleComponent} from './article.component';

@NgModule({
  imports: [
    BrowserModule,
    UpgradeModule,
  ],
  declarations: [
    RootComponent,
    ArticleComponent
  ],
  bootstrap: [
    RootComponent
  ]
})
export class Ng2AppModule {
  constructor(public upgrade: UpgradeModule){}
}
```

This connects the component declaration to the Angular 2 context, but Angular 1 still has no concept of how to interface with it. For this, you'll need to use downgradeComponent() to define the Angular 2 component as an Angular 1 directive. Give the Angular 1 directive a different HTML tag to render inside so you can be certain that it's Angular 1 doing the rendering and not Angular 2:

```
[main.ts]

import {Component, Input} from '@angular/core';
import {downgradeComponent} from '@angular/upgrade/static';
import {Ng1AppModule} from './ng1.module';

@Component({
  selector: 'ng2-article',
  template: `
    <h1>{{title}}</h1>
    <p>Written by: {{author}}</p>
  `
})
export class ArticleComponent {
  @Input() author:string
  title:string = 'Unicycle Jousting Recognized as Olympic Sport';
}

Ng1AppModule.directive(
  'ng1Article',
  downgradeComponent({component: ArticleComponent}));
```

Finally, since this component has an input, you'll need to pass this value via a binding attribute. Even though the component is still being declared as an Angular 1 directive, you'll use the Angular 2 binding syntax:

```
[index.html]

<!DOCTYPE html>
<html>
  <head>
    <!-- Angular 2 scripts -->
    <script src="zone.js "></script>
    <script src="reflect-metadata.js"></script>
    <script src="system.js"></script>
    <script src="system-config.js"></script>
  </head>
  <body>
    <div ng-init="authorName='Jake Hsu'">
      <ng1-article [author]="authorName"></ng1-article>
    </div>
    <root></root>
  </body>
</html>
```

The input and output must be explicitly declared at the time of conversion:

```
[app/article.component.ts]

import {Component, Input} from '@angular/core';
import {downgradeComponent} from '@angular/upgrade/static';
import {Ng1AppModule} from './ng1.module';

@Component({
  selector: 'ng2-article',
  template: `
    <h1>{{title}}</h1>
    <p>Written by: {{author}}</p>
  `
})
export class ArticleComponent {
  @Input() author:string
  title:string = 'Unicycle Jousting Recognized as Olympic Sport';
}

Ng1AppModule.directive(
  'ng1Article',
  downgradeComponent({
    component: ArticleComponent,
    inputs: ['author']
```

```
}));
```

These are all the steps required. If done properly, you should see the component render along with the author's name being interpolated inside the Angular 2 component through Angular 1's `ng-init` definition.

How it works...

You are giving Angular 1 the ability to direct Angular 2 to a certain element in the DOM and say, "*I need you to render here.*" Angular 2 still controls the component view and operation, and in every sense, the main thing we really care about is a full Angular 2 component adapted for use in an Angular 1 template.

 `downgradeComponent()` takes an object specifying the component as an argument and returns the function that Angular 1 is expecting for the directive definition.

See also

- *Connecting Angular 1 and Angular 2 with UpgradeModule* shows you how to run Angular 1 and 2 frameworks together
- *Downgrade Angular 2 providers to Angular 1 services with downgradeInjectable* demonstrates how to use an Angular 2 service inside an Angular 1 application

Downgrade Angular 2 providers to Angular 1 services with downgradeInjectable

If you have followed the steps in *Connecting Angular 1 and Angular 2 with UpgradeModule*, you should now have a hybrid application that is capable of sharing different elements with the opposing framework. If you are unfamiliar with Angular 2 providers, it is recommended that you go through the dependency injection chapter before you proceed.

Like with templated components, interchangeability is also offered to service types. It is possible to define a service type in Angular 2 and then inject it into an Angular 1 context.

The code, links, and a live example in relation to this recipe are available at `http://ngcookbook.herokuapp.com/2824/`.

Getting ready

Begin with the code written in *Connecting Angular 1 and Angular 2 with UpgradeModule*.

How to do it...

First, define the service you would like to inject into an Angular 1 component:

```
[app/article.service.ts]

import {Injectable} from '@angular/core';

@Injectable()
export class ArticleService {
  article:Object = {
    title: 'Research Shows Moon Not Actually Made of Cheese',
    author: 'Jake Hsu'
  };
}
```

Next, define the Angular 1 component that should inject it:

```
[app/article.component.ts]

export const ng1Article = {
  template: `
    <h1>{{article.title}}</h1>
    <p>{{article.author}}</p>
  `,
  controller: (ArticleService, $scope) => {
    $scope.article = ArticleService.article;
  }
};
```

`ArticleService` won't be injected yet though, since Angular 1 has no idea that this service exists. Doing this is very simple, however. First, you'll list the service provider in the Angular 2 module definition as you normally would:

```
[app/ng2.module.ts]

import {NgModule} from '@angular/core';
import {BrowserModule} from '@angular/platform-browser';
import {UpgradeModule} from '@angular/upgrade/static';
import {RootComponent} from './root.component';
import {ArticleService} from './article.service';

@NgModule({
  imports: [
    BrowserModule,
    UpgradeModule,
  ],
  declarations: [
    RootComponent
  ],
  providers: [
    ArticleService
  ],
  bootstrap: [
    RootComponent
  ]
})
export class Ng2AppModule {
  constructor(public upgrade: UpgradeModule){}
}
```

Still, Angular 1 does not understand how to use the service.

In the same way you convert an Angular 2 component definition into an Angular 1 directive, convert an Angular 2 service into an Angular 1 factory. Use `downgradeInjectable` and add the Angular 1 component and the converted service to the Angular 1 module definition:

```
[app/ng1.module.ts]

import 'angular';
import {ng1Article} from './article.component';
import {ArticleService} from './article.service';
import {downgradeInjectable} from '@angular/upgrade/static';

export const Ng1AppModule = angular.module('Ng1AppModule', [])
  .component('ng1Article', ng1Article)
  .factory('ArticleService', downgradeInjectable(ArticleService));
```

That's all! You should be able to see the Angular 1 component render with the data passed from the Angular 2 service.

See also

- *Connecting Angular 1 and Angular 2 with UpgradeModule* shows you how to run Angular 1 and 2 frameworks together
- *Downgrading Angular 2 components to Angular 1 directives with downgradeComponent* demonstrates how to use an Angular 2 component inside an Angular 1 application

2
Conquering Components and Directives

Your objective is to iterate through this and display the article title only if it is set as active. This chapter will cover the following recipes:

- Using decorators to build and style a simple component
- Passing members from a parent component to a child component
- Binding to native element attributes
- Registering handlers on native browser events
- Generating and capturing custom events using EventEmitter
- Attaching behavior to DOM elements with Directives
- Projecting nested content using ngContent
- Using ngFor and ngIf structural directives for model-based DOM control
- Referencing elements using template variables
- Attribute property binding
- Utilizing component life cycle hooks
- Referencing a parent component from a child component
- Configuring mutual parent-child awareness with ViewChild and forwardRef
- Configuring mutual parent-child awareness with ContentChild and forwardRef

Introduction

Directives as you came to know them in Angular 1 have been done away with. In their place, we have two new entities: components and the new version of directives. Angular 2 applications are now component-driven; with further exposure, you will discover why this style is superior.

Much of the syntax is entirely new and may seem strange at first. Fear not! The underpinnings of the Angular 2 style are elegant and marvelous once completely understood.

Using decorators to build and style a simple component

When writing an application component in TypeScript, there are several new paradigms that you must become familiar and comfortable with. Though possibly intimidating initially, you will find that you'll be able to carry over much of your comprehension of Angular 1 directives.

 The code and a live example of this are available at
`http://ngcookbook.herokuapp.com/6577/`.

Getting ready

One of the simplest imaginable components we can build is a template element that interpolates some values into its template. In Angular 1, one way this could be achieved was by creating an element directive, attaching some data to the scope inside the link function, and a template that would reference the data. I selected this description specifically because nearly all those concepts have been binned.

Suppose you want to create a simple article component with a pseudo template as follows:

```
<p>{{date}}</p>
<h1>{{title}}</h1>
<h3>Written by: {{author}}</h3>
```

You want to create a component that will live inside its own HTML tag, render the template, and interpolate the values.

How to do it…

The elemental building block of Angular 2 applications is the component. This component could generally be defined with two pieces: the core class definition and the class decoration.

Writing the class definition

All Angular 2 components begin as a class. This class is used to instantiate the component, and any data required inside the component template will be accessible from the class's properties. Thus, the foundational class for the component would appear as follows:

```
[app/article.component.ts]

export class ArticleComponent {
  currentDate:date;
  title:string;
  author:string;
  constructor() {
    this.currentDate = new Date();
    this.title = `
      Flight Security Restrictions to Include
      Insults, Mean Faces
    `;
    this.author = 'Jake';
  }
};
```

Here are a few things to note for those who are new to TypeScript or ES6 in general:

- You will note the class definition is prefixed with an `export` keyword. This is adherence to the new ES6 module convention, which naturally is also part of TypeScript. Assuming the `Article` class is defined in the `foo.ts` file, it can be imported to a different module using the `import` keyword, and the path to that module would be `import {Article} from './foo';` (this assumes that the importing file is in the same directory as `foo.ts`).
- The title definition uses the new ES6 template string syntax, a pair of backticks (` `` `) instead of the traditional set of quotes (`''`). You will find you become quite fond of this, as it means the `'' + '' + ''` messiness formerly used to define multiline templates would no longer be necessary.

- All the properties of this class are typed. TypeScript's typing syntax takes the form of `propertyName:propertyType = optionalInitValue`. JavaScript is, of course, a loosely typed language, and JavaScript is what the browser is interpreting in this case. However, writing your application in TypeScript allows you to utilize type safety at compile time, which will allow you to avoid undesirable and unanticipated behavior.
- All ES6 classes come with a predefined `constructor()` method, which is invoked upon instantiation. Here, you are using the constructor to instantiate the properties of the class, which is a perfectly fine strategy for member initialization. Having the member property definition outside the constructor is allowed, since it is useful for adding types to properties; thus, here you are simply obviating the use of the constructor since you are able to add a type and assign the value in the same line. A more succinct style could be as follows:

```
[app/article.component.ts]

export class ArticleComponent {
  currentDate:date = new Date();
  title:string = `
    Flight Security Restrictions to Include
    Insults, Mean Faces
  `;
  author:string = 'Jake';
}
```

- The TypeScript compiler will automatically move the member initialization process inside the class constructor, so this version and the previous one are behaviorally identical.

Writing the component class decorator

Although you have created a class that has information associated with it, it does not yet have any way to interface with the DOM. Furthermore, this class is yet to be assigned with any meaning in the context of Angular 2. You can accomplish this with decorators.

Decorators are a feature of TypeScript but not by any means unique to the language. Python developers, among many others, should be quite familiar with the concept of class modulation via explicit decoration. Generally speaking, it allows you to have a regularized modification of the defined classes using separately defined decorators. However, in Angular 2, you will largely be utilizing the decorators provided to you by the framework to declare the various framework elements. Decorators such as `@Component` are defined in the Angular source code as a `Component` function, and the function is applied as a decorator using the @ symbol.

An @ prefix signals that the imported function should be applied as a decorator. These decorators are visually obvious but will usually not exist by themselves or with an empty object literal. This is because Angular 2 decorators are generally made useful by their **decorator metadata**. This concept can be made more concrete here by using the predefined `Component` decorator.

Nothing is available for free in Angular 2. In order to use the component decorator, it must be imported from the Angular 2 `core` module into the module that wishes to use it. You can then prepend this `Component` to the class definition:

```
[app/article.component.ts]

import {Component} from '@angular/core';

@Component({})
export class ArticleComponent {
  currentDate:date = new Date();
  title:string = `
    Flight Security Restrictions to Include
    Insults, Mean Faces
  `;
  author:string = 'Jake';
}
```

As mentioned before, the `@Component` decorator accepts a `ComponentMetadata` object, which in the preceding code is just an empty object literal (note that the preceding code will not compile). Conceptually, this metadata object is very similar to the directive definition object in Angular 1. Here, you want to provide the decorator metadata object with two properties, namely `selector` and `template`:

```
[app/article.component.ts]

import {Component} from '@angular/core';

@Component({
```

```
    selector: 'article',
    template: `
      <p>{{currentDate|date}}</p>
      <h1>{{title}}</h1>
      <h3>Written by: {{author}}</h3>
    `
})
export class ArticleComponent {
  currentDate:date = new Date();
  title:string = `
    Flight Security Restrictions to Include
    Insults, Mean Faces
  `;
  author:string = 'Jake';
}
```

Note that `selector` is the string that will be used to find where the component should be inserted in the DOM, and `template` is obviously the stringified HTML template.

With all this, you will be able to see your article component in action with the `<article></article>` tag.

How it works...

The class definition has supplanted the Angular 1 concept of having a controller. The component instances of this class have member properties that can be interpolated and bound into the template, similar to `$scope` in Angular 1.

In the template, the interpolation and data binding processes seem to occur much in the same way, they did in Angular 1. This is not actually the case, which is visited in greater detail later in this chapter. The built-in `date` modifier, which resembles an Angular 1 filter, is now dubbed with a `pipe` although it works in a very similar fashion.

The `selector` metadata property is a string representing a CSS selector. In this definition, you target all the occurrences of an `article` tag, but the selector specificity and detail is of course able to handle a great deal of additional complexity. Use this to your advantage.

There's more...

The concept that must be internalized for Angular 2 neophytes is the total encapsulation of a component. This book will go into further detail about the different abilities of the `ComponentMetadata` object, but the paradigm they and all class decorators introduce is the concept that *Angular 2 components are self-describing*. By examining the class definition, you can wholly reason the data, service, class, and injectable dependencies. In Angular 1, this was not possible because of the "scope soup" pattern.

One could argue that in Angular 1, CSS styling was a second-class citizen. This is no longer the case with components, as the metadata object offers robust support for complex styling. For example, to italicize the author in your `Article` component, use this code:

```
[app/article.component.ts]

import {Component} from '@angular/core';

@Component({
  selector: 'article',
  template: `
    <p>{{currentDate|date}}</p>
    <h1>{{title}}</h1>
    <h3>Written by: {{author}}</h3>
  `,
  styles: [`
    h3 {
      font-style: italic;
    }
  `]
})
export class ArticleComponent {
  currentDate:date = new Date();
  title:string = `
    Flight Security Restrictions to Include
    Insults, Mean Faces
  `;
  author:string = 'Jake';
}
```

Angular 2 will use this `styles` property and compile it into a generated style sheet, which it will then apply to only this component. You do not have to worry about the rest of the HTML `h3` tags being inadvertently styled. This is because Angular 2's generated style sheet will ensure that only this component—and its children—are subject to the CSS rules listed in the metadata object.

This is intended to emulate the total modularity of web components. However, since web components do not yet have universal support, Angular 2's design essentially performs a polyfill for this behavior.

See also

- *Passing members from a parent component into a child component* goes through the basics of downward data flow between components
- *Using ngFor and ngIf structural directives for model-based DOM control* instructs you on how to utilize some of Angular 2's core built-in directives
- *Utilizing component lifecycle hooks* gives an example of how you can integrate with Angular 2's component rendering flow

Passing members from a parent component into a child component

With the departure of the Angular 1.x concept of $scope inheritance, mentally (partially or entirely) remodeling how information would be passed around your application is a must. In its place, you have an entirely new system of propagating information throughout the application's hierarchy.

Gone also is the concept of defaulting to bidirectional data binding. Although it made for an application that was simpler to reason about, bidirectional data binding incurs an unforgivably expensive drag on performance. This new system operates in an asymmetric fashion: members are propagated downwards through the component tree, but not upwards unless explicitly performed.

The code, links, and a live example of this are available at http://ngcookbook.herokuapp.com/6543/.

Getting ready

Suppose you had a simple application that intended to (but currently cannot) pass data from a parent ArticleComponent to a child AttributionComponent:

```
[app/components.ts]

import {Component} from '@angular/core';

@Component({
  selector: 'attribution',
  template: `
    <h3>Written by: {{author}}</h3>
  `
})
export class AttributionComponent {
  author:string;
}
 @Component({
  selector: 'article',
  template: `
    <h1>{{title}}</h1>
    <attribution></attribution>
  `
})
export class ArticleComponent {
  title:string = 'Belching Choir Begins World Tour';
  name:string = 'Jake';
}
```

How to do it...

In this initial implementation, the components defined here are not yet aware of each other, and the `<attribution></attribution>` tag will remain inert in the DOM. This is a good thing! It means these two components are completely decoupled, and you are able to only introduce connection logic as necessary.

Connecting the components

First, since the `<attribution></attribution>` tag appears inside the `Article` component, you must make the component aware of the existence of `AttributionComponent`. This is accomplished by introducing the component in the module in which `ArticleComponent` is also declared:

```
[app/app.module.ts]

import {NgModule} from '@angular/core';
import {BrowserModule} from '@angular/platform-browser';
import {ArticleComponent, AttributionComponent}
```

```
    from './components';

@NgModule({
  imports: [
    BrowserModule
  ],
  declarations: [
    ArticleComponent,
    AttributionComponent
  ],
  bootstrap: [
    ArticleComponent
  ]
})
export class AppModule {}
```

 For the purpose of this recipe, don't concern yourself just yet with the details of what NgModule is doing. In the example in this recipe, the entire application is just an instance of ArticleComponent with AttributionComponent inside it. So, all the component declarations can be done inside the same module.

With this, you will see that ArticleComponent is able to match the <attribution></attribution> tag with the AttributionComponent definition.

Inside a single module, the order of the definition could matter a lot. ES6 and TypeScript class declarations are not hoisted, so you cannot reference them at all before the declaration without generating errors. In this recipe, since ArticleComponent is defined before AttributionComponent, the former cannot directly reference the latter inside its definition.

 If you were to instead define AttributionComponent inside a separate module and import it with the module loader, the order issue becomes irrelevant. As you will notice, this is one of the excellent benefits of having a highly modular application structure.

One caveat to this is that Angular does make it possible to do out-of-order class references using a forwardRef. However, if solving the order problem is possible by splitting it into separate modules, that is preferred over forwardRef.

This being the case, go ahead and split your component file into two separate modules and import them accordingly:

```
[app/app.module.ts]

import {NgModule} from '@angular/core';
import {BrowserModule} from '@angular/platform-browser';
import {ArticleComponent} from './article.component';
import {AttributionComponent} from './attribution.component';

@NgModule({
  imports: [
    BrowserModule
  ],
  declarations: [
    ArticleComponent,
    AttributionComponent
  ],
  bootstrap: [
    ArticleComponent
  ]
})
export class AppModule {}

[app/article.component.ts]

import {Component} from '@angular/core';

@Component({
  selector: 'article',
  template: `
    <h1>{{title}}</h1>
    <attribution></attribution>
  `
})
export class ArticleComponent {
  title:string = 'Belching Choir Begins World Tour';
  name:string = 'Jake';
}

[app/attribution.component.ts]

import {Component} from '@angular/core';

@Component({
  selector: 'attribution',
  template: `
    <h3>Written by: {{author}}</h3>
```

```
})
export class AttributionComponent {
  author:string;
}
```

Declaring inputs

Similar to the Angular 1 directive's scope property object, in Angular 2, you must declare the members of the parent component to bring them down to the child component. In Angular 1, this could be done implicitly with an inherited `$scope`, but this is no longer the case. Angular 2 component inputs must be explicitly defined.

Another important difference between Angular 1 and Angular 2 is that `@Input` in Angular 2 is a unidirectional data binding feature. Data updates will flow downwards, and the parent will not be updated unless explicitly notified.

The process of declaring inputs in a child component is done through the `Input` decorator, but the decorator is invoked inside the class definition instead of doing so in front of it. `Input` is imported from the core module and invoked inside the class definition that is paired with a member.

Don't let this confuse you. The implementation of the actual decorating function is hidden from you since it is imported as a single target, so don't think much about what the `@Input()` syntax is doing. There is a defined `Input` function in the Angular source, and you are certainly invoking this method here. However, for your purposes, it is merely declaring the member that follows it as the one that will be passed in explicitly from the parent component. You use it in the same way as the Component decorator, just in a different place.

```
[app/attribution.component.ts]

import {Component, Input} from '@angular/core';

@Component({
  selector: 'attribution',
  template: `
    <h3>Written by: {{author}} </h3>
  `
})
export class AttributionComponent {
  @Input() author:string;
```

}

Next, you must pass the value bound to the child component tag to the parent component. In the context of this recipe, you want to pass the `name` property of the `Article` component object to the `author` property of the `Attribution` component object. One way of accomplishing this is by using the square bracket notation on the tag attribute, which specifies the attribute string as bound data:

```
[app/article.component.ts]

import {Component} from '@angular/core';

@Component({
  selector: 'article',
  template: `
    <h1>{{title}}</h1>
    <attribution [author]="name"></attribution>
  `
})
export class ArticleComponent {
  title:string = 'Belching Choir Begins World Tour';
  name:string = 'Jake';
}
```

With this, you have successfully passed a member property down, from a parent to a child component!

How it works...

Recall that the starting point of this example was that we had two components that didn't know the other exists, even though they are defined and exported inside the same module. The process demonstrated in this recipe is to provide the child component to the parent component, configure the child component to expect that a member will be bound to an input attribute, and finally provide that member in the template of the parent component.

There's more...

Some people have an issue with the square bracket notation. It is valid HTML, but some developers feel it is unintuitive and looks odd.

Additionally, the bracket notation is not valid XML. Developers using HTML generated through XSLT will not be able to utilize the new syntax. Fortunately, everywhere the new Angular 2 syntax utilizes new new `[]` or `()` syntax, there is an equivalent syntax that the framework supports which will behave identically.

Instead of using pairs of square brackets, you can prefix the attribute name with `bind-` and it will behave identically:

```
[app/article.component.ts]

import {Component, Input} from '@angular/core';

@Component({
  selector: 'article',
  template: `
    <h1>{{ title }}</h1>
    <attribution bind-author="name"></attribution>
  `
})
export class ArticleComponent {
  title:string = 'Belching Choir Begins World Tour';
  name:string = 'Jake';
}
```

Angular expressions

Note that the value of the attribute `name` is not a string but an expression. Angular knows how to evaluate this expression in the context of the parent component. As is the case with Angular expressions though, you are more than welcome to provide a static value and Angular will happily evaluate it and provide it to the child component.

For example, the following change would hardcode the child component to assign the string `"Mike Snifferpippets"` as the `author` property:

```
[app/article.component.ts]

import {Component, Input} from '@angular/core';
import {AttributionComponent} from './attribution.component';

@Component({
  selector: 'article',
  template: `
    <h1>{{title}}</h1>
    <attribution [author]="'Mike Snifferpippets'"></attribution>
```

```
    `,
  directives: [AttributionComponent]
})
export class ArticleComponent {
  title:string = 'Belching Choir Begins World Tour';
  name:string = 'Jake';
}
```

Unidirectional data binding

The data binding you have set up in this recipe is actually unidirectional. More specifically, changes in the parent component member will propagate downwards to the child component, but changes to the child component member will not propagate upwards. This will be explored further in another recipe, but it is important to keep in mind that the Angular 2 data flow is, by default, downwards through the component tree.

Member methods

Angular doesn't care about the nature of the bound value. TypeScript will enforce type correctness should you deviate from the declared type, but you are welcome to pass parent methods to the child with this strategy as well.

Keep in mind that passing a method bound in this way does not enforce the context in which it is evaluated. If the parent component passes a member method that utilizes the `this` keyword and the child component evaluates it, `this` will refer to the child component instance and not the parent component. Therefore, if the method tries to access the member data on the parent component, it will not be available.

There are a number of ways to mitigate this problem. Generally though, if you find you are passing a parent member method down to the child component and invoking it, there is probably a better way to design your application.

See also

- *Using decorators to build and style a simple component* describes the building blocks of implementing an Angular 2 component

- *Binding to native element attributes* shows how Angular 2 interfaces with HTML element attributes
- *Registering handlers on native browser events* demonstrates how you can easily attach behavior to browser events.
- *Generating and capturing custom events using EventEmitter* details how to propagate information upwards between components.
- *Using ngFor and ngIf structural directives for model-based DOM control* instructs you on how to utilize some of Angular 2's core built-in directives.

Binding to native element attributes

In Angular 1, it was expected that the developer would utilize the built-in replacement directives for element attributes that had meaningful DOM behavior attached to them. This was due to the fact that many of these attributes had behavior that was incompatible with how Angular 1 data binding operated. In Angular 2, these special attribute directives are done away with, and the binding behavior and syntax is subsumed into the normal binding behavior.

 The code, links, and a live example of this are available at `http://ngcookbook.herokuapp.com/8313/`.

How to do it...

Binding to the native attribute is as simple as placing square brackets around the attribute and treating it as normal bound data:

```
[app/logo.component.ts]

import {Component} from '@angular/core';

@Component({
  selector: 'logo',
  template: '<img [src]="logoUrl">'
})
export class LogoComponent {
  logoUrl:string =
    '//angular.io/resources/images/logos/standard/logo-nav.png';
}
```

With this setup, the `<img>` element will dutifully fetch and show the image when it is provided by Angular.

How it works...

This is a different solution to the same problem that `ng-src` solved in Angular 1. The browser is looking for an `src` attribute on the tag. Since the square brackets are included as part of the attribute string, the browser will not find one and therefore not make a request. `[src]` will only make an image request once the value is filled and provided to the element.

See also

- *Passing members from a parent component into a child component* goes through the basics of downward data flow between components.
- *Registering handlers on native browser events* demonstrates how you can easily attach behavior to browser events.
- *Attaching behavior to DOM elements with directives* demonstrates how to attach behavior to elements with attribute directives.
- *Referencing elements using template variables* demonstrates Angular 2's new template variable construct.
- *Attribute property binding* shows Angular 2's clever way of deep referencing element properties.

Registering handlers on native browser events

In Angular 2, the other hemisphere of binding that is needed for a fully functioning application is event binding. The Angular 2 event binding syntax is similar to that of data binding.

 The code, links, and a live example of this are available at `http://ngcookbook.herokuapp.com/4437/`.

Getting ready

Suppose you wanted to create an article application that counted shares, and you began with the following skeleton:

```
[app/article.component.ts]
import {Component} from '@angular/core';

@Component({
  selector: 'article',
  template: `
    <h1>{{title}}</h1>
    <p>Shares: {{shareCt}}</p>
    <button>Share</button>
  `
})
export class ArticleComponent {
  title:string = 'Police Apprehend Tiramisu Thieves';
  shareCt:number = 0;
}
```

How to do it...

The Angular 2 event binding syntax is accomplished with a pair of parentheses surrounding the event type. In this case, events that you wish to listen for will have a type property of click, and this is what they will be bound against. The value of the bound event attribute is an expression, so you can invoke the method as a handler within it:

```
[app/article.component.ts]

import {Component} from '@angular/core';

@Component({
  selector: 'article',
  template: `
    <h1>{{title}}</h1>
    <p>Shares: {{shareCt}}</p>
    <button (click)="share()">Share</button>
  `
})
export class ArticleComponent {
  title:string = 'Police Apprehend Tiramisu Thieves';
  shareCt:number = 0;
  share():void {
    ++this.shareCt;
  }
```

```
    }
```

How it works...

Angular watches for the event binding syntax (click) and adds a click listener to ArticleComponent, bound to the share() handler. When this event is observed, it evaluates the expression attached to the event, which in this case will invoke a method defined on the component.

There's more...

Since capturing the event must occur in an expression, you are provided with an $event parameter in the expression, which will usually be passed as an argument to the handler method. This is similar to the process in Angular 1. Inspecting this $event object reveals it as the vanilla click event generated by the browser:

```
[app/article.component.ts]

import {Component} from '@angular/core';

@Component({
  selector: 'article',
  template: `
    <h1>{{title}}</h1>
    <p>Shares: {{shareCt}}</p>
    <button (click)="share($event)">Share</button>
  `
})
export class ArticleComponent {
  title:string = 'Police Apprehend Tiramisu Thieves';
  shareCt:number = 0;
  share(e:Event):void {
    console.log(e);   // MouseEvent
    ++this.shareCt;
  }
}
```

You will also note that the share() method here is demonstrating how typing can be applied to the parameters and the return value of the method:

```
myMethod(arg1:arg1type, arg2:arg2type, ...):returnType
```

As with member binding, you are also able to use an alternate event binding syntax if you do not care to use a set of parentheses. Prefixing `on-` to the event attribute will provide you with identical behavior:

```
import {Component} from '@angular/core';

@Component({
  selector: 'article',
  template: `
    <h1>{{title}}</h1>
    <p>Shares: {{shareCt}}</p>
    <button on-click="share($event)">Share</button>
  `
})
export class Article {
  title:string = 'Police Apprehend Tiramisu Thieves';
  shareCt:number = 0;
  share(e:Event):void {
    ++this.shareCt;
  }
}
```

See also

- *Binding to native element attributes* shows how Angular 2 interfaces with HTML element attributes.
- *Generating and capturing custom events using EventEmitter* details how to propagate information upwards between components.
- *Attaching behavior to DOM elements with directives* demonstrates how to attach behavior to elements with attribute directives.
- *Attribute property binding* shows Angular 2's clever way of deep referencing element properties.

Generating and capturing custom events using EventEmitter

In the wake of the disappearance of `$scope`, Angular was left with a void for propagating information up the component tree. This void is filled in part by custom events, and they represent the Yin to the downward data binding Yang.

The code, links, and a live example of this are available at
http://ngcookbook.herokuapp.com/8611/.

Getting ready

Suppose you had an Article application as follows:

```
[app/text-editor.component.ts]

import {Component} from '@angular/core';

@Component({
  selector: 'text-editor',
  template: `
    <textarea></textarea>
  `
})
export class TextEditorComponent {}

[app/article.component.ts]

import {Component} from '@angular/core';

@Component({
  selector: 'article',
  template: `
    <h1>{{title}}</h1>
    <p>Word count: {{wordCount}}</p>
    <text-editor></text-editor>
  `
})
export class ArticleComponent {
  title:string = `
    Maternity Ward Resorts to Rock Paper Scissors Following
    Baby Mixup`;
  wordCount:number = 0;

  updateWordCount(e:number):void {
    this.wordCount = e;
  }
}
```

This application will ideally be able to read the content of `textarea` when there is a change, and also count the number of words and report it to the parent component to be interpolated. As is the case, none of this is implemented.

How to do it...

A developer thinking in terms of Angular 1 would attach `ng-model` to `textarea`, use `$scope.$watch` on the model data, and pass the data to the parent via `$scope` or some other means. Unfortunately for such a developer, these constructs are radically different or non-existent in Angular 2. Fear not! The new implementation is more expressive, more modular, and much cleaner.

Capturing the event data

`ngModel` still exists in Angular 2, and it would certainly be suitable here. However, you don't actually need to use `ngModel` at all, and in this case, it allows you to be more explicit about when your application takes action. First, you must retrieve the text from the `textarea` element and make it usable in `TextEditorComponent`:

```
[app/text-editor.component.ts]

import {Component} from '@angular/core';

@Component({
  selector: 'text-editor',
  template: `
    <textarea (keyup)="emitWordCount($event)"></textarea>
  `
})
export class TextEditorComponent {
  emitWordCount(e:Event):void {
    console.log(
      (e.target.value.match(/\S+/g) || []).length);
  }
}
```

Excellent! As claimed, you don't need to use `ngModel` to acquire the element's contents. What's more, you are now able to utilize native browser events to explicitly define when you want `TextEditorComponent` to take action.

With this, you are setting a listener on the native browser's `keyup` event, fired from the `textarea` element. This event has a `target` property that exposes the value of the text in the element, which is exactly what you want to use. The component then uses a simple regular expression to count the number of non-whitespace sequences. This is your word count.

Emitting a custom event

`console.log` does not help to inform the parent component of the word count you are calculating. To do this, you need to create a custom event and emit it upwards:

```
[app/text-editor.component.ts]

import {Component, EventEmitter, Output} from '@angular/core';

@Component({
  selector: 'text-editor',
  template: `
    <textarea (keyup)="emitWordCount($event)"></textarea>
  `
})
export class TextEditorComponent {
  @Output() countUpdate = new EventEmitter<number>();

  emitWordCount(e:Event):void {
    this.countUpdate.emit(
      (e.target.value.match(/\S+/g) || []).length);
  }
}
```

Using the `@Output` decorator allows you to instantiate an `EventEmitter` member on the child component that the parent component will be able to listen to. This `EventEmitter` member, like any other class member, is available as `this.countUpdate`. The child component is able to send events upward by invoking the `emit()` method on this member, and the argument to this method is the value which you wish to send to the event. Here, since you want to send an integer count of words, you instantiate the `EventEmitter` member by typing it as a `<number>` emitter.

Listening for custom events

So far, you are through with only half the implementation, as these custom events are being fired off into the ether of the browser with no listeners. Since the method you need to use is already defined on the parent component, all you need to do is hook into the event listener to that method.

The ( ) template syntax is used to add listeners to events, and Angular does not discriminate between native browser events and events that originate from EventEmitters. Thus, since you declared the child component's EventEmitter as @Output, you will be able to add a listener for events that come from it on the parent component, as follows:

```
[app/article.component.ts]

import {Component } from 'angular2/core';

@Component({
  selector: 'article',
  template: `
    <h1>{{title}}</h1>
    <p>Word count: {{wordCount}}</p>
    <text-editor (countUpdate)="updateWordCount($event)">
    </text-editor>
  `
})
export class ArticleComponent {
  title:string = `
    Maternity Ward Resorts to Rock Paper Scissors Following
    Baby Mixup`;
  wordCount:number = 0;

  updateWordCount(e:number):void {
    this.wordCount = e;
  }
}
```

With this, your application should correctly count the words in the TextEditor component and update the value in the Article component.

How it works...

Using `@Output` in conjunction with `EventEmitter` allows you to create child components that expose an API for the parent component to hook into. The `EventEmitter` sends the events upward with its `emit` method, and the parent component can subscribe to them by binding to the emitter output.

The flow of this example is as follows:

1. The keystroke inside `textarea` causes the native browser's `keyup` event.
2. The `TextEditor` component has a listener set on this event, so the attached expression is evaluated, which will invoke `emitWordCount`.
3. The `emitWordCount` inspects the `Event` object and extracts the text from the associated DOM element. It parses the text for the number of contained words and invokes the `EventEmitter.emit` method.
4. The `EventEmitter` method emits an event associated with the declared `countUpdate` `@Output` member.
5. The `ArticleComponent` sees this event and invokes the attached expression. The expression invokes `updateWordCount`, passing in the event value.
6. The `ArticleComponent` property is updated, and since this value is interpolated in the view, Angular honors the data binding process by updating the view.

There's more...

The name `EventEmitter` is a bit deceiving. If you're paying attention, you will notice that the parent component member method invoked in the handler does not have a typed parameter. You will also notice that you are directly assigning that parameter to the member typed as `number`. This should seem odd as the template expression invoking the method is passing `$event`, which you used earlier as a browser `Event` object. This seems like a mismatch because it *is* a mismatch. If you bind to native browser events, the event you will observe can only be the native browser event object. If you bind to custom events, the event you will observe is whatever was passed when `emit` was invoked. Here, the parameter to `updateWordCount()` is simply the integer you provided with `this.countUpdate.emit()`.

Also note that you are not required to provide a value for the emitted event. You can still use `EventEmitter` to signal to a parent component that an event has occurred and that it should evaluate the bound expression. To do this, you simply create an untyped emitter with `new EventEmitter()` and invoke `emit()` with no arguments. `$event` should be `undefined`.

It is not possible to pass multiple values as custom events. To send multiple pieces of data, you need to combine them into an object or array.

See also

- *Binding to native element attributes* shows how Angular 2 interfaces with HTML element attributes.
- *Registering handlers on native browser events* demonstrates how you can easily attach behavior to browser events.

Attaching behavior to DOM elements with directives

In the course of creating applications, you will often find it useful to be able to attach component-style behavior to DOM elements, but without the need to have templating. If you were to attempt to construct an Angular 2 component without providing a template in some way, you will meet with a stern error telling you that some form of template is required.

Here lies the difference between Angular 2 components and directives: components have views (which can take the form of a `template`, `templateUrl`, or `@View` decorator), whereas directives do not. They otherwise behave identically and provide you with the same behavior.

 The code, links, and a live example of this are available at `http://ngcookbook.herokuapp.com/3292/`.

Getting ready

Suppose you have the following application:

```
[app/article.component.ts]

import {Component} from '@angular/core';

@Component({
  selector: 'article',
  template: `<h1>{{title}}</h1>`,
  styles: [`
    h1 {
      text-overflow: ellipsis;
      white-space: nowrap;
      overflow: hidden;
      max-width: 300px;
    }
  `]
})
export class ArticleComponent {
  title:string = `Presidential Candidates Respond to
    Allegations Involving Ability to Dunk`;
}
```

Currently, this application is using CSS to truncate the article title with an ellipsis. You would like to expand this application so that the Article component reveals the entire title when clicked by simply adding an HTML attribute.

How to do it...

Begin by defining the basic class that will power the attribute directive and add it to the application module:

```
[app/click-to-reveal.directive.ts]

export class ClickToRevealDirective {
  reveal(target) {
    target.style['white-space'] = 'normal';
  }
}

[app/app.module.ts]

import {NgModule} from '@angular/core';
import {BrowserModule} from '@angular/platform-browser';
```

```
import {ArticleComponent} from './article.component';
import {ClickToRevealDirective}
  from './click-to-reveal.directive';

@NgModule({
  imports: [
    BrowserModule
  ],
  declarations: [
    ArticleComponent,
    ClickToRevealDirective
  ],
  bootstrap: [
    ArticleComponent
  ]
})
export class AppModule {}
```

First, you must decorate the `ClickToRevealDirective` class as `@Directive` and use it inside the Article component:

```
[app/click-to-reveal.directive.ts]

import { Directive} from '@angular/core';

@Directive({
  selector: '[click-to-reveal]'
})
export class ClickToRevealDirective {
  reveal(target) {
    target.style['white-space'] = 'normal';
  }
}
```

Next, add the attribute to the element that you wish to apply the directive to:

```
[app/article.component.ts]

import {Component} from '@angular/core';

@Component({
  selector: 'article',
  template: `<h1 click-to-reveal>{{ title }}</h1>`,
  styles: [`
    h1 {
      text-overflow: ellipsis;
      white-space: nowrap;
      overflow: hidden;
```

```
      max-width: 300px;
    }
  `]
})
export class ArticleComponent {
  title: string;
  constructor() {
    this.title = `Presidential Candidates Respond to
      Allegations Involving Ability to Dunk`;
  }
}
```

 Note that the Directive is using an attribute CSS selector to associate itself with any elements that have click-to-reveal. This of course approximates an Angular 1 attribute's directive behavior, but this form is far more flexible since it can wield the innate matchability of selectors.

Now that the Article component is aware of ClickToRevealDirective, you must provide it the ability to attach itself to click events.

Attaching to events with HostListeners

An attentive developer will have noticed that up until this point in the chapter, you have created components that listen to the events generated by the children. This is no problem since you can expressively set listeners in a parent component template on the child tag.

However, in this situation, you are looking to add a listener to the same element that the directive is being attached to. What's more, you do not have a good way of adding an event binding expression to the template from inside a directive. Ideally, you would like to not have to expose this method from inside the directive. How should you proceed then?

The solution is to utilize a new Angular construct called HostListener. Simply put, it allows you to capture self-originating events and handle them internally:

```
[app/click-to-reveal.directive.ts]

import { Directive, HostListener} from '@angular/core';

@Directive({
  selector: '[click-to-reveal]'
})
export class ClickToRevealDirective {
  @HostListener('click', ['$event.target'])
  reveal(target) {
    target.style['white-space'] = 'normal';
```

```
    }
  }
```

With this, `click` events on the `<h1>` element should successfully invoke the `reveal()` method.

How it works...

The directive needs a way to attach to native click events. Furthermore, it needs a way to capture objects such as $event that Angular provides to you; these objects would normally be captured in the binding expression.

`@HostListener` decorates a directive method to act as the designated event handler. The first argument in its invocation is the event identification string (here, `click`, but it could just as easily be a custom event from `EventEmitter`), and the second argument is an array of string arguments that are evaluated as expressions.

There's more...

You are not restricted to one `HostListener` inside a directive. Using it merely associates an event with a directive method. So you are able to stack multiple `HostListener` declarations on a single handler, for example, to listen for both a `click` and `mouseover` event.

See also

- *Using decorators to build and style a simple component* describes the building blocks of implementing an Angular 2 component
- *Passing members from a parent component into a child component* goes through the basics of downward data flow between components
- *Using ngFor and ngIf structural directives for model-based DOM control* instructs you in how to utilize some of Angular 2's core built-in directives
- *Attribute property binding* shows Angular 2's clever way of deep referencing element properties

Projecting nested content using ngContent

Utilizing components as standalone tags that are self-contained and wholly manage their contents is a clean pattern, but you will frequently find that your component tags demand that they enclose content.

 The code, links, and a live example of this are available at
`http://ngcookbook.herokuapp.com/6172/`.

Getting ready

Suppose you had the following application:

```
[app/ad-section.component.ts]

import {Component} from '@angular/core';

@Component({
  selector: 'ad-section',
  template: `
    <a href="#">{{adText}}</a>
  `
})
export class AdSectionComponent {
  adText:string = 'Selfie sticks 40% off!';
}

[app/article.component.ts]

import {Component} from '@angular/core';

@Component({
  selector: 'article',
  template: `
    <h1>{{title}}</h1>
    <p>U.S. senators are up in arms following the recent ruling
       stripping them of their beloved selfie sticks.</p>
    <p>A bipartisan committee drafted a resolution to smuggle
       selfie sticks onto the floor by any means necessary.</p>
  `
})
export class ArticleComponent {
  title:string = 'Selfie Sticks Banned from Senate Floor';
```

```
}
```

Your objective here is to modify this so that the AdSection component can be incorporated into the Article component without interfering with its content.

How to do it...

The AdSection component wants to incorporate an extra element around the existing Article content. This is easy to accomplish:

```
[app/article.component.ts]

import {Component} from '@angular/core';

@Component({
  selector: 'article',
  template: `
    <h1>{{title}}</h1>
    <ad-section>
      <p>U.S. senators are up in arms following the recent ruling
          stripping them of their beloved selfie sticks.</p>
      <p>A bipartisan committee drafted a resolution to smuggle
          selfie sticks onto the floor by any means necessary.</p>
    </ad-section>
  `
})
export class ArticleComponent {
  title:string = 'Selfie Sticks Banned from Senate Floor';
}
```

You will notice though that this is a destructive operation. When rendering AdSectionComponent, Angular is not concerned about any content that is inside it. It sees that AdSectionComponent has a template associated with it, and it dutifully supplants the element's contents with it; this template is defined in the @Component decorator. In this case, that wipes out the <p> tags that you want to retain.

To preserve them, you must instruct Angular how it should manage wrapped content. This can be accomplished with an <ng-content> tag:

```
[app/ad-section.component.ts]

import {Component} from '@angular/core';

@Component({
  selector: 'ad-section',
```

```
  template: `
    <a href="#">{{adText}}</a>
    <ng-content select="p"></ng-content>
  `
})
export class AdSectionComponent {
  adText:string = 'Selfie sticks 40% off!';
}
```

With this, the ad anchor element is inserted before the wrapped content.

How it works...

Similar to how `ng-transclude` worked in Angular 1, `ng-content` serves to interpolate the component tag's wrapped content into its template. The difference here is that `ng-content` uses a `select` attribute to target the wrapped elements. This is simply a CSS selector, operating in the same way in which `@Component` decorators handle the `selector` property in `ComponentMetadata`.

There's more...

The `select` attribute in this example was superfluous, as it ended up selecting the entirety of the wrapped content. Of course, if the select value only matched some of the wrapped content, it would tease out only those elements and interpolate them. `<ng-content>` will by default insert the entirety of the wrapped content if you decline to provide it with a select value.

Also note that the select attribute is a limited CSS selector. It is not capable of performing complex selections such as `:nth-child`, and it is only able to target top-level elements inside the wrapping tags. For example, in this application, the paragraph tag inside `<div><p>Blah</p></div>` would not be included with a `select="p"` attribute value.

See also

- *Referencing a parent component from a child component* describes how a component can gain a direct reference to its parent via injection
- *Configuring mutual parent-child awareness with ViewChild and forwardRef* instructs you on how to properly use `ViewChild` to reference child component object instances

- *Configuring Mutual Parent-Child Awareness with ContentChild and forwardRef* instructs you on how to properly use ContentChild to reference child component object instances

Using ngFor and ngIf structural directives for model-based DOM control

Any developer that has used a client framework is intimately familiar with two basic operations in an application: iterative rendering from a collection and conditional rendering. The new Angular 2 implementations look a bit different but operate in much the same way.

The code, links, and a live example are available at
`http://ngcookbook.herokuapp.com/3211/`.

Getting ready

Suppose you had the following application:

```
[app/article-list.component.ts]

import {Component} from '@angular/core';

@Component({
  selector: 'article-list',
  template: ''
})
export class ArticleListComponent {
  articles:Array<Object> = [
    {title: 'Foo', active: true},
    {title: 'Bar', active: false},
    {title: 'Baz', active: true}
  ];
}
```

Your objective is to iterate through this and display the article title only if it is set as active.

How to do it...

Similar to Angular 1, Angular 2 provides you with directives to accomplish this task. ngFor is used to iterate through the articles collection:

```
[app/article-list.component.ts]

import {Component} from '@angular/core';

@Component({
  selector: 'article-list',
  template: `
    <div *ngFor="let article of articles; let i = index">
      <h1>
        {{i}}: {{article.title}}
      </h1>
    </div>
  `
})
export class ArticleListComponent {
  articles:Array<Object> = [
    { title: 'Foo', active: true },
    { title: 'Bar', active: false },
    { title: 'Baz', active: true }
  ];
}
```

Similar to ngFor, ngIf can be incorporated as follows:

```
[app/article-list.component.ts]

import {Component} from 'angular2/core';

@Component({
  selector: 'article-list',
  template: `
    <div *ngFor="let article of articles; let i = index">
      <h1 *ngIf="article.active">
        {{i}}: {{ article.title }}
      </h1>
    </div>
  `
})
export class ArticleListComponent {
  articles:Array<Object> = [
    {title: 'Foo', active: true},
    {title: 'Bar', active: false},
    {title: 'Baz', active: true}
```

```
    ];
  }
```

With this, you will see that only the objects in the `articles` array with `active:true` are rendered.

How it works...

At first, the asterisk and pound sign notation could be confusing for many developers. For most applications, you will not need to know how this syntactic sugar actually works behind the scenes.

In reality, Angular decomposes all the structural directives prefixed with * to utilize a template. First, Angular breaks down `ngFor` and `ngIf` to use the template directives on the same element. The syntax does not change much yet:

```
[app/article-list.component.ts]

import {Component} from '@angular/core';

@Component({
  selector: 'article-list',
  template: `
    <div template="ngFor let article of articles; let i = index">
      <h1 template="ngIf article.active">
        {{i}}: {{ article.title }}
      </h1>
    </div>
  `
})
export class ArticleList {
  articles: Array<Object>,
  constructor() {
    this.articles = [
      { title: 'Foo', active: true },
      { title: 'Bar', active: false },
      { title: 'Baz', active: true }
    ];
  }
}
```

Following this, Angular decomposes this `template` directive into a wrapping `<template>` element:

```
[app/article-list.component.ts]
```

```
import {Component} from '@angular/core';

@Component({
  selector: 'article-list',
  template: `
    <template ngFor let-article [ngForOf]="articles" let-i="index">
      <div>
        <template [ngIf]="article.active">
          <h1>
            {{i}}: {{article.title}}
          </h1>
        </template>
      </div>
    </template>
  `
})
export class ArticleList {
  articles: Array<Object>,
  constructor() {
    this.articles = [
      { title: 'Foo', active: true },
      { title: 'Bar', active: false },
      { title: 'Baz', active: true }
    ];
  }
}
```

Note that both the versions displayed here—either using the `template` directive or the `<template>` element—will behave identically to using the original structural directives. That being said, there generally will not be a reason to ever do it this way; this is merely a demonstration to show you how Angular understands these directives behind the scenes.

When inspecting the actual DOM of these examples using `ngFor` and `ngIf`, you will be able to see Angular's automatically added HTML comments that describe how it interprets your markup and translates it into template bindings.

There's more...

The `template` element is born out of the Web Components' specification. Templates are a definition of how a DOM subtree can eventually be defined as a unit, but the elements that appear within it are not created or active until the template is actually used to create an instance from that template. Not all web browsers support web components, so Angular 2 does a polyfill to emulate proper template behavior.

In this way, the `ngFor` directive is actually creating a web component template that utilizes the subordinate `ngForOf` binding, which is a property of `NgFor`. Each instance in `articles` will use the template to create a DOM section, and within this section, the `article` and `index` template variables will be available for interpolation.

See also

- *Using decorators to build and style a simple component* describes the building blocks of implementing an Angular 2 component
- *Passing members from a parent component into a child component* goes through the basics of downward data flow between components
- *Binding to native element attributes* shows how Angular 2 interfaces with HTML element attributes
- *Attaching behavior to DOM elements with directives* demonstrates how to attach behavior to elements with attribute directives
- *Attribute property binding* shows Angular 2's clever way of deep referencing element properties
- *Utilizing component lifecycle hooks* gives an example of how you can integrate with Angular 2's component rendering flow.

Referencing elements using template variables

Many developers will begin with Angular 2 and reach for something that resembles the trustworthy `ng-model` in Angular 1. `NgModel` exists in Angular 2, but there is a new way of referencing elements in the template: local template variables.

The code, links, and a live example of this are available at
`http://ngcookbook.herokuapp.com/5094/`.

Getting ready

Suppose you had the following application and wanted to directly access the `input` element:

```
[app/article.component.ts]

import {Component} from '@angular/core';

@Component({
  selector: 'article',
  template: `
    <input>
    <h1>{{title}}</h1>
  `
})
export class ArticleComponent {}
```

How to do it...

Angular 2 allows you to have a # assignment within the template itself, which can consequently be referenced from inside the template. For example, refer to the following code:

```
[app/article.component.ts]

import {Component} from '@angular/core';

@Component({
  selector: 'article',
  template: `
    <input #title>
    <h1>{{title}}</h1>
  `
})
export class ArticleComponent {}
```

With this, you will see [object HTMLInputElement] (or something similar, depending on your browser) interpolated into the <h1> tag. This means that the #title inside the <input> tag is now directly referencing the element object, which of course means that the value of the element should be available for you.

Don't get too excited just yet! If you attempt to interpolate title.value and then manipulate the input field, you will not see the browser update. This is because Angular 2 no longer supports bidirectional data binding in this way. Fear not, for the solution to this problem lies within the new Angular 2 data binding pattern.

Angular will decline to update the DOM until it thinks it needs to. This need is determined by what behavior in the application might cause the interpolated data to change. A bound event, which will propagate upwards through the component tree, may cause a data change. Thus, you can create an event binding on an element, and the mere presence of this event binding will trigger Angular to update the template:

```
[app/article.component.ts]

import {Component} from '@angular/core';

@Component({
  selector: 'article',
  template: `
    <input #title (keyup)="0">
    <h1>{{title.value}}</h1>
  `
})
export class ArticleComponent {}
```

Here, the keyup event from the text input is bound to an expression that is effectively a no-op. Since the event will trigger an update of the DOM, you can successfully pull out the latest value property from the title input element object. With this, you have successfully bound the input value to the interpolated string.

There's more...

If you aren't crazy about the # notation, you can always replace it with val- and still achieve identical behavior:

```
[app/article.component.ts]

import {Component} from '@angular/core';

@Component({
```

```
  selector: 'article',
  template: `
    <input val-title (keyup)="0">
    <h1>{{title.value}}</h1>
    `
})
export class ArticleComponent {}
```

Also, it's important to recall that these template variables are only accessible within the template. If you want to pass them back to the controller, you'll have to use it as a handler argument:

```
[app/article.component.ts]

import {Component} from '@angular/core';

@Component({
  selector: 'article',
  template: `
    <input #title (keyup)="setTitle(title.value)">
    <h1>{{myTitle}}</h1>
    `
})
export class ArticleComponent {
  myTitle:string;

  setTitle(val:string):void {
    this.myTitle = val;
  }
}
```

See also

- *Referencing a parent component from a child component* describes how a component can gain a direct reference to its parent via injection
- *Configuring mutual parent-child awareness with ViewChild and forwardRef* instructs you on how to properly use ViewChild to reference child component object instances

- *Configuring mutual parent-child awareness with ContentChild and forwardRef instructs you on how to properly use* `ContentChild` *to reference child component object instances*

Attribute property binding

One of the great new benefits of the new Angular binding style is that you are able to more accurately target what you are binding to. Formerly, the HTML attribute that was used as a directive or data token was simply used as a matching identifier. Now, you are able to use property bindings within the binding markup for both the input and output.

 The code, links, and a live example of this is available at `http://ngcookbook.herokuapp.com/8565/`.

Getting ready

Suppose you had the following application:

```
[app/article.component.ts]

import {Component} from '@angular/core';

@Component({
  selector: 'article',
  template: `
    <input #title (keydown)="setTitle(title.value)">
    <h1>{{myTitle}}</h1>
  `
})
export class ArticleComponent {
  myTitle:string;

  setTitle(val:string):void {
    this.myTitle = val;
  }
}
```

Your objective is to modify this so that it exhibits the following behavior:

- The `<h1>` tag is not updated with the value of the input field until the user strikes the *Enter* key.
- If the `<h1>` value does not match the value in the title input (call this state "stale"), the text color should be red. If it does match, it should be green.

How to do it...

Both of these behaviors can be achieved with Angular 2's attribute property binding. First, you can change the event binding so that only an *Enter* key will invoke the callback:

```
[app/article.component.ts]

import {Component} from '@angular/core';

@Component({
  selector: 'article',
  template: `
    <input #title (keydown.enter)="setTitle(title.value)">
    <h1>{{myTitle}}</h1>
  `
})
export class ArticleComponent {
  myTitle:string;

  setTitle(val:string):void {
    this.myTitle = val;
  }
}
```

Next, you can use Angular's style binding to directly assign a value to a `style` property. This requires adding a Boolean to the controller object to maintain the state:

```
[app/article.component.ts]

import {Component} from '@angular/core';

@Component({
  selector: 'article',
  template: `
    <input #title (keydown.enter)="setTitle(title.value)">
    <h1 [style.color]="isStale ? 'red' : 'green'">{{myTitle}}</h1>
  `
})
export class ArticleComponent {
  myTitle:string = '';
```

```
    isStale:boolean = false;
    setTitle(val:string):void {
      this.myTitle = val;
    }
  }
```

Closer, but this still provides no way of reaching a stale state. To achieve this, add another keydown event binding:

```
[app/article.component.ts]

import {Component} from '@angular/core';

@Component({
  selector: 'article',
  template: `
    <input #title
           (keyup.enter)="setTitle(title.value)"
           (keyup)="checkStale(title.value)">
    <h1 [style.color]="isStale ? 'red' : 'green'">
      {{myTitle}}
    </h1>
  `
})
export class ArticleComponent {
  myTitle:string = '';
  private isStale:boolean = false;

  setTitle(val:string):void {
    this.myTitle = val;
  }
  checkStale(val:string):void {
    this.isStale = val !== this.myTitle;
  }
}
```

With this, the color of the <h1> tag should correctly keep track of whether the data is stale or not!

How it works…

The simple explanation is that Angular provides you with a lot of syntactical sugar, but at a very basic level without involving a lot of complexity. If you were to inspect the `keyup` event, you would of course notice that there is no `enter` property available. Angular offers you a number of these pseudo properties so that checking the `keyCode` of the pressed key is not necessary.

In a similar way, Angular also allows you to bind to and access `style` properties directly. It is inferred that the style being accessed refers to the host element.

There's more…

Note here that you have assigned two handlers to what is essentially the same event. Not only this, but rearranging the order of the binding markup will break this application's desired behavior.

 When two handlers are assigned to the same event, Angular will execute the handlers in the order that they are defined in the markup.

See also

- *Binding to native element attributes* shows how Angular 2 interfaces with HTML element attributes
- *Registering handlers on native browser events* demonstrates how you can easily attach behavior to browser events
- *Generating and capturing custom events using EventEmitter* details how to propagate information upwards between components
- *Attaching behavior to DOM elements with directives* demonstrates how to attach behavior to elements with attribute directives

Utilizing component lifecycle hooks

Angular's component rendering process has a large number of facets, and different types of data and references will become available at different times. To account for this, Angular 2 allows components to set callbacks, which will be executed at different points in the component's life cycle.

 The code, links, and a live example of this are available at
`http://ngcookbook.herokuapp.com/2048/`.

Getting ready

Suppose you began with the following application, which simply allows the addition and removal of articles from a single input:

```
[app/article-list.component.ts]

import {Component} from '@angular/core';

@Component({
  selector: 'article-list',
  template: `
    <input (keyup.enter)="add($event)">
    <article *ngFor="let title of titles; let i = index"
             [articleTitle]="title">
      <button (click)="remove(i)">X</button>
    </article>
  `
})
export class ArticleListComponent {
  titles:Array<string> = [];
  add(e:Event):void {
    this.titles.push(e.target.value);
    e.target.value = '';
  }
  remove(index:number) {
    this.titles.splice(index, 1);
  }
}
[app/article.component.ts]

import {Component, Input} from '@angular/core';
```

```
@Component({
  selector: 'article',
  template: `
    <h1>
      <ng-content></ng-content>{{articleTitle}}
    </h1>
    `
})
export class ArticleComponent {
  @Input() articleTitle:string;
}
```

Your objective is to use life cycle hooks to keep track of the process of adding and removing operations.

How to do it...

Angular allows you to import hook interfaces from the core module. These interfaces are manifested as class methods, which are invoked at the appropriate time:

```
[app/article.component.ts]

import {Component, Input, ngOnInit, ngOnDestroy}
  from '@angular/core';

@Component({
  selector: 'article',
  template: `
    <h1>
      <ng-content></ng-content>{{articleTitle}}
    </h1>
    `
})
export class ArticleComponent implements OnInit, OnDestroy {
  @Input() articleTitle:string;
  ngOnInit() {
    console.log('created', this.articleTitle);
  }
  ngOnDestroy() {
    console.log('destroyed', this.articleTitle);
  }
}
```

With this, you should see logs each time a new ArticleComponent is added or removed.

How it works...

Different hooks have different semantic meanings, but they will occur in a well-defined order. Each hook's execution guarantees that a certain behavior of a component is just completed.

The hooks that are currently available to you in the order of execution are as follows:

- ngOnChanges
- ngOnInit
- ngDoCheck
- ngAfterContentInit
- ngAfterContentChecked
- ngAfterViewInit
- ngAfterContentChecked
- ngOnDestroy

It is also possible for third-party libraries to extend these and add their own hooks.

There's more...

Using hooks is optional, and Angular will only invoke them if you have defined them. The use of the implements interface declaration is optional, but it will signal to the TypeScript compiler that a corresponding method should be expected, which is obviously a good practice.

See also

- *Referencing a parent component from a child component* describes how a component can gain a direct reference to its parent via injection
- *Configuring mutual parent-child awareness with ViewChild and forwardRef* instructs you on how to properly use ViewChild to reference child component object instances
- *Configuring mutual parent-child awareness with ContentChild and forwardRef* instructs you on how to properly use ContentChild to reference child component object instances

Referencing a parent component from a child component

In the course of building an application, you may encounter a scenario where it would be useful to reference a parent component from a child component, such as to inspect member data or invoke public methods. In Angular 2, this is actually quite easy to accomplish.

 The code, links, and a live example of this are available at
`http://ngcookbook.herokuapp.com/4907/`.

Getting ready

Suppose you begin with the following `ArticleComponent`:

```
[app/article.component.ts]

import {Component} from '@angular/core';

@Component({
  selector: 'article',
  template: `
    <feedback [val]="likes"></feedback>
  `
})
export class ArticleComponent {
  likes:number = 0;
  incrementLikes():void {
    this.likes++;
  }
}
```

Your objective is to implement the feedback component so that it displays the number of likes passed to it, but the parent component controls the actual like count and passes that value in.

How to do it...

Begin by implementing the basic structure of the child component:

```
[app/feedback.component.ts]

import {Component, Input} from '@angular/core';

@Component({
  selector: 'feedback',
  template: `
    <h1>Number of likes: {{ val }}</h1>
    <button (click)="likeArticle()">Like this article!</button>
  `
})
export class FeedbackComponent {
  @Input() val:number;
  likeArticle():void {}
}
```

So far, none of this should sound surprising. Clicking on the button invokes an empty method, and you want this method to invoke a method from the parent component. However, you currently lack a reference to do this. Listing the component in the child component constructor will make it available to you:

```
[app/feedback.component.ts]

import {Component, Input} from '@angular/core';
import {ArticleComponent} from './article.component';

@Component({
  selector: 'feedback',
  template: `
    <h1>Number of likes: {{ val }}</h1>
    <button (click)="like()">Like this article!</button>
  `
})
export class FeedbackComponent {
  @Input() val:number;
  private articleComponent:ArticleComponent;
  constructor(articleComponent:ArticleComponent) {
    this.articleComponent = articleComponent;
  }
  like():void {
    this.articleComponent.incrementLikes();
  }
}
```

With a reference to the parent component now available, you are easily able to invoke its public method, namely `incrementLikes()`. At this point, the two components should communicate correctly.

How it works...

Very simply, Angular 2 recognizes that you are injecting a component that is typed in the same way as the parent, and it will provide that parent for you. This is the full parent instance, and you are free to interact with it as you would normally interact with any component instance.

Notice that it is required that you store a reference to the component inside the constructor. Unlike when you inject a service, the child component will not automatically make the `ArticleComponent` instance available to you as `this.articleComponent`; you need to do this manually.

There's more...

An astute developer will notice that this creates a very rigid dependency from the child component to the parent component. This is indeed the case, but not necessarily a bad thing. Often, it is useful to allow components to more easily interact with each other at the expense of their modularity. And generally, this will be a judgment call on your part.

See also

- *Passing members from a parent component into a child component* goes through the basics of downward data flow between components
- *Registering handlers on native browser events* demonstrates how you can easily attach behavior to browser events
- *Generating and capturing custom events using EventEmitter* details how to propagate information upwards between components
- *Configuring mutual parent-child awareness with ViewChild and forwardRef* instructs you on how to properly use `ViewChild` to reference child component object instances

- *Configuring mutual parent-child awareness with ContentChild and forwardRef* instructs you on how to properly use `ContentChild` to reference child component object instances

Configuring mutual parent-child awareness with ViewChild and forwardRef

Depending on your application's separation of concerns, it might make sense for a child component in your application to reference a parent, and at the same time, for the parent to reference the child. There are two similar implementations that allow you to accomplish this: using `ViewChild` and `ContentChild`. This recipe will discuss them both.

 The code, links, and a live example of this are available at `http://ngcookbook.herokuapp.com/1315/`.

Getting ready

Begin with the recipe setup shown in *Referencing a parent component from a child component*. Your objective is to add the ability to enable and disable the like button from the parent component.

How to do it...

The initial setup only gives the child access to the parent, which is only half of what you need. The other half is to give the parent access to the child.

Getting a reference to `FeedbackComponent` that you see in the `ArticleComponent` template view can be done in two ways, and the first way demonstrated here will use `ViewChild`.

Configuring a ViewChild reference

Using `ViewChild` will allow you to extract a component reference from inside the view. More plainly, in this example, using `ViewChild` will give you the ability to reference the `FeedbackComponent` instance from inside the `ArticleComponent` code.

First, configure `ArticleComponent` so that it will retrieve the component reference:

```
[app/article.component.ts]

import {Component, ViewChild} from '@angular/core';
import {FeedbackComponent} from './feedback.component';

@Component({
  selector: 'article',
  template: `
    <input type="checkbox"
            (click)="changeLikesEnabled($event)">
    <feedback [val]="likes"></feedback>
  `
})
export class ArticleComponent {
  @ViewChild(FeedbackComponent)
    feedbackComponent:FeedbackComponent;
  likes:number = 0;
  incrementLikes():void {
    this.likes++;
  }
  changeLikesEnabled(e:Event):void {
    this.feedbackComponent.setLikeEnabled(e.target.checked);
  }
}
```

The main theme in this new code is that the `ViewChild` decorator implicitly understands that it should target the view of this component, find the instance of `FeedbackComponent` that is being rendered there, and assign it to the `feedbackCompnent` member of the `ArticleComponent` instance.

Correcting the dependency cycle with forwardRef

At this point, you should be seeing your application throwing new errors, most likely about being unable to resolve the parameters for `FeedbackComponent`. This occurs because you have set up a cyclic dependency: `FeedbackComponent` depends on `ArticleComponent` and `ArticleComponent` depends on `FeedbackComponent`. Thankfully, this problem exists in the domain of Angular dependency injection, so you don't really need the module, just a token that represents it. For this purpose, Angular 2 provides you with `forwardRef`, which allows you to use a module dependency inside your class definition before it is defined. Use it as follows:

```
[app/feedback.component.ts]
```

```
import {Component, Input, Inject, forwardRef}
   from '@angular/core';
import {ArticleComponent} from './article.component';

@Component({
  selector: 'feedback',
  template: `
    <h1>Number of likes: {{ val }}</h1>
    <button (click)="likeArticle()">
      Like this article!
    </button>
  `
})
export class FeedbackComponent {
  @Input() val:number;
  private articleComponent:ArticleComponent;
  constructor(@Inject(forwardRef(() => ArticleComponent))
      articleComponent:ArticleComponent) {

    this.articleComponent = articleComponent;
  }
  likeArticle():void {
    this.articleComponent.incrementLikes();
  }
}
```

Adding the disable behavior

With the cycle problem resolved, add the setLikeEnabled() method that the parent component is invoking:

```
[app/feedback.component.ts]

import {Component, Input, Inject, forwardRef}
   from '@angular/core';
import {ArticleComponent} from './article.component';

@Component({
  selector: 'feedback',
  template: `
    <h1>Number of likes: {{ val }}</h1>
    <button (click)="likeArticle()"
            [disabled]="!likeEnabled">
      Like this article!
    </button>
  `
})
```

```
export class FeedbackComponent {
  @Input() val:number;
  private likeEnabled:boolean = false;
  private articleComponent:ArticleComponent;
  constructor(@Inject(forwardRef(() => ArticleComponent))
      articleComponent:ArticleComponent) {

    this.articleComponent = articleComponent;
  }
  likeArticle():void {
    this.articleComponent.incrementLikes();
  }
  setLikeEnabled(newEnabledStatus:boolean):void {
    this.likeEnabled = newEnabledStatus;
  }
}
```

With this, toggling the checkbox should enable and disable the like button.

How it works...

`ViewChild` directs Angular to find the first instance of `FeedbackComponent` present inside the `ArticleComponent` view and assign it to the decorated class member. The reference will be updated along with any view updates. This decorated member will refer to the child component instance and can be interacted with like any normal object instance.

 It's important to remember the duality of the component instance and its representation in the template. For example, `FeedbackComponent` is represented by a feedback tag (pre-render) and a header tag and a button (post-render), but neither of these form the actual component. The `FeedbackComponent` instance is a JavaScript object that lives in the memory, and this is the object you want access to. If you just wanted a reference to the template elements, this could be accomplished by a template variable, for example.

There's more...

Since Angular performs hierarchical rendering, `ViewChild` will not be ready until the view is initialized, but rather, after the `AfterViewInit` life cycle hook. This can be demonstrated as follows:

```
[app/article.component.ts]
```

```
import {Component, ViewChild, ngAfterViewInit}
   from '@angular/core';
import {FeedbackComponent} from './feedback.component';

@Component({
  selector: 'article',
  template: `
    <input type="checkbox"
           (click)="changeLikesEnabled($event)">
    <feedback [val]="likes"></feedback>
  `
})
export class ArticleComponent implements AfterViewInit {
  @ViewChild(FeedbackComponent)
     feedbackComponent:FeedbackComponent;
  likes:number = 0;
  constructor() {
    console.log(this.feedbackComponent);
  }
  ngAfterViewInit() {
    console.log(this.feedbackComponent);
  }
  incrementLikes():void {
    this.likes++;
  }
  changeLikesEnabled(e:Event):void {
    this.feedbackComponent.setLikeEnabled(e.target.checked);
  }
}
```

This will first log undefined inside the constructor as the view, and therefore, FeedbackComponent does not yet exist. Once the AfterViewInit life cycle hook occurs, you will be able to see FeedbackComponent logged to the console.

ViewChildren

If you would like to get a reference to multiple components, you can perform an identical reference acquisition using ViewChildren, which will provide you with a QueryList of all the matching components in the view.

 A QueryList can be used like an array with its toArray() method. It also exposes a changes property, which emits an event every time a member of QueryList changes.

See also

- *Utilizing component lifecycle hooks* gives an example of how you can integrate with Angular 2's component rendering flow
- *Referencing a parent component from a child component* describes how a component can gain a direct reference to its parent via injection
- *Configuring mutual parent-child awareness with ContentChild and forwardRef* instructs you on how to properly use `ContentChild` to reference child component object instances

Configuring mutual parent-child awareness with ContentChild and forwardRef

The companion to Angular's `ViewChild` is `ContentChild`. It performs a similar duty; it retrieves a reference to the target child component and makes it available as a member of the parent component instance. The difference is that `ContentChild` retrieves the markup that exists inside the parent component's selector tags, whereas `ViewChild` retrieves the markup that exists inside the parent component's view.

The difference is best demonstrated by a comparison of behavior, so this recipe will convert the example from *Configuring Mutual Parent-Child Awareness with ViewChild and forwardRef* to use `ContentChild` instead.

 The code, links, and a live example of this are available at `http://ngcookbook.herokuapp.com/7386/`.

Getting ready

Begin with the code from the *Configuring mutual parent-child awareness with ViewChild and forwardRef* recipe.

How to do it...

Before you begin the conversion, you'll need to nest the `ArticleComponent` tags inside another root component, as `ContentChild` will not work for the root-level bootstrapped application component. Create a wrapped `RootComponent`:

```
[app/root.component.ts]

import {Component} from '@angular/core';

@Component({
  selector: 'root',
  template: `
    <article></article>
  `
})
export class RootComponent {}
```

Converting to ContentChild

`ContentChild` is introduced to components in essentially the same way as `ViewChild`. Inside `ArticleComponent`, perform this conversion and replace the `<feedback>` tag with `<ng-content>`:

```
[app/article.component.ts]

import {Component, ContentChild} from '@angular/core';
import {FeedbackComponent} from './feedback.component';

@Component({
  selector: 'article',
  template: `
    <input type="checkbox"
           (click)="changeLikesEnabled($event)">
    <ng-content></ng-content>
  `
})
export class ArticleComponent {
  @ContentChild(FeedbackComponent)
    feedbackComponent:FeedbackComponent;
  likes:number = 0;
  incrementLikes():void {
    this.likes++;
  }
  changeLikesEnabled(e:Event):void {
    this.feedbackComponent.setLikeEnabled(e.target.checked);
```

```
        }
    }
```

Of course, this will only be able to find the child component if the `<article></article>` tag has content inside of it:

```
[app/root.component.ts]

import {Component} from '@angular/core';

@Component({
  selector: 'root',
  template: `
    <article>
      <feedback></feedback>
    </article>
  `
})
export class RootComponent {}
```

 You'll notice that the like count value being passed to the child component as an input has been removed. Very simply, that convention will not work anymore, as binding it here would draw the like count from `RootComponent`, which does not have this information.

Correcting data binding

The `FeedbackComponent` will need to retrieve the like count directly:

```
[app/feedback.component.ts]

import {Component, Inject, forwardRef} from '@angular/core';
import {ArticleComponent} from './article.component';

@Component({
  selector: 'feedback',
  template: `
    <h1>Number of likes: {{ val }}</h1>
    <button (click)="likeArticle()"
            [disabled]="!likeEnabled">
      Like this article!
    </button>
  `
})
export class FeedbackComponent {
  private val:number;
```

```
    private likeEnabled:boolean = false;
    private articleComponent:ArticleComponent;
    constructor(@Inject(forwardRef(() => ArticleComponent))
        articleComponent:ArticleComponent) {

      this.articleComponent = articleComponent;
      this.updateLikes();
    }
    updateLikes() {
      this.val = this.articleComponent.likes;
    }
    likeArticle():void {
      this.articleComponent.incrementLikes();
      this.updateLikes();
    }
    setLikeEnabled(newEnabledStatus:boolean):void {
      this.likeEnabled = newEnabledStatus;
    }
  }
}
```

That's it! The application should behave identically to the setup from the *Getting ready* section of the recipe.

How it works...

ContentChild does nearly the same thing as ViewChild; it just looks in a different place. ContentChild directs Angular to find the first instance of FeedbackComponent present inside the ArticleComponent tags. Here, this step refers to anything that is interpolated by <ng-content>. It then assigns the found component instance to the decorated class member. The reference is updated along with any view updates. This decorated member will refer to the child component instance and can be interacted with like any normal object instance.

There's more...

Since Angular performs hierarchical rendering, ContentChild will not be ready until the view is initialized, but rather, after the AfterContentInit life cycle hook. This can be demonstrated as follows:

```
[app/article.component.ts]

import {Component, ContentChild, ngAfterContentInit}
  from '@angular/core';
```

```
import {FeedbackComponent} from './feedback.component';

@Component({
  selector: 'article',
  template: `
    <input type="checkbox"
           (click)="changeLikesEnabled($event)">
    <ng-content></ng-content>
  `
})
export class ArticleComponent implements AfterContentInit {
  @ContentChild(FeedbackComponent)
    feedbackComponent:FeedbackComponent;
  likes:number = 0;
  constructor() {
    console.log(this.feedbackComponent);
  }
  ngAfterContentInit() {
    console.log(this.feedbackComponent);
  }
  incrementLikes():void {
    this.likes++;
  }
  changeLikesEnabled(e:Event):void {
    this.feedbackComponent.setLikeEnabled(e.target.checked);
  }
}
```

This will first log undefined inside the constructor as the content, and therefore `FeedbackComponent` does not yet exist. Once the `AfterContentInit` life cycle hook occurs, you will be able to see `FeedbackComponent` logged to the console.

ContentChildren

If you would like to get a reference to multiple components, you can perform an identical reference acquisition process using `ContentChildren`, which will provide you with `QueryList` of all the matching components inside the component's tags.

A `QueryList` can be used like an array with its `toArray()` method. It also exposes a changes property, which emits an event every time a member of `QueryList` changes.

See also

- *Utilizing component lifecycle hooks* gives an example of how you can integrate with Angular 2's component rendering flow.
- *Referencing a parent component from a child component* describes how a component can gain a direct reference to its parent via injection.
- *Configuring mutual parent-child awareness with ViewChild and forwardRef* instructs you on how to properly use `ViewChild` to reference child component object instances.

3
Building Template-Driven and Reactive Forms

This chapter will cover the following recipes:

- Implementing simple two-way data binding with ngModel
- Implementing basic field validation with a FormControl
- Bundling FormControls with a FormGroup
- Bundling FormControls with a FormArray
- Implementing basic forms with ngForm
- Implementing basic forms with FormBuilder and formControlName
- Creating and using a custom validator
- Creating and using a custom asynchronous validator with Promises

Introduction

Forms are important elemental constructs for nearly every web application, and they have been reimagined for the better in Angular 2. Angular 1 forms were very useful, but they were totally dependent on the conventions of ngModel. Angular 2's newfound conventions remove it from ngModel dependence and offer a fresh approach to form and information management that ultimately feels cleaner and more approachable.

Fundamentally, it is important to understand where and why forms are useful. There are many places in an application where multitudinous input demands association, and forms are certainly useful in this context. Angular 2 forms are best used when validating the said input, especially so when multiple-field and cross-field validation is required. Additionally, Angular forms maintain the state of various form elements, allowing the user to reason the "history" of an input field.

It is also critical to remember that the Angular 2 form behavior, much in the same way as its event and data binding, is getting integrated with the already robust browser form behavior. Browsers are already very capable of submitting data, recalling data upon a page reload, simple validation, and other behaviors that pretty much all forms rely upon. Angular 2 doesn't redefine these; rather, it integrates with these behaviors in order to link in other behaviors and data that are part of either a framework or your application.

In this chapter, be aware of the duality of the use of `FormsModule` and `ReactiveFormsModule`. They behave very differently and are almost always used separately when it comes to form construction.

Implementing simple two-way data binding with ngModel

Angular 2 still has two-way data binding, but the way it behaves is a bit different than what you're used to. This recipe will begin with a very simple example and then break it down into pieces to describe what it's actually doing.

The code, links, and a live example related to this recipe are available at `http://ngcookbook.herokuapp.com/0771/`.

How to do it...

Two-way data binding uses the `ngModel` directive, which is included in `FormsModule`. Add this directive to your application module:

```
[app/app.module.ts]

import {NgModule} from '@angular/core';
import {BrowserModule} from '@angular/platform-browser';
```

```
import {FormsModule} from '@angular/forms';
import {ArticleEditorComponent} from './article-editor.component';

@NgModule({
  imports: [
    BrowserModule,
    FormsModule
  ],
  declarations: [
    ArticleEditorComponent
  ],
  bootstrap: [
    ArticleEditorComponent
  ]
})
export class AppModule {}
```

Next, flesh out your component, which will have two instances of input bound to the same component member using ngModel:

```
[app/article-editor.component.ts]

import {Component} from '@angular/core';

@Component({
  selector: 'article-editor',
  template: `
    <input [(ngModel)]="title">
    <input [(ngModel)]="title">
    <h2>{{title}}</h2>
  `
})
export class ArticleEditorComponent {
  title:string;
}
```

That's all that's required! You should see input modifications instantly reflected in the other input as well as in <h2> itself.

How it works...

What you're really doing is binding to the event and property that ngModel associates with this input. When the component's title member changes, the input is bound to that value and will update its own value. When the input's value changes, it emits an event, which ngModel will bind to and extract the value from before propagating it to the component's title member.

 The *banana-in-a-box* syntax [()] is simply indicative of the binding done to both the input property with [] and the input events with ().

In reality, this is shorthand for the following:

```
[app/article-editor.component.ts]

import {Component} from '@angular/core';

@Component({
  selector: 'article-editor',
  template: `
    <input [ngModel]="title" (ngModelChange)="title=$event">
    <input [ngModel]="title" (ngModelChange)="title=$event">
    <h2>{{title}}</h2>
  `
})
export class ArticleEditorComponent {
  title:string;
}
```

You will find that this behaves identically to what we discussed before.

There's more...

You might still find that there's a bit too much syntactical sugar happening here for your taste. You're binding to ngModel, but somehow, it is equivalent to the input value. Similarly, you're binding to ngModelChange events, which are all emitting a $event that appears to be only a string.

This is indeed correct. The ngModel directive understands what it is a part of and is able to integrate [ngModel] and (ngModelChange) correctly to associate the desired bindings.

The core of these bindings is essentially doing the following:

```
[app/article-editor.component.ts]

import {Component} from '@angular/core';

@Component({
  selector: 'article-editor',
  template: `
    <input [value]="title" (input)="title=$event.target.value">
    <input [value]="title" (input)="title=$event.target.value">
    <h2>{{title}}</h2>
  `
})
export class ArticleEditorComponent {
  // Initialize title, otherwise you'll get "undefined"
  title:string = '';
}
```

See also

- *Implementing simple two-way data binding with ngModel* demonstrates the new way in Angular 2 to control bidirectional data flow
- *Implementing basic field validation with a FormControl* details the basic building block of an Angular form
- *Bundling FormControls with a FormGroup* shows how to combine FormControls
- *Bundling FormControls with a FormArray* shows how to handle iterable form elements
- *Implementing basic forms with ngForm* demonstrates Angular's declarative form construction
- *Implementing basic forms with FormBuilder and formControlName* shows how to use the FormBuilder service to quickly put together nested forms
- *Creating and using a custom validator* demonstrates how to create a custom directive that behaves as input validation
- *Creating and using a custom asynchronous validator with Promises* shows how Angular allows you to have a delayed evaluation of a form state

Implementing basic field validation with a FormControl

The simplest form behavior imaginable would be the validation of a single input field. Most of the time, utilizing `<form>` tags and going through the rest of the boilerplate is good practice, but for the purpose of checking a single input, it's preferable to distill this down to the bare minimum required in order to use input checking.

 The code, links, and a live example related to this recipe are available at `http://ngcookbook.herokuapp.com/4076/`.

Getting ready

Suppose the following is your initial setup:

```
[app/article-editor.component.ts]

import {Component} from '@angular/core';

@Component({
  selector: 'article-editor',
  template: `
    <p>Article title (required):</p>
    <input required>
    <button>Save</button>
    <h1>{{title}}</h1>
  `
})
export class ArticleEditorComponent {
  title:string;
}
```

Your goal is to change this in a way that clicking the save button will validate the input and update the `title` member only if it is valid.

How to do it...

The most elemental component of Angular forms is the `FormControl` object. In order to be able to assess the state of the field, you first need to instantiate this object inside the component and associate it with the field using the `formControl` directive. `FormControl` lives inside `ReactiveFormsModule`. Add it as a module import:

```
[app/app.module.ts]

import {NgModule} from '@angular/core';
import {BrowserModule} from '@angular/platform-browser';
import {ReactiveFormsModule} from '@angular/forms';
import {ArticleEditorComponent} from './article-editor.component';

@NgModule({
  imports: [
    BrowserModule,
    ReactiveFormsModule
  ],
  declarations: [
    ArticleEditorComponent
  ],
  bootstrap: [
    ArticleEditorComponent
  ]
})
export class AppModule {}
```

With this, you can use `FormControl` inside `ArticleEditorComponent`. Instantiate `FormControl` inside the component and bind the input element to it using the `formControl` directive:

```
[app/article-editor.component.ts]

import {Component} from '@angular/core';
import {FormControl} from '@angular/forms';

@Component({
  selector: 'article-editor',
  template: `
    <p>Article title (required):</p>
    <input [formControl]="titleControl" required>
    <button>Save</button>
    <h1>{{title}}</h1>


  `
})
```

```
export class ArticleEditorComponent  {
  title:string;
  titleControl:FormControl = new FormControl();
}
```

Now that you have created a `FormControl` object and associated it with an input field, you will be able to use its validation API to check the state of the field. All that is left is to use it inside the submit click handler:

```
[app/article-editor.component.ts]

import {Component} from '@angular/core';
import {FormControl} from '@angular/forms';

@Component({
  selector: 'article-editor',
  template: `
    <p>Article title (required):</p>
    <input [formControl]="titleControl" required>
    <button (click)="submitTitle()">Save</button>
    <h1>{{title}}</h1>

    `
})
export class ArticleEditorComponent  {
  title:string;
  titleControl:FormControl = new FormControl();
  submitTitle():void {
    if(this.titleControl.valid) {
      this.title = this.titleControl.value;
    } else {
      alert("Title required");
    }
  }
}
```

With this, the submit click handler will be able to check the input's validation state and value with the same object.

How it works...

The `formControl` directive serves only to bind an existing `FormControl` object to a DOM element. The `FormControl` object that you instantiate inside the component constructor can either utilize validation attributes inside an HTML tag (as is done in this example), or accept Angular validators when initialized; or, it can do both.

It's extremely important to note that just because the `FormControl` object is instantiated, it does not mean that it is able to validate the input immediately.

Without an initialized value, an empty input field will begin its life with a value of `null`, which in the presence of a `required` attribute is of course invalid. However, in this example, if you were to check whether the `FormControl` object becomes valid immediately after you instantiate it in the constructor, the `FormControl` object would dutifully inform you that the state is valid since it has not been bound to the DOM element yet, and therefore, no validations are being violated. Since the input element's `formControl` binding will not occur until the component template becomes part of the actual DOM, you will not be able to check the input state until the binding is complete or inside the `ngAfterContentChecked` life cycle hook. Note that this pertains to the example under consideration.

Once the `formControl` directive completes the binding, the `FormControl` object will exist as an input wrapper, allowing you to use its `valid` and `value` members.

There's more...

This recipe uses `ReactiveFormsModule`, which is simpler to understand since all of the setup is explicit. When you use `FormsModule` instead, you discover that a lot of what is accomplished in this recipe could be done automatically for you, such as the instantiation and binding of `FormControl` objects. It also revolves around the presence of a `<form>` tag, which is the de facto top-level `FormControl` container. This recipe serves to demonstrate one of the simplest forms of Angular form behavior.

Validators and attribute duality

As mentioned in this recipe, validation definitions can come from two places. Here, you used a standardized HTML tag attribute that Angular recognizes and automatically incorporates into the `FormControl` validation specification. You could have just as easily elected to utilize an Angular `Validator` to accomplish the same task instead. This can be accomplished by importing Angular's default `Validators` and initializing the `FormControl` object with the `required` validator:

```
[app/article-editor.component.ts]

import {Component} from '@angular/core';
```

```
import {FormControl, Validators} from '@angular/forms';

@Component({
  selector: 'article-editor',
  template: `
    <p>Article title (required):</p>
    <input [formControl]="titleControl">
    <button (click)="submitTitle()">Save</button>
    <h1>{{title}}</h1>


  `
})
export class ArticleEditorComponent  {
  title:string;
  // First argument is the default input value
  titleControl:FormControl =
    new FormControl(null, Validators.required);

  submitTitle():void {
    if(this.titleControl.valid) {
      this.title = this.titleControl.value;
    } else {
      alert("Title required");
    }
  }
}
```

Tagless controls

As you might suspect, there is no reason a `FormControl` must be bound to a DOM element. `FormControl` is an elemental piece of form logic that acts as an atomic piece of stateful information, whether or not this information is derived from `<input>`. Say you wanted to add a `FormControl` that would prevent quick form submission by only becoming valid after 10 seconds. You could explicitly create a `FormControl` object that would tie into the combined form validation but would not be associated with a DOM element.

See also

- *Implementing simple two-way data binding with ngModel* demonstrates the new way in Angular 2 to control bidirectional data flow
- *Bundling FormControls with a FormGroup* shows how to combine FormControl objects

- *Bundling FormControls with a FormArray* shows how to handle iterable form elements

Bundling controls with a FormGroup

Naturally, forms in applications frequently exist to aggregate multiple instances of input into a unified behavior. One common behavior is to assess whether a form is valid, which of course requires that all of its subfields are valid. This will most commonly be achieved by bundling multiple `FormControl` objects into a `FormGroup`. This can be done in different ways, with varying degrees of explicitness. This recipe covers an entirely explicit implementation, that is, everything here will be created and "joined" manually.

 The code, links, and a live example related to this recipe are available at `http://ngcookbook.herokuapp.com/3052`.

Getting ready

Suppose you began with the following skeleton application:

```
[app/article-editor.component.ts]

import {Component} from '@angular/core';

@Component({
  selector: 'article-editor',
  template: `
    <p>Title: <input></p>
    <p>Text: <input></p>
    <p><button (click)="saveArticle()">Save</button></p>
    <hr />
    <p>Preview:</p>
    <div style="border:1px solid #999;margin:50px;">
      <h1>{{article.title}}</h1>
      <p>{{article.text}}</p>
    </div>
  `
})
export class ArticleEditorComponent {
  article:{title:string, text:string} = {};
```

```
    saveArticle():void {}
  }
```

Your goal is to update the `article` object (and consequently the template) only if all the input fields are valid.

How to do it...

First, add the necessary code to attach new `FormControl` objects to each input field and validate them with the built-in `required` validator:

```
[app/article-editor.component.ts]

import {Component} from '@angular/core';
import {FormControl, Validators}
  from '@angular/forms';

@Component({
  selector: 'article-editor',
  template: `
    <p>Title: <input [formControl]="titleControl"></p>
    <p>Text: <input [formControl]="textControl"></p>
    <p><button (click)="saveArticle()">Save</button></p>
    <hr />
    <p>Preview:</p>
    <div style="border:1px solid #999;margin:50px;">
      <h1>{{article.title}}</h1>
      <p>{{article.text}}</p>
    </div>
  `
})
export class ArticleEditorComponent {
  article:{title:string, text:string} = {};
  titleControl:FormControl
    = new FormControl(null, Validators.required);
  textControl:FormControl
    = new FormControl(null, Validators.required);

  saveArticle():void {}
}
```

At this point, you could individually inspect each input's `FormControl` object and check whether it is valid. However, if this form grows to 100 fields, it would become unbearably tedious to maintain them. Therefore, you can bundle these `FormControl` objects into a single `FormGroup` instead:

```
[app/article-editor.component.ts]

import {Component} from '@angular/core';
import {FormControl, FormGroup, Validators}
  from '@angular/forms';

@Component({
  selector: 'article-editor',
  template: `
    <p>Title: <input [formControl]="titleControl"></p>
    <p>Text: <input [formControl]="textControl"></p>
    <p><button (click)="saveArticle()">Save</button></p>
    <hr />
    <p>Preview:</p>
    <div style="border:1px solid #999;margin:50px;">
      <h1>{{article.title}}</h1>
      <p>{{article.text}}</p>
    </div>
    `
})
export class ArticleEditorComponent {
  article:{title:string, text:string} = {};
  titleControl:FormControl
    = new FormControl(null, Validators.required);
  textControl:FormControl
    = new FormControl(null, Validators.required);
  articleFormGroup:FormGroup = new FormGroup({
    title: this.titleControl,
    text: this.textControl
  });

  saveArticle():void {}
}
```

`FormGroup` **objects also expose valid and value members, so you can use these to verify and assign directly from the object:**

```
[app/article-editor.component.ts]

import {Component} from '@angular/core';
import {FormControl, FormGroup, Validators}
  from '@angular/forms';

@Component({
  selector: 'article-editor',
  template: `
    <p>Title: <input [formControl]="titleControl"></p>
    <p>Text: <input [formControl]="textControl"></p>
```

```
      <p><button (click)="saveArticle()">Save</button></p>
      <hr />
      <p>Preview:</p>
      <div style="border:1px solid #999;margin:50px;">
        <h1>{{article.title}}</h1>
        <p>{{article.text}}</p>
      </div>
      `
})
export class ArticleEditorComponent {
  article:{title:string, text:string} = {};
  titleControl:FormControl
    = new FormControl(null, Validators.required);
  textControl:FormControl
    = new FormControl(null, Validators.required);
  articleFormGroup:FormGroup = new FormGroup({
    title: this.titleControl,
    text: this.textControl
  });

  saveArticle():void {
    if (this.articleFormGroup.valid) {
      this.article = this.articleFormGroup.value;
    } else {
      alert("Missing field(s)!");
    }
  }
}
```

With this addition, your form should now be working fine.

How it works...

Both `FormControl` and `FormGroup` inherit from the abstract base class called `AbstractControl`. What this means for you is that both of them expose the same base class methods, but `FormGroup` will aggregate its composition of `AbstractControl` objects to be read from its own members. As you can see in the preceding code, `valid` acts as a logical AND operator for all the children (meaning every single child must return `true` for it to return `true`); `value` returns an object of the same topology as the one provided at the instantiation of `FormGroup`, but with each `FormControl` value instead of the `FormControl` object.

As you might expect, since `FormGroup` expects an object with `AbstractControl` properties, you are free to nest a `FormGroup` inside another `FormGroup`.

There's more…

You are able to access a `FormGroup`'s contained `FormControl` members via the `controls` property. The string that you used to key the `FormControl` members—either upon `FormGroup` instantiation, or with the `addControl` method—is used to retrieve it. In this example, the `text FormControl` object could be retrieved inside a component method via `this.articleCtrlGroup.controls.text`.

 The Angular documentation warns you to specifically not to modify the underlying `FormControl` collection directly. This may lead to an undefined data binding behavior. So, always be sure to use the `FormGroup` member methods `addControl` and `removeControl` instead of directly manipulating the collection of `FormControl` objects that you pass upon instantiation.

FormGroup validators

Like `Control`, a `FormGroup` can have its own validators. These can be provided when the `FormGroup` is instantiated, and they behave in the same way that a `FormControl` validator would behave. By adding validators at the `FormGroup` level, `FormGroup` can override the default behavior of only being valid when all its components are valid or adding extra validation clauses.

Error propagation

Angular validators not only have the ability to determine whether they are valid or not, but they are also capable of returning error messages describing what is wrong. For example, when the input fields are empty, if you were to examine the `errors` property of the `text FormControl` object via `this.articleCtrlGroup.controls.text.errors`, it would return `{required: true}`. This is the default error message of the built-in required validator. However, if you were to inspect the `errors` property on the parent `FormGroup` via `this.articleCtrlGroup.errors`, you will find it to be `null`.

This may be counter-intuitive, but it is not a mistake. Error messages will only appear on the `FormControl` instance that is causing them. If you wish to aggregate error messages, you will have to traverse the nested collections of `FormControl` objects manually.

See also

- *Implementing simple two-way data binding with ngModel* demonstrates the new way in Angular 2 to control bidirectional data flow
- *Implementing basic field validation with a FormControl* details the basic building block of an Angular form
- *Bundling FormControls with a FormArray* shows how to handle iterable form elements

Bundling FormControls with a FormArray

You will most likely find that `FormGroups` are more than capable of serving your needs for the purpose of combining many `FormControl` objects into one container. However, there is one very common pattern that makes its sister type, the `FormArray`, extremely useful: variable length cloned inputs.

 The code, links, and a live example related to this recipe are available at `http://ngcookbook.herokuapp.com/2816/`.

Getting ready

Suppose you had the following skeleton application:

```
[app/article-editor.component.ts]

import {Component} from '@angular/core';
import {FormControl, Validators}
  from '@angular/forms';

@Component({
  selector: 'article-editor',
  template: `
    <p>Tags:</p>
```

```
    <ul>
      <li *ngFor="let t of tagControls; let i = index">
        <input [formControl]="t">
      </li>
    </ul>
    <p><button (click)="addTag()">+</button></p>
    <p><button (click)="saveArticle()">Save</button></p>
  `
})
export class ArticleEditorComponent {
  tagControls:Array<FormControl> = [];
  addTag():void {}
  saveArticle():void {}
}
```

Your objective is to modify this component so that an arbitrary number of tags can be added and so all the tags can be validated together.

How to do it...

In many ways, a `FormArray` behaves more or less identically to a `FormGroup`. It is imported in the same way and inherited from `AbstractControl`. Also, it is instantiated in a similar way and can add and remove `FormControl` instances. First, add the boilerplate to your application; this will allow you to instantiate an instance of a `FormArray` and pass it the array of `FormControl` objects already inside the component. Since you already have a button that is meant to invoke the `addTag` method, you should also configure this method to push a new `FormControl` on to `tagControl`:

```
[app/article-editor.component.ts]

import {Component} from '@angular/core';
import {FormControl, FormArray, Validators}
  from '@angular/forms';

@Component({
  selector: 'article-editor',
  template: `
    <p>Tags:</p>
    <ul>
      <li *ngFor="let t of tagControls; let i = index">
        <input [formControl]="t">
      </li>
    </ul>
    <p><button (click)="addTag()">+</button></p>
    <p><button (click)="saveArticle()">Save</button></p>
```

```
})
export class ArticleEditorComponent {
  tagControls:Array<FormControl> = [];
  tagFormArray:FormArray = new FormArray(this.tagControls);
  addTag():void {
    this.tagFormArray
      .push(new FormControl(null, Validators.required));
  }
  saveArticle():void {}
}
```

 At this point, it's important that you don't confuse yourself with what you are working with. Inside this ArticleEditor component, you have an array of FormControl objects (tagControls) and you also have a single instance of FormArray (tagFormArray). The FormArray instance is initialized by being passed the array of FormControl objects, which it will then be able to manage.

Now that your FormArray is managing the tag's FormControl objects, you can safely use its validator:

```
[app/article-editor.component.ts]

import {Component} from '@angular/core';
import {FormControl, FormArray, Validators}
  from '@angular/forms';

@Component({
  selector: 'article-editor',
  template: `
    <p>Tags:</p>
    <ul>
      <li *ngFor="let t of tagControls; let i = index">
        <input [formControl]="t">
      </li>
    </ul>
    <p><button (click)="addTag()">+</button></p>
    <p><button (click)="saveArticle()">Save</button></p>
  `
})
export class ArticleEditorComponent {
  tagControls:Array<FormControl> = [];
  tagFormArray:FormArray = new FormArray(this.tagControls);
  addTag():void {
    this.tagFormArray
      .push(new FormControl(null, Validators.required));
```

```
    }
    saveArticle():void {
      if (this.tagFormArray.valid) {
        alert('Valid!');
      } else {
        alert('Missing field(s)!');
      }
    }
  }
```

How it works...

Because the template is reacting to the `click` event, you are able to use Angular data binding to automatically update the template. However, it is extremely important that you note the asymmetry in this example. The template is iterating through the `tagControls` array. However, when you want to add a new `FormControl` object, you push it to `tagFormArray`, which will in turn push it to the `tagControls` array. The `FormArray` object acts as the manager of the collection of `FormControl` objects, and all modifications of this collection should go through the manager, not the collection itself.

The Angular documentation warns you to specifically not modify the underlying `FormControl` collection directly. This may lead to undefined data binding behavior, so always be sure to use the `FormArray` members `push`, `insert`, and `removeAt` instead of directly manipulating the array of `FormControl` objects that you pass upon instantiation.

There's more...

You can take this example one step further by adding the ability to remove from this list as well. Since you already have the index inside the template repeater and `FormArray` offers index-based removal, this is simple to implement:

```
[app/article-editor.component.ts]

import {Component} from '@angular/core';
import {FormControl, FormArray, Validators}
  from '@angular/forms';

@Component({
  selector: 'article-editor',
  template: `
    <p>Tags:</p>
```

[117]

```
        <ul>
          <li *ngFor="let t of tagControls; let i = index">
            <input [formControl]="t">
            <button (click)="removeTag(i)">X</button>
          </li>
        </ul>
        <p><button (click)="addTag()">+</button></p>
        <p><button (click)="saveArticle()">Save</button></p>
      `
})
export class ArticleEditorComponent {
  tagControls:Array<FormControl> = [];
  tagFormArray:FormArray = new FormArray(this.tagControls);
  addTag():void {
    this.tagFormArray
      .push(new FormControl(null, Validators.required));
  }
  removeTag(idx:number):void {
    this.tagFormArray.removeAt(idx);
  }
  saveArticle():void {
    if (this.tagFormArray.valid) {
      alert('Valid!');
    } else {
      alert('Missing field(s)!');
    }
  }
}
```

This allows you to cleanly insert and remove FormControl instances while letting Angular data binding do all of the work for you.

See also

- *Implementing simple two-way data binding with ngModel* demonstrates the new way in Angular 2 to control bidirectional data flow
- *Implementing basic forms with ngForm* demonstrates Angular's declarative form construction
- *Implementing basic forms with FormBuilder and formControlName* shows how to use the FormBuilder service to quickly put together nested forms

Implementing basic forms with NgForm

The basic denominations of Angular forms are `FormControl`, `FormGroup`, and `FormArray` objects. However, it is often not directly necessary to use these objects at all; Angular provides mechanisms with which you can implicitly create and assign these objects and attach them to the form's DOM elements.

 The code, links, and a live example related to this recipe are available at `http://ngcookbook.herokuapp.com/5116/`.

Getting ready

Suppose you began with the following skeleton application:

```
[app/article-editor.component.ts]

import {Component} from '@angular/core';

@Component({
  selector: 'article-editor',
  template: `
    <p><input placeholder="Article title"></p>
    <p><textarea placeholder="Article text"></textarea></p>
    <p><button (click)="saveArticle()">Save</button></p>
  `
})
export class ArticleEditorComponent {
  saveArticle():void {}
}
```

Your objective is to collect all of the form data and submit it using Angular's form constructs.

How to do it...

You should begin by reorganizing this into an actual browser form. Angular gives you a lot of directives and components for this, and importing the `FormsModule` will give you access to all the ones you need most of the time:

```
[app/app.module.ts]
```

```
import {NgModule} from '@angular/core';
import {BrowserModule} from '@angular/platform-browser';
import {FormsModule} from '@angular/forms';
import {ArticleEditorComponent} from './article-editor.component';

@NgModule({
  imports: [
    BrowserModule,
    FormsModule
  ],
  declarations: [
    ArticleEditorComponent
  ],
  bootstrap: [
    ArticleEditorComponent
  ]
})
export class AppModule {}
```

In addition, you should reconfigure the button so it becomes an actual `submit` button. The handler should be triggered when the form is submitted, so you can reattach the listener to the form's native `submit` event instead of the button's `click` event. Angular provides an `ngSubmit EventEmitter` on top of this event, so go ahead and attach the listener to this:

```
[app/article-editor.component.ts]

import {Component} from '@angular/core';

@Component({
  selector: 'article-editor',
  template: `
    <form (ngSubmit)="saveArticle()">
      <p><input placeholder="Article title"></p>
      <p><textarea placeholder="Article text"></textarea></p>
      <p><button type="submit">Save</button></p>
    </form>
  `
})
export class ArticleEditorComponent {
  saveArticle():void {}
}
```

Next, you should configure the form to pass the form data to the handler through a template variable.

The form element will have an `NgForm` object (and inside this, a `FormGroup`) automatically associated with it when you import `FormsModule` into the encompassing module. Angular creates and associates the `NgForm` instance behind the scenes.

One way you can access this instance is by assigning the `ngForm` directive as a template variable. It's a bit of syntactical magic, but using `#f="ngForm"` signals to Angular that you want to be able to reference the form's `NgForm` from the template using the `f` variable.

Once you declare the template variable, you are able to pass the `ngForm` instance to the submit handler as an argument, specifically as `saveArticle(f)`.

This leaves you with the following:

```
[app/article-editor.component.ts]
import {Component} from '@angular/core';
import {NgForm} from '@angular/forms';

@Component({
  selector: 'article-editor',
  template: `
    <form #f="ngForm"
          (ngSubmit)="saveArticle(f)">
      <p><input placeholder="Article title"></p>
      <p><textarea placeholder="Article text"></textarea></p>
      <p><button type="submit">Save</button></p>
    </form>
    `
})
export class ArticleEditorComponent {
  saveArticle(f:NgForm):void {
    console.log(f);
  }
}
```

When you test this manually, you should see your browser logging an `NgForm` object every time you click on the Save button. Inside this object, you should see a shiny new `FormGroup` and also the `ngSubmit EventEmitter` that you are listening to. So far, so good!

Declaring form fields with ngModel

You may have noticed that none of the form fields have been collected. This, of course, is because Angular has not been instructed to pay attention to them. For this, FormsModule provides you with ngModel, which will do certain things for you:

- Instantiate a FormControl object.
- Attach it to the DOM element that incorporates the ngModel attribute.
- Locate the FormGroup that the element lives inside and add to it the FormControl it just created. The string value of the name attribute will be its key inside the FormGroup.

 This last bullet is important, as attempting to use ngModel without an encompassing form control construct to attach itself to will result in errors. This form control construct can be the form's FormGroup itself, or it can even be a child FormGroup instance.

With this, go ahead and add ngModel to each of the text input fields:

```
import {Component} from '@angular/core';
import {NgForm} from '@angular/forms';

@Component({
  selector: 'article-editor',
  template: `
    <form #f="ngForm"
          (ngSubmit)="saveArticle(f)">
      <p><input ngModel
                name="title"
                placeholder="Article title"></p>
      <p><textarea ngModel
                   name="text"
                   placeholder="Article text"></textarea></p>
      <p><button type="submit">Save</button></p>
    </form>
  `
})
export class ArticleEditorComponent {
  saveArticle(f:NgForm):void {
    console.log(f);
  }
}
```

Your form should now be fully functional. In the submit handler, you can verify that `FormGroup` has two `FormControl` objects attached to it by inspecting `f.form.controls`, which should give you the following:

```
{
  text: FormControl { ... },
  title: FormControl { ... }
}
```

How it works...

In essence, you are using the hierarchical nature of the DOM to direct how your `FormControl` architecture is structured. The topmost `NgForm` instance is coupled with a `FormGroup`; inside this, the rest of the form's `FormControl` objects will reside.

Each `ngModel` directs its referenced `FormControl` to the `FormGroup` owned by the `NgForm` instance. With this nested structure now assembled, it is possible to read and reason the state of the entire form from the `NgForm` object. This being the case, passing this object to the submit handler will allow you to manage every aspect of form inspection and validation.

There's more...

If, instead, you wanted to group some of these fields together, this can be accomplished by simply wrapping them with an `ngModelGroup` directive. Similar to `ngModel`, this automatically instantiates a `FormGroup` and attaches it to the parent `FormGroup`; also, it will add any enclosed `FormControl` or `FormGroup` objects to itself. For example, refer to the following:

```
[app/article.component.ts]

import {Component} from '@angular/core';
import {NgForm} from '@angular/forms';

@Component({
  selector: 'article-editor',
  template: `
    <form #f="ngForm"
          (ngSubmit)="saveArticle(f)">
      <div ngModelGroup="article">
        <p><input ngModel
                  name="title"
```

```
                        placeholder="Article title"></p>
            <p><textarea ngModel
                        name="text"
                        placeholder="Article text"></textarea></p>
        </div>
        <p><button type="submit">Save</button></p>
    </form>
    `
})
export class ArticleEditorComponent {
    saveArticle(f:NgForm):void {
        console.log(f);
    }
}
```

Now, inspecting `f.form.controls` will reveal that it has a single `FormGroup` keyed by article:

```
{
    article: FormGroup: {
        controls: {
            text: FormControl { ... },
            title: FormControl { ... }
        },
        ...
    }
}
```

Since this matches the structure you set up in the template, it checks out.

See also

- *Implementing simple two-way data binding with ngModel* demonstrates the new way in Angular 2 to control bidirectional data flow
- *Implementing basic forms with FormBuilder and formControlName* shows how to use the FormBuilder service to quickly put together nested forms

Implementing basic forms with FormBuilder and formControlName

Out of the box, Angular provides a way for you to put together forms that don't rely on the template hierarchy for definition. Instead, you can use `FormBuilder` to explicitly define how you want to structure the form objects and then manually attach them to each input.

 The code, links, and a live example related to this recipe are available at `http://ngcookbook.herokuapp.com/9302/`.

Getting ready

Suppose you began with the following skeleton application:

```
[app/article-editor.component.ts]

import {Component} from '@angular/core';

@Component({
  selector: 'article-editor',
  template: `
    <p><input placeholder="Article title"></p>
    <p><textarea placeholder="Article text"></textarea></p>
    <p><button (click)="saveArticle()">Save</button></p>
  `
})
export class ArticleEditorComponent {
  constructor() {}
  saveArticle():void {}
}
```

Your objective is to collect all of the form data and submit it using Angular's form constructs.

How to do it...

`FormBuilder` is included in `ReactiveFormsModule`, so you will need to import these targets into the application module:

```
[app/app.module.ts]
```

```
import {NgModule} from '@angular/core';
import {BrowserModule} from '@angular/platform-browser';
import {ReactiveFormsModule} from '@angular/forms';
import {ArticleEditorComponent} from './article-editor.component';

@NgModule({
  imports: [
    BrowserModule,
    ReactiveFormsModule
  ],
  declarations: [
    ArticleEditorComponent
  ],
  bootstrap: [
    ArticleEditorComponent
  ]
})
export class AppModule {}
```

Additionally, you will need to inject it into your component to make use of it. In Angular 2, this can simply be accomplished by listing it as a typed constructor parameter. The `FormBuilder` uses the `group()` method to return the top-level `FormGroup`, which you should assign to your component instance. For now, you will pass an empty object as its only argument.

With all this, you can integrate the `articleGroup` `FormGroup` into the template by attaching it inside a `form` tag using the `formGroup` directive:

```
[app/article-editor.component.ts]

import {Component, Inject} from '@angular/core';
import {FormBuilder, FormGroup} from '@angular/forms';

@Component({
  selector: 'article-editor',
  template: `
    <form [formGroup]="articleGroup"
          (ngSubmit)="saveArticle()">
      <p><input placeholder="Article title"></p>
      <p><textarea placeholder="Article text"></textarea></p>
      <p><button type="submit">Save</button></p>
    </form>
  `
})
export class ArticleEditorComponent {
  articleGroup:FormGroup;
```

```
    constructor(@Inject(FormBuilder) formBuilder:FormBuilder) {
      this.articleGroup = formBuilder.group({});
    }
    saveArticle():void {}
  }
```

With all this, you have successfully created the structure for your form, but `FormGroup` is still not connected to the multiple input. For this, you will first set up the structure of the controls inside the builder and consequently attach them to each `input` tag with `formControlName`, as follows:

```
[app/article-editor.component.ts]

import {Component, Inject} from '@angular/core';
import {FormBuilder, FormGroup, Validators} from '@angular/forms';

@Component({
  selector: 'article-editor',
  template: `
    <form [formGroup]="articleGroup"
          (ngSubmit)="saveArticle()">
      <p><input formControlName="title"
                placeholder="Article title"></p>
      <p><textarea formControlName="text"
                   placeholder="Article text"></textarea></p>
      <p><button type="submit">Save</button></p>
    </form>
  `
})
export class ArticleEditorComponent {
  articleGroup:FormGroup;

  constructor(@Inject(FormBuilder) formBuilder:FormBuilder) {
    this.articleGroup = formBuilder.group({
      title: [null, Validators.required],
      text: [null, Validators.required]
    });
  }
  saveArticle():void {
    console.log(this.articleGroup);
  }
}
```

With this, your form will have two `FormControl` objects instantiated inside it, and they will be associated with proper `input` elements. When you click on **Submit**, you will be able to see the input `FormControls` inside `FormGroup`. However, you may prefer to namespace these `FormControl` objects inside an `article` designation, and you can easily do this by introducing an `ngFormGroup` and a corresponding level of indirection inside the `formBuilder` definition:

```
[app/article-editor.component.ts]

import {Component, Inject} from '@angular/core';
import {FormBuilder, FormGroup, Validators} from '@angular/forms';

@Component({
  selector: 'article-editor',
  template: `
    <form [formGroup]="articleGroup"
          (ngSubmit)="saveArticle()">
      <div formGroupName="article">
        <p><input formControlName="title"
                  placeholder="Article title"></p>
        <p><textarea formControlName="text"
                     placeholder="Article text"></textarea></p>
      </div>
      <p><button type="submit">Save</button></p>
    </form>
  `
})
export class ArticleEditorComponent {
  articleGroup:FormGroup;
  constructor(@Inject(FormBuilder) formBuilder:FormBuilder) {
    this.articleGroup = formBuilder.group({
      article: formBuilder.group({
        title: [null, Validators.required],
        text: [null, Validators.required]
      })
    });
  }
  saveArticle():void {
    console.log(this.articleGroup);
  }
}
```

Now, the `title` and `text` `FormControl` objects will exist nested inside an article `FormGroup` and they can be successfully validated and inspected in the submit handler.

How it works…

As you might suspect, the arrays living inside the `formBuilder.group` definitions will be applied as arguments to a `FormControl` constructor. This is nice since you can avoid the `new FormControl()` boilerplate when creating each control. The string that keys the `FormControl` is linked to it with `formControlName`. Because you are using `formControlName` and `formGroupName`, you will need to have the `formBuilder` nested structure match *exactly* to what is there in the template.

There's more…

It is totally understandable that having to duplicate the structure in the template and the `FormBuilder` definition is a little annoying. This is especially true in this case, as the presence of `formGroup` doesn't really add any valuable behavior since it is attached to an inert `div` element. Instead, you might want to be able to do this article namespace grouping without modifying the template. This behavior can be accomplished with `formControl`, whose behavior is similar to `formModel` (it binds to an existing instance on the component).

 Note the paradigm that is being demonstrated with these different kinds of form directives. With things such as `ngForm`, `formGroup`, `formArray`, and `formControl`, Angular is implicitly creating and linking these instances. If you choose to not use `FormBuilder` to define how `FormControls` behave, this can be accomplished by adding validation directives to the template. On the other hand, you also have `formModel` and `formControl`, which bind to the instances of these control objects that you must manually create on the component.

`[app/article-editor.component.ts]`

```
import {Component, Inject} from '@angular/core';
import {FormBuilder, FormControl, FormGroup, Validators}
  from '@angular/forms';

@Component({
  selector: 'article-editor',
  template: `
    <form [formGroup]="articleGroup"
        (ngSubmit)="saveArticle()">
      <p><input [formControl]="titleControl"
               placeholder="Article title"></p>
      <p><textarea [formControl]="textControl"
                 placeholder="Article text"></textarea></p>
```

```
        <p><button type="submit">Save</button></p>
      </form>
      `
})
export class ArticleEditorComponent {
  titleControl:FormControl
    = new FormControl(null, Validators.required);
  textControl:FormControl
    = new FormControl(null, Validators.required);
  articleGroup:FormGroup;
  constructor(@Inject(FormBuilder) formBuilder:FormBuilder) {
    this.articleGroup = formBuilder.group({
      article: formBuilder.group({
        title: this.titleControl,
        text: this.textControl
      })
    });
  }
  saveArticle():void {
    console.log(this.articleGroup);
  }
}
```

Importantly, note that you have created an identical output of the one you created earlier. title and text are bundled inside an article FormGroup. However, the template doesn't need to have any reference to this intermediate FormGroup.

See also

- *Implementing simple two-way data binding with ngModel* demonstrates the new way in Angular 2 to control bidirectional data flow
- *Implementing basic field validation with a FormControl* details the basic building block of an Angular form
- *Implementing basic forms with ngForm* demonstrates Angular's declarative form construction

Creating and using a custom validator

The basic built-in validators that Angular provides will get you off the ground, but if your application relies on forms, you will undoubtedly come to a point where you will want to define your own validator logic.

 The code, links, and a live example related to this recipe are available at `http://ngcookbook.herokuapp.com/8574/`.

Getting ready

Suppose you had started with the following skeleton application:

```
[app/article-editor.component.ts]

import {Component} from '@angular/core';
import {FormControl, Validators} from '@angular/forms';

@Component({
  selector: 'article-editor',
  template: `
    <h2>Psych Study on Humility Wins Major Award</h2>
    <textarea [formControl]="bodyControl"
              placeholder="Article text"></textarea>
    <p><button (click)="saveArticle()">Save</button></p>
  `
})
export class ArticleEditorComponent {
  articleBody:string = '';
  bodyControl:Control
    = new FormControl(null, Validators.required);

  saveArticle():void {
    if (this.bodyControl.valid) {
      alert('Valid!');
    } else {
      alert('Invalid!');
    }
  }
}
```

Your objective is to add an additional validation to the `textarea` that will limit it to 10 words. (The editorial staff is big on brevity.)

How to do it...

If you look at the function signature of an `AbstractControl`, you will notice that the validator argument is just a `ValidatorFn`. This validator function can be any function that accepts an `AbstractControl` object as its sole argument and returns an object keyed with `strings` for the error object. This error object acts as a dictionary of errors, and a validator can return as many errors as applicable. The value of the dictionary entry can (and should) contain metadata about what is causing the error. If there are no errors found by the custom validator, it should just return `null`.

The simplest way to implement this is by adding a member method to the component:

```
[app/article-editor.component.ts]
export class ArticleEditor {
  articleBody:string
  bodyCtrl:Control
  constructor() {
    this.articleBody = '';
    this.bodyCtrl = new Control('', Validators.required);
  }
  wordCtValidator(c:Control): {[key: string]: any} {
    let wordCt:number = (c.value.match(/\S+/g) || []).length;
    return wordCt <= 10 ?
      null :
      { 'maxwords': { 'limit':10, 'actual':wordCt } };
  }
  saveArticle() {
    if (this.bodyCtrl.valid) {
      alert('Valid!');
    } else {
      alert('Invalid!');
    }
  }
}
```

Here, you're using a regular expression to match any non-whitespace strings, which can be treated as a "word." You also need to initialize the `FormControl` object to an empty string since you are using the `string` prototype's `match` method. Since this regular expression will return null when there are no matches, a fallback `|| []` clause is added to always yield something that has a `length` method.

Now that the validator method is defined, you need to actually use it on `FormControl`. Angular allows you to bundle an array of validators into a single validator, evaluating them in order:

```
[app/article-editor.component.ts]

import {Component} from '@angular/core';
import {FormControl, Validators} from '@angular/forms';

@Component({
  selector: 'article-editor',
  template: `
    <h2>Psych Study on Humility Wins Major Award</h2>
    <textarea [formControl]="bodyControl"
              placeholder="Article text"></textarea>
    <p><button (click)="saveArticle()">Save</button></p>
  `
})
export class ArticleEditorComponent {
  articleBody:string = '';
  bodyControl:FormControl = new FormControl(null,
    [Validators.required, this.wordCtValidator]);

  wordCtValidator(c:FormControl):{[key: string]: any} {
    let wordCt:number
      = ((c.value || '').match(/\S+/g) || []).length;
    return wordCt <= 10 ?
      null :
      {maxwords: {limit:10, actual:wordCt}};
  }

  saveArticle():void {
    if (this.bodyControl.valid) {
      alert('Valid!');
    } else {
      alert('Invalid!');
    }
  }
}
```

With this, your `FormControl` should now only be valid when there are 10 words or fewer and the input is not empty.

How it works...

A `FormControl` expects a `ValidatorFn` with a specified return type, but it does not care where it comes from. Therefore, you were able to define a method inside the component class and just pass it along when `FormControl` was instantiated.

The `FormControl` object associated with a given input must be able to have validators associated with it. In this recipe, you first implemented custom validation using explicit association via the instantiation arguments and defining the validator as a simple standalone `ValidationFn`.

There's more...

Your inner software engineer should be totally dissatisfied with this solution. The validator you just defined cannot be used outside this component without injecting the entire component, and explicitly listing every validator when instantiating the `FormControl` is a major pain.

Refactoring into validator attributes

A superior solution is to implement a formal `Validator` class. This has several benefits: you will be able to import/export the class and use the validator as an attribute in the template, which obviates the need for bundling validators with `Validators.compose`.

Your strategy should be to create a directive that can function not only as an attribute, but also as something that Angular can recognize as a formal `Validator` and automatically incorporate it as such. This can be accomplished by creating a directive that implements the `Validator` interface and also bundles the new `Validator` directive into the existing `NG_VALIDATORS` token.

 For now, don't worry about the specifics of what is happening with the `providers` array inside the directive metadata object. This will be covered in depth in the chapter on dependency injection. All that you need to know here is that this code is allowing the `FormControl` object bound to `textarea` to associate the custom validator you are building with it.

First, move the validation method to its own directive by performing the steps mentioned in the preceding paragraph:

```
[app/max-word-count.validator.ts]
```

```
import {Directive} from '@angular/core';
import {Validator, FormControl, NG_VALIDATORS}
  from '@angular/forms';

@Directive({
  selector: '[max-word-count]',
  providers: [{
    provide:NG_VALIDATORS,
    useExisting: MaxWordCountValidator,
    multi: true
  }]
})
export class MaxWordCountValidator implements Validator {
  validate(c:FormControl):{[key:string]:any} {
    let wordCt:number = ((c.value || '')
          .match(/\S+/g) || []).length;
    return wordCt <= 10 ?
      null :
      {maxwords: {limit:10, actual:wordCt}};
  }
}
```

Next, add this directive to the application module:

```
[app/app.module.ts]

import {NgModule} from '@angular/core';
import {BrowserModule} from '@angular/platform-browser';
import {ReactiveFormsModule} from '@angular/forms';
import {ArticleEditorComponent} from './article-editor.component';
import {MaxWordCountValidator} from './max-word-count.validator';

@NgModule({
  imports: [
    BrowserModule,
    ReactiveFormsModule
  ],
  declarations: [
    ArticleEditorComponent,
    MaxWordCountValidator
  ],
  bootstrap: [
    ArticleEditorComponent
  ]
})
export class AppModule {}
```

This makes it available to all the components in this module. What's more, the provider configuration you specified before allows you to simply add the directive attribute to any input, and Angular will be able to incorporate its validation function into that `FormControl`. The integration is as follows:

```
[app/article-editor.component.ts]

import {Component} from '@angular/core';
import {FormControl} from '@angular/forms';

@Component({
  selector: 'article-editor',
  template: `
    <h2>Psych Study on Humility Wins Major Award</h2>
    <textarea [formControl]="bodyControl"
              required
              max-word-count
              placeholder="Article text"></textarea>
    <p><button (click)="saveArticle()">Save</button></p>
  `
})
export class ArticleEditorComponent {
  articleBody:string = '';
  bodyControl:FormControl = new FormControl();

  saveArticle():void {
    if (this.bodyControl.valid) {
      alert('Valid!');
    } else {
      alert('Invalid!');
    }
  }
}
```

This is already far superior. The `MaxWordCount` directive can now be imported and used anywhere in our application by simply listing it as a directive dependency in a component. There's no need for the `Validator.compose` nastiness when instantiating a `FormControl` object.

This is especially useful when you are implicitly creating these `FormControl` objects with `formControl` and other built-in form directives, which for many applications will be the primary form utilization method. Building your custom validator as an attribute directive will integrate seamlessly in these situations.

You should still be dissatisfied though, as the validator is hardcoded to check for 10 words. You would instead like to leave this up to the input that is using it. Therefore, you should change the directive to accept a single parameter, which will take the form of the attribute's value:

```
[app/max-word-count.validator.ts]

import {Directive} from '@angular/core';
import {Validator, FormControl, NG_VALIDATORS}
  from '@angular/forms';

@Directive({
  selector: '[max-word-count]',
  inputs: ['rawCount: max-word-count'],
  providers: [{
    provide:NG_VALIDATORS,
    useExisting: MaxWordCountValidator,
    multi: true
  }]
})
export class MaxWordCountValidator implements Validator {
  rawCount:string;
  validate(c:FormControl):{[key:string]:any} {
    let wordCt:number =
      ((c.value || '').match(/\S+/g) || []).length;
    return wordCt <= this.maxCount ?
      null :
      {maxwords: {limit:this.maxCount, actual:wordCt}};
  }
  get maxCount():number {
    return parseInt(this.rawCount);
  }
}
[app/article-editor.component.ts]

import {Component} from '@angular/core';
import {FormControl} from '@angular/forms';

@Component({
  selector: 'article-editor',
  template: `
    <h2>Psych Study on Humility Wins Major Award</h2>
    <textarea [formControl]="bodyControl"
              required
              max-word-count="10"
              placeholder="Article text"></textarea>
    <p><button (click)="saveArticle()">Save</button></p>
  `
```

```
})
export class ArticleEditorComponent {
  articleBody:string = '';
  bodyControl:FormControl = new FormControl();

  saveArticle():void {
    if (this.bodyControl.valid) {
      alert('Valid!');
    } else {
      alert('Invalid!');
    }
  }
}
```

Now you have defined the value of the attribute as an input to the validator, which you can then use to configure how the validator will operate.

See also

- *Creating and using a custom asynchronous validator with Promises* shows how Angular allows you to have a delayed evaluation of the form state

Creating and using a custom asynchronous validator with Promises

A standard validator operates under the assumption that the validity of a certain input can be calculated in a short amount of time that the application can wait to get over with before it continues further. What's more, Angular will run this validation every time the validator is invoked, which might be quite often if form validation is bound to rapid-fire events such as keypresses.

Therefore, it makes good sense that a construct exists that will allow you to smoothly handle the validation procedures that take an arbitrary amount of time to execute or procedures that might not return at all. For this, Angular offers `async Validator`, which is fully compatible with `Promises`.

The code, links, and a live example related to this recipe are available at `http://ngcookbook.herokuapp.com/7811/`.

Getting ready

Suppose you had started with the following skeleton application:

```
[app/article-editor.component.ts]

import {Component} from '@angular/core';
import {FormControl} from '@angular/forms';

@Component({
  selector: 'article-editor',
  template: `
    <h2>New York-Style Pizza Actually Saucy Cardboard</h2>
    <textarea [formControl]="bodyControl"
              placeholder="Article text">
    </textarea>
    <p><button (click)="saveArticle()">Save</button></p>
  `
})
export class ArticleEditorComponent {
  articleBody:string = '';
  bodyControl:FormControl = new FormControl();
  saveArticle():void {
    if (this.bodyControl.valid) {
      alert('Valid!');
    } else {
      alert('Invalid!');
    }
  }
}
```

Your objective is to configure this form in a way that it will become valid only 5 seconds after the user enters the input in order to deter simple spambots.

How to do it…

First, create your validator class, and inside it, place a static validation method. This is similar to a synchronous validation method, but it will instead return a `Promise` object, passing the result data to the `resolve` method. The `FormControl` object accepts the async `Validator` as its third argument. If you weren't using any normal `Validators`, you could leave it as `null`.

As you would combine several `Validators` into one using `Validators.compose`, **async** `Validators` can be combined using `Validators.composeAsync`.

Create the validator skeleton in its own file:

```
[app/delay.validator.ts]

import {FormControl, Validator} from '@angular/forms';

export class DelayValidator implements Validator {
  static validate(c:FormControl):Promise<{[key:string]:any}> {
  }
}
```

Though the validator does not yet do anything, you may still add it to the component:

```
[app/article-editor.component.ts]

import {Component} from '@angular/core';
import {FormControl, Validators} from '@angular/forms';
import {DelayValidator} from './delay.validator';

@Component({
  selector: 'article-editor',
  template: `
    <h2>New York-Style Pizza Actually Saucy Cardboard</h2>
    <textarea [formControl]="bodyControl"
              placeholder="Article text">
    </textarea>
    <p><button (click)="saveArticle()">Save</button></p>
  `
})
export class ArticleEditorComponent {
  articleBody:string = '';
  bodyControl:FormControl =
    new FormControl(null, null, DelayValidator.validate);
  saveArticle():void {
    if (this.bodyControl.valid) {
      alert('Valid!');
    } else {
      alert('Invalid!');
    }
  }
}
```

The validator must return a promise, but this promise doesn't ever need to be resolved. Furthermore, you'd like to set the delay to only one time per rendering. So in this case, you can just attach the promise to the `FormControl`:

```
[app/delay.validator.ts]

import {FormControl, Validator} from '@angular/forms';

export class DelayValidator implements Validator {
  static validate(c:FormControl):Promise<{[key:string]:any}> {
    if (c.pristine && !c.value) {
      return new Promise;
    }
    if (!c.delayPromise) {
      c.delayPromise = new Promise((resolve) => {
        setTimeout(() => {
          console.log('resolve');
          resolve();
        }, 5000);
      });
    }
    return c.delayPromise;
  }
}
```

With this addition, the form will remain invalid until 5 seconds after the first time the value of the `textarea` is changed.

How it works...

Asynchronous validators are handled independently via regular (synchronous) validators, but other than their internal latency differences, they ultimately behave in nearly the exact same way. The important difference is that an async `Validator`, apart from the valid and invalid states that it shares with a normal `Validator`, has a pending state. The `FormControl` will remain in this state until a promise is made indicating the `Validator` will return either resolves or rejects.

 A `FormControl` in a `pending` state is treated as invalid for the purpose of checking the validity of aggregating constructs, such as `FormGroup` or `FormArray`.

In the `Validator` you just created, checking the `pristine` property of `FormControl` is a fine way of ascertaining whether or not the form is "fresh." Before the user modifies the input, `pristine` is `true`; following any modification (even removing all of the entered text), `pristine` becomes `false`. Therefore, it is a perfect tool in this example, as it allows us to have the `FormControl` maintain the form state without overcomplicating the `Validator`.

There's more...

It's critical to note the form that this validator takes. The validation method inside the `DelayValidator` class is a static method and nowhere is the `DelayValidator` class being instantiated. The purpose of the class is merely to house the validator. Therefore, you are unable to store information inside this class, since there are no instances in which you can do so.

 In this example, you might be tempted to add member data to the validator since you want to track whether the input has been modified yet. Doing so is very much an anti-pattern! The `FormControl` object should act as your sole source of stateful information in this scenario. A `FormControl` object is instantiated for each input field, and therefore it is the ideal "datastore" with which you can track what the input is doing.

Validator execution

If you were to inspect when the validator method is being called, you would find that it executes only on a keypress inside `textarea`. This may seem arbitrary, but the default `FormControl`/input assignment is to evaluate the validators of `FormControl` on a `change` event emitted from the input. `FormControl` objects expose a `registerOnChange` method, which lets you hook onto the same point that the validators will be evaluated.

See also

- *Creating and using a custom validator* demonstrates how to create a custom directive that behaves as input validation

4
Mastering Promises

This chapter will cover the following recipes:

- Understanding and implementing basic Promises
- Chaining Promises and Promise handlers
- Creating Promise wrappers with Promise.resolve() and Promise.reject()
- Implementing Promise barriers with Promise.all()
- Canceling asynchronous actions with Promise.race()
- Converting a Promise into an Observable
- Converting an HTTP service Observable into ZoneAwarePromise

Introduction

In Angular 1, promises acted as strange birds. They were essential for building robust asynchronous applications, but using them seemed to come at a price. Their implementation by way of the $q service and the duality of promise and deferred objects seemed bizarre. Nonetheless, once you were able to master them, it was easy to see how they could be the foundation of extremely robust implementations in the single-threaded event-driven world of JavaScript.

Fortunately, for developers everywhere, ES6 formally embraces the Promise feature as a central component. Since TypeScript is a superset of ES6, you will be pleased to know that you can wield promises everywhere in Angular without extra baggage. Although Observables subsume a lot of the utility offered by promises, there is still very much a place for them in your toolkit.

Being able to use Promises natively is a privilege of TypeScript to a JavaScript transpilation. As of now, some browsers support Promises natively, while some do not. Good news is that if you're writing your applications in TypeScript and are transpiling them properly, you don't have to worry about this! Really, the only time you would need to consider the actual transpilation mechanics is when you need information related to the performance or payload size benefits of native implementations versus their respective polyfills, and this should never be an issue for nearly all applications.

Understanding and implementing basic Promises

Promises are very useful in many of the core aspects of Angular. Although they are no longer bound to the core framework service, they still manifest themselves throughout Angular's APIs. The implementation is considerably simpler than Angular 1, but the main rhythms have remained consistent.

You can refer to the code, links, and a live example of this at `http://ngcookbook.herokuapp.com/5195`.

Getting ready

Before you start using promises, you should first understand the problem they are trying to solve. Without worrying too much about the internals, you can classify the concept of a Promise into three distinct stages:

- **Initialization**: I have a piece of work that I want to accomplish, and I want to define what should happen when this work is completed. I do not know whether this work will be ever completed; also, the work may either fail or succeed.
- **Pending**: I have started the work, but it has not been completed yet.
- **Completed**: The work is finished, and the promise assumes a final state. The "completed" state assumes two forms: resolved and rejected. These correspond to success and failure, respectively.

There is more nuance to how promises work, but for now, this is sufficient to get into some of the code.

How to do it...

A promise implementation in one of its simplest forms is as follows:

```
// promises are instantiated with the 'new' keyword
var promise = new Promise(() => {});
```

The function passed to the `Promise` constructor is the piece of work that is expected to execute asynchronously. The formal term for this function is `executor`.

The `Promise` constructor doesn't care at all about how the `executor` function behaves. It merely provides it with the two `resolve` and `reject` functions. It is left up to the `executor` function to utilize them appropriately. Note that the `executor` function doesn't need to be asynchronous at all; however, if it isn't asynchronous, then you might not need a Promise for what you are trying to accomplish.

When this function is executed, internally it understands when it is completed; however, on the outside, there is no construct that represents the concept of "run this when the `executor` function is completed". Therefore, its first two parameters are the `resolve` and `reject` functions. The promise wrapping the `executor` function is in the `pending` state until one of these is invoked. Once invoked, the promise irreversibly assumes the respective state.

The `executor` function is invoked immediately when the promise is instantiated. Just as importantly, it is invoked before the promise instantiation is returned. This means that if the promise reaches either a `fulfilled` or `rejected` state inside the executor synchronously, then the return value of `new Promise(...)` will be the freshly constructed Promise with a `resolved` or `rejected` status, skipping the `pending` state entirely.

The return value of `executor` is unimportant. No matter what it returns, the `promise` constructor will always return the freshly created promise.

The following code demonstrates five different examples of ways that a promise can be instantiated, resolved, or rejected:

```
// This executor is passed resolve and reject, but is
// effectively a no-op, so the promise p2 will forever
// remain in the 'pending' state.
const p1 = new Promise((resolve, reject) => {});

// This executor invokes 'resolve' immediately, so
// p2 will transition directly to the 'fulfilled' state.
const p2 = new Promise((resolve, reject) => resolve());

// This executor invokes 'reject' immediately, so
// p3 will transition directly to the 'rejected' state.
// A transition to the 'rejected' state will also throw
// an exception. This exception is thrown after the
// executor completes, so any logic following the
// invocation of reject will still be executed.
const p3 = new Promise((resolve, reject) => {
  reject();
  // This log() prints before the exception is thrown
  console.log('I got rejected!');
});

// This executor invokes 'resolve' immediately, so
// p4 will transition directly to the 'fulfilled' state.
// Once a promise exits the 'pending' state, it cannot change
// again, so even though reject is invoked afterwards, the
// final state of p4 is still 'fulfilled'.
const p4 = new Promise((resolve, reject) => {
  resolve();
  reject();
});

// This executor assigns its resolve function to a variable
// in the encompassing lexical scope so it can be called
// outside the promise definition.
var outerResolve;
const p5 = new Promise((resolve, reject) => {
  outerResolve = resolve();
});
// State of p5 is 'pending'

outerResolve();
// State of p5 is 'fulfilled'
```

With what you've done so far, you will not find the promise construct to be of much use; this is because all that the preceding code accomplishes is the setting up of the state of a single promise. The real value emerges when you set the subsequent state handlers. A Promise object's API exposes a then() method, which allows you to set handlers to be executed when the Promise reaches its final state:

```
// p1 is a simple promise to which you can attach handlers
const p1 = new Promise((resolve, reject) => {});

// p1 exposes a then() method which accepts a
// resolve handler (onFulfilled), and a
// reject handler (onRejected)
p1.then(
  // onFulfilled is invoked when resolve() is invoked
  () => {},
  // onRejected is invoke when reject() is invoked
  () => {});
// If left here, p1 will forever remain "pending"


// Using the 'new' keyword still allows you to call a
// method on the returned instance, so defining the
// then() handlers immediately is allowed.
//
// Instantly resolves p2
const p2 = new Promise((resolve, reject) => resolve())
  .then(
    // This method will immediately be invoked following
    // the p2 executor invoking resolve()
    () => console.log('resolved!'));
// "resolved!"


// Instantly rejects p3
const p3 = new Promise((resolve, reject) => reject())
  .then(
    () => console.log('resolved!'),
    // This second method will immediately be invoked following
    // the p3 executor invoking reject()
    () => console.log('rejected!'));
// "rejected!"


const p4 = new Promise((resolve, reject) => reject())
  // If you don't require use of the resolve handler,
  // catch() allows you to define just the error handling
  .catch(() => console.log('rejected!'));


// executor parameters can be captured outside its lexical
// scope for later invocation
var outerResolve;
```

```
const p5 = new Promise((resolve, reject) => {
  outerResolve = resolve;
}).then(() => console.log('resolved!'));

outerResolve();
// "resolved!"
```

How it works...

Promises in JavaScript confer to the developer the ability to write asynchronous code in parallel with synchronous code more easily. In JavaScript, this was formerly solved with nested callbacks, colloquially referred to as "callback hell." A single callback-oriented function might be written as follows:

```
// a generic asynchronous callback function
function asyncFunction(data, successCallback, errorCallback) {
  // asyncFunction will perform some operation that may succeed,
  // may fail, or may not return at all, any of which
  // occurs in an unknown amount of time

  // this pseudo-response contains a success boolean,
  // and the returned data if successful
  asyncOperation(data, function(response) {
    if (response.success === true) {
      successCallback(response.data);
    } else {
      errorCallback();
    }
  });
};
```

If your application does not demand any semblance of in-order or collective completion, then the following will suffice:

```
function successCallback(data) {
  // asyncFunction succeeded, handle data appropriately
};
function errorCallback() {
  // asyncFunction failed, handle appropriately
};

asyncFunction(data1, successCallback, errorCallback);
asyncFunction(data2, successCallback, errorCallback);
asyncFunction(data3, successCallback, errorCallback);
```

This is almost never the case though. Often, your application will either demand that this data is acquired in a sequence, or that an operation that requires multiple asynchronously acquired pieces of data executes once all of the data has been successfully acquired. In this case, without access to promises, the callback hell emerges:

```
asyncFunction(data1, (foo) => {
  asyncFunction(data2, (bar) => {
    asyncFunction(data3, (baz) => {
      // foo, bar, baz can now all be used together
      combinatoricFunction(foo, bar, baz);
    }, errorCallback);
  }, errorCallback);
}, errorCallback);
```

This so-called callback hell here is really just an attempt to serialize three asynchronous calls, but the parametric topology of these asynchronous functions forces the developer to subject their application to this ugliness.

There's more...

An important point to remember about promises is that they allow you to break apart a calculation into two parts: the part that understands when the promise's "execution" has been completed and the part that signals to the rest of the program that the execution has been completed.

Decoupled and duplicated Promise control

Because a promise can give away the control of who decides where the Promise will be made ready, multiple foreign parts of the code can set the state of the promise.

A promise instance can be either resolved or rejected at multiple places inside the executor::

```
const p = new Promise((resolve, reject) => {
  // the following are pseudo-methods, each of which can be called
  // independently and asynchronously, or not at all
  function canHappenFirst() { resolve(); };
  function mayHappenFirst() { resolve(); }
  function mightHappenFirst() { reject(); };
});
```

A promise instance can also be resolved at multiple places outside the executor:

```
var outerResolve;
const p = new Promise((resolve, reject) => {
```

```
    outerResolve = resolve;
});

// the following are pseudo-methods, each of which can be called
// independently and asynchronously, or not at all
function canHappenFirst() { outerResolve (); };
function mayHappenFirst() { outerResolve (); }
function mightHappenFirst() { outerResolve (); };
```

 Once a Promise's state becomes `fulfilled` or `rejected`, attempts to reject or resolve that promise further will be silently ignored. A promise state transition occurs only once, and it cannot be altered or reversed.

Resolving a Promise to a value

Part of the central concept of promise constructs is that they are able to "promise" that there will be a value available when the promise is resolved.

States do not necessarily have a data value associated with them; they only confer to the promise a defined state of evaluation:

```
var resolveHandler = () => {},
    rejectHandler = () => {};
const p0 = new Promise((resolve, reject) => {
  // state can be defined with any of the following:
  // resolve();
  // reject();
  // resolve(myData);
  // reject(myData);
}).then(resolveHandler, rejectHandler);
```

An evaluated promise (resolved or rejected) is associated with a handler for each of the states. This handler is invoked upon the promise's transition into that respective state. These handlers can access the data returned by the resolution or rejection:

```
const p1 = new Promise((resolve, reject) => {
  // console.info is the resolve handler,
  // console.error is the reject handler
  resolve(123);
}).then(console.info, console.error);

// (info) 123

// reset to demonstrate reject()
const p2 = new Promise((resolve, reject) => {
```

```
  // console.info is the resolve handler,
  // console.error is the reject handler
  reject(456);
}).then(console.info, console.error);

// (error) 456
```

Delayed handler definition

Unlike callbacks, handlers can be defined at any point in the promise life cycle, including after the promise state has been defined:

```
const p3 = new Promise((resolve, reject) => {
  // immediately resolve the promise
  resolve(123);
});

// subsequently define a handler, will be immediately
// invoked since promise is already resolved
p3.then(console.info);

// (info) 123
```

Multiple handler definition

Similar to how a single deferred object can be resolved or rejected at multiple places in the application, a single promise can have multiple handlers that can be bound to a single state. For example, a single promise with multiple resolved handlers attached to it will invoke all the handlers if the resolved state is reached; the same is true for rejected handlers:

```
const p4 = new Promise((resolve, reject) => {
  // Invoke resolve() after 1 second
  setTimeout(() => resolve(), 1000);
});

const cb = () => console.log('called');

p4.then(cb);
p4.then(cb);

// After 1 second:
// "called"
// "called"
```

Private Promise members

An extremely important departure from Angular 1 is that the state of a promise is totally opaque to the execution. Formerly, you were able to tease out the state of the promise using the pseudo-private `$$state` property. With the formal ES6 `Promise` implementation, the state cannot be inspected by your application. You can, however, glean the state of a promise from the console. For example, inspecting a promise in Google Chrome yields something like the following:

```
Promise {
  [[PromiseStatus]]: "fulfilled",
  [[PromiseValue]]: 123
}
```

PromiseStatus and PromiseValue are private Symbols, which are a new construct in ES6. Symbol can be thought of as a unique key that is useful for setting properties on objects that shouldn't be easily accessed from elsewhere. For example, if a promise were to use the 'PromiseStatus' string to key a property, it could be easily used outside the object, even if the property was supposed to remain private. With ES6 private symbols, however, a symbol is unique when generated, and there is no good way to access it inside the instance.

See also

- *Chaining Promises and Promise handlers* details how you can wield this powerful chaining construct to serialize asynchronous operations
- *Creating Promise wrappers with Promise.resolve() and Promise.reject()* demonstrates how to use the core Promise utilities

Chaining Promises and Promise handlers

Much of the purpose of promises is to allow the developer to serialize and reason about independent asynchronous actions. This can be accomplished by utilizing the Promise chaining feature.

The code, links, and a live example of this are available at `http://ngcookbook.herokuapp.com/6828/`.

How to do it...

The promise handler definition method `then()` returns another promise, which can have further handlers defined upon it—in a handler called chain:

```
var successHandler = () => { console.log('called'); };

var p = new Promise((resolve, reject) => { resolve(); })
  .then(successHandler)
  .then(successHandler)
  .then(successHandler);

// called
// called
// called
```

Chained handlers' data handoff

Chained handlers can pass data to their subsequent handlers in the following manner:

```
var successHandler = (val) => {
  console.log(val);
  return val+1;
};

var p = new Promise((resolve, reject) => { resolve(0); })
  .then(successHandler)
  .then(successHandler)
  .then(successHandler);

// 0
// 1
// 2
```

Rejecting a chained handler

Returning normally from a promise handler (not the executor) will, by default, signal child promise states to become resolved. However, if either the executor or the subsequent handlers throw an uncaught exception, they will, by default, reject; this will serve to catch the exception:

```
const p = new Promise((resolve, reject) => {
  // executor will immediately throw an exception, forcing
  // a reject
  throw 123;
```

```
})
.then(
  // child promise resolved handler
  data => console.log('resolved', data),
  // child promise rejected handler
  data => console.log('rejected', data));

// "rejected", 123
```

 Note that the exception, here a number primitive, is the data that is passed to the rejection handler.

How it works...

A Promise reaching a final state will trigger child promises to follow it in turn. This simple but powerful concept allows you to build broad and fault-tolerant promise structures that elegantly mesh collections of dependent asynchronous actions.

There's more...

The topology of promises lends itself to some interesting utilization patterns.

Promise handler trees

Promise handlers will execute in the order that the promises are defined. If a promise has multiple handlers attached to a single state, then that state will execute all its handlers before resolving the following chained promise:

```
const incr = val => {
  console.log(val);
  return ++val;
};

var outerResolve;
const firstPromise = new Promise((resolve, reject) => {
  outerResolve = resolve;
});

// define firstPromise's handler
firstPromise.then(incr);
```

```
// append another handler for firstPromise, and collect
// the returned promise in secondPromise
const secondPromise = firstPromise.then(incr);
// append another handler for the second promise, and collect
// the returned promise in thirdPromise
const thirdPromise = secondPromise.then(incr);

// at this point, invoking outerResolve() will:
// resolve firstPromise; firstPromise's handlers executes
// resolve secondPromise; secondPromises's handler executes
// resolve thirdPromise; no handlers defined yet

// additional promise handler definition order is
// unimportant; they will be resolved as the promises
// sequentially have their states defined
secondPromise.then(incr);
firstPromise.then(incr);
thirdPromise.then(incr);

// the setup currently defined is as follows:
// firstPromise -> secondPromise -> thirdPromise
// incr()          incr()          incr()
// incr()          incr()
// incr()

outerResolve(0);
// 0
// 0
// 0
// 1
// 1
// 2
```

 Since the return value of a handler decides whether or not the promise state is resolved or rejected, any of the handlers associated with a promise is able to set the state—which, as you may recall, can only be set once. The defining of the parent promise state will trigger the child promise handlers to be executed.

It should now be apparent how the trees of the promise functionality can be derived from the combination of promise chaining and handler chaining. When used properly, they can yield extremely elegant solutions for difficult and ugly asynchronous action serializations.

catch()

The `catch()` method is a shorthand for `promise.then(null, errorCallback)`. Using it can lead to slightly cleaner promise definitions, but it is nothing more than syntactical sugar:

```
var outerReject;
const p = new Promise((resolve, reject) => {
  outerReject = reject;
})
.catch(() => console.log('rejected!'));

outerReject();
// "rejected"
```

It is also possible to chain `p.then().catch()`. An error thrown by the original promise will propagate through the promise created by `then()`, cause it to reject, and reach the promise created by `catch()`. It creates one extra level of promise indirection, but to an outside observer, it will behave the same.

See also

- *Understanding and implementing basic Promises* gives an extensive rundown of how and why to use Promises
- *Creating Promise wrappers with Promise.resolve() and Promise.reject()* demonstrates how to use the core Promise utilities

Creating Promise wrappers with Promise.resolve() and Promise.reject()

It is useful to have the ability to create promise objects that have already reached a final state with a defined value, and also to be able to normalize JavaScript objects into promises. `Promise.resolve()` and `Promise.reject()` afford you the ability to perform both these actions.

The code, links, and a live example of this are available at
`http://ngcookbook.herokuapp.com/9315/`.

How to do it...

Like all other static Promise methods, `Promise.resolve()` and `Promise.reject()`
return a promise object. In this case, there is no `executor` definition.

If one of these methods is provided with a non-promise argument, the returned promise
will assume either a `fulfilled` or `rejected` state (corresponding to the invoked method).
This method will pass the argument to `Promise.resolve()` and `Promise.reject()`,
along with any corresponding handlers:

```
Promise.resolve('foo');
// Promise {[[PromiseStatus]]: "resolved", [[PromiseValue]]: "foo"}

Promise.reject('bar');
// Promise {[[PromiseStatus]]: "rejected", [[PromiseValue]]: "bar"}
// (error) Uncaught (in promise) bar
```

The preceding code is behaviorally equivalent to the following:

```
new Promise((resolve, reject) => resolve('foo'));
// Promise {[[PromiseStatus]]: "resolved", [[PromiseValue]]: "foo"}

new Promise((resolve, reject) => reject ('bar'));
>> Promise {[[PromiseStatus]]: "rejected", [[PromiseValue]]: "bar"}
// (error) Uncaught (in promise) bar
```

Promise normalization

`Promise.resolve()` will uniquely handle scenarios where it is passed with a promise
object as its argument. `Promise.resolve()` will effectively operate as a no-op, returning
the initial promise argument without any modification. It will not make an attempt to
coerce the argument promise's state:

```
const a = Promise.resolve('baz');
console.log(a);
// Promise {status: 'resolved', value: 'baz'}

const b = Promise.resolve(a);
```

```
console.log(b);
// Promise {status: 'resolved', value: 'baz'}

console.log(a === b);
// true

const c = Promise.reject('qux');
// Error qux
console.log(c)
// Promise {status: 'rejected', value: 'qux'}

const d = Promise.resolve(c);
console.log(d);
// Promise {status: 'rejected', value: 'qux'}

console.log(c === d);
// true
```

How it works...

When thinking about `Promises` in the context of them "promising" to eventually assume a value, these methods are simply ameliorating any latent period separating the pending and final states.

The dichotomy is very simple:

- `Promise.reject()` will return a rejected promise no matter what its argument is. Even if it is a promise object, the value of the returned promise will be that of the promise object.
- `Promise.resolve()` will return a fulfilled promise with the wrapped value if that value is not a promise. If it is a promise, it behaves as a no-op.

There's more...

Importantly, the behavior of `Promise.resolve()` is nearly the same as how `$q.when()` operated in Angular 1. `$q.when()` was able to normalize promise objects, but it would always return a newly created promise object:

```
// Angular 1
const a = $q(() => {});
console.log(a);
// Promise {...}
```

```
const b = $q.when(a);
console.log(b);
// Promise {...}

console.log(a === b);
// false
```

See also

- *Understanding and implementing basic Promises* gives an extensive rundown of how and why to use Promises
- *Implementing Promise barriers with Promise.all()* show you how Promises can be composable
- *Canceling asynchronous actions with Promise.race()* guides you through the process of implementing a zero-failure-tolerant Promise system

Implementing Promise barriers with Promise.all()

You may find your application requires the use of promises in an all-or-nothing type of situation. That is, it will need to collectively evaluate a group of promises, and this collection will resolve as a single promise if and only if all of the contained promises are resolved; if any one of them is rejected, the aggregate promise will be rejected.

 The code, links, and a live example of this are available at
`http://ngcookbook.herokuapp.com/8496/`.

How to do it...

The `Promise.all()` method accepts an iterable collection of promises (for example, an array of `Promise` objects or an object with a number of promise properties), and it will attempt to resolve all of them as a single aggregate promise. The parameter of the aggregate resolved handler will be an array or object that matches the resolved values of the contained promises:

```
var outerResolveA, outerResolveB;
```

```
const promiseA = new Promise((resolve, reject) => {
  outerResolveA = resolve;
});
const promiseB = new Promise((resolve, reject) => {
  outerResolveB = resolve;
});

const multiPromiseAB = Promise.all([promiseA, promiseB])
  .then((values) => console.log(values));

outerResolveA(123);
outerResolveB(456);

// [123, 456]
```

If any of the promises in the collection are rejected, the aggregate promise will be rejected. The parameter of the aggregate rejected handler will be the returned value of the rejected promise:

```
var outerResolveC, outerRejectD;
const promiseC = new Promise((resolve, reject) => {
  outerResolveC = resolve;
});
const promiseD = new Promise((resolve, reject) => {
  outerRejectD = reject;
});

const multiPromiseCD = Promise.all([promiseC, promiseD])
  .then(
    values => console.log(values),
    rejectedValue => console.error(rejectedValue));

// resolve a collection promise, no handler execution
outerResolveC(123);
// reject a collection promise, rejection handler executes
outerRejectD(456);

// (error) 456
```

How it works...

As demonstrated, the aggregate promise will reach the final state only when all of the enclosed promises are resolved, or when a single enclosed promise is rejected. Using this type of promise is useful when the collection of promises do not need to reason about one another, but collective completion is the only metric of success for the group.

In the case of a contained rejection, the aggregate promise will not wait for the remaining promises to complete, but those promises will not be prevented from reaching their final state. Only the first promise to be rejected will be able to pass rejection data to the aggregate promise rejection handler.

There's more...

`Promise.all()` is in many ways extremely similar to an operating-system-level process synchronization barrier. A process barrier is a common point in the thread instruction execution that a collection of processes will reach independently and at different times, and no process can proceed further until all have reached this point. In the same way, `Promise.all()` will not proceed unless either all of the contained promises have been resolved—reached the barrier—or a single contained rejection will prevent that state from ever being achieved, in which case the failover handler logic will take over.

Since `Promise.all()` allows you to have a recombination of promises, it also allows your application's Promise chains to become a **directed acyclic graph (DAG)**. The following is an example of a promise progression graph that diverges first and converges later:

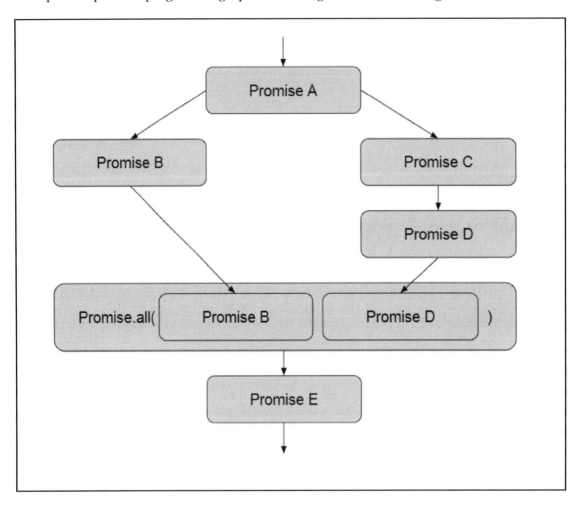

This level of complexity is uncommon, but it is available for use should your application require it.

See also

- *Creating Promise Wrappers with Promise.resolve() and Promise.reject()* demonstrates how to use the core Promise utilities
- *Canceling asynchronous actions with Promise.race()* guides you through the implementation of a zero-failure-tolerant Promise system

Canceling asynchronous actions with Promise.race()

ES6 introduces `Promise.race()`, which is absent from the $q spec in Angular 1. Like `Promise.all()`, this static method accepts an iterable collection of promise objects; whichever one resolves or rejects first will become the result of the promise wrapping the collection. This may seem like unusual behavior, but it becomes quite useful when you're building a cancellation behavior into the system.

 The code, links, and a live example of this are available at
`http://ngcookbook.herokuapp.com/4362/`.

Getting ready

Suppose you started with a simple promise that resolves to a value after 3 seconds:

```
const delayedPromise = new Promise((resolve, reject) =>
  setTimeout(resolve.bind(null, 'foobar'), 3000))
.then(val => console.log(val));
```

You would like to have the ability to detach a part of your application from waiting for this promise.

How to do it…

A simple solution would be to expose the promise's reject handler and just invoke it from whatever is to perform the cancelation. However, it is preferable to stop waiting for this promise instead of destroying it.

A concrete example of this would be a slow but critical HTTP request that your application makes. You might not want the UI to wait for it to complete, but you may have resolve handlers attached to the request that you still want to handle the result, once it is returned.

Instead, you can take advantage of `Promise.race()` and introduce a cancellation promise alongside the original one:

```
// Use this method to capture the cancellation function
var cancel;

const cancelPromise = new Promise((resolve, reject) => {
  cancel = reject;
});
const delayedPromise = new Promise((resolve, reject) =>
  setTimeout(resolve.bind(null, 'foobar'), 3000));

// Promise.race() creates a new promise
Promise.race([cancelPromise, delayedPromise])
.then(
  val => console.log(val),
  () => console.error('cancelled!'));

// If you invoke cancel() before 3 seconds elapses
// (error) "cancelled!"


// Instead, if 3 seconds elapses
// "foobar"
```

Now, if `delayedPromise` resolves first, the promise created by `Promise.race()` will log the value passed to it here, `foobar`. If, however, you invoke `cancel()` before it happens, then that same Promise will print a `cancelled!` error.

How it works...

`Promise.race()` just waits for any of its inner promises to arrive at the final state. It creates and returns a new promise that is beholden to the state of the contained promises. When it observes that any of them transitions to the final state, the new promise also assumes this state.

In this example, the executor of `cancelPromise` and `delayedPromise` are invoked before `Promise.race()` is called. Since promises only care about the state of other promises, it isn't important that the promises passed to `Promise.race()` need to be already technically started.

Note that the use of `Promise.race()` doesn't affect the implementation of `delayedPromise`. Even when `cancel()` is invoked, `delayedPromise` will still be resolved and its handlers will still be executed normally, unaware that the surrounding `Promise.race()` has already been rejected. You can prove this to yourself by adding a resolve handler to `delayedPromise`, invoking `cancel()` and seeing the resolve handler of `delayedPromise` being executed anyway:

```
var cancel;
const cancelPromise = new Promise((resolve, reject) => {
  cancel = reject;
});
const delayedPromise = new Promise((resolve, reject) =>
  setTimeout(resolve.bind(null, 'foobar'), 3000))
.then(() => console.log('still resolved!'));

Promise.race([ cancelPromise, delayedPromise ])
.then(
  val => console.log(val),
  () => console.error('cancelled!'));

cancel();
// (error) cancelled!

// After 3 seconds elapses
// "still resolved!"
```

See also

- *Creating Promise wrappers with Promise.resolve() and Promise.reject()* demonstrates how to use the core Promise utilities
- *Implementing Promise barriers with Promise.all()* show you how Promises can be composable

Converting a Promise into an Observable

Observables and Promises serve different purposes and are good at different things, but in a specific part of an application, you will almost certainly want to be dealing with a single denomination. This means converting observables into promises and vice versa. Thanks to RxJS, this is quite simple.

> For more on RxJS Observables, refer to `Chapter 5`, *ReactiveX Observables*, which covers them in depth.

> The code, links, and a live example of this are available at `http://ngcookbook.herokuapp.com/5244/`.

How to do it...

There is a good deal of parity between Promise and Observable. There are discrete success and error cases, and the concept of successful completion only corresponds to the success case.

RxJS observables expose a `fromPromise` method, which wraps Promise as an Observable:

```
import {Observable} from 'rxjs/Rx';

var outerResolve, outerReject;

const p1 = new Promise((resolve, reject) => {
  outerResolve = resolve;
  outerReject = reject;
});

var o1 = Observable.fromPromise(p1);
```

Now that you have an `Observable` instance, you can utilize its `subscribe()` events, which correspond to the state of the `Promise` instance:

```
import {Observable} from 'rxjs/Rx';

var outerResolve, outerReject;

const p1 = new Promise((resolve, reject) => {
```

```
    outerResolve = resolve;
    outerReject = reject;
});

var o1 = Observable.fromPromise(p1);

o1.subscribe(
  // onNext handler
  () => console.log('resolved!'),
  // onError handler
  () => console.log('rejected'),
  // onCompleted handler
  () => console.log('finished!'));
outerResolve();
// "resolved!"
// "finished!"
```

How it works...

The new `Observable` instance doesn't replace the promise. It just attaches itself to the Promise's resolved and rejected states. When this happens, it emits events and invokes the respective callbacks. The `Observable` instance is bound to the state of the Promise, but `Promise` is not aware that anything has been attached to it since it blindly exposes its resolve and reject hooks.

 Note that only a resolved Promise will invoke the `onCompleted` handler; rejecting the promise will not invoke it.

There's more...

Observables and Promises are interchangeable if you are so inclined, but do consider that they are both appropriate in different situations.

Observables are good at stream-type operations, where the length of the stream is indeterminate. It is certainly possible to have an Observable that only ever emits one event, but an Observable will not broadcast this state to listeners that are attached later, unless you configure it to do so (such as `BehaviorObservable`).

Promises are good at masking asynchronous behavior. They allow you to write code and set handlers upon the Promise as if the promised state or value was realized at the time of execution. Of course it's not, but the ability to define a handler synchronously at runtime and have the Promise instance decide when it's appropriate to execute it, as well as the ability to chain these handlers, is extremely valuable.

See also

- *Understanding and implementing basic Promises* gives an extensive rundown of how and why to use Promises
- *Converting an HTTP service Observable into ZoneAwarePromise* gives you an Angular-centric view of how Promises, Observables, and Zones integrate inside an Angular application

Converting an HTTP service Observable into a ZoneAwarePromise

In Angular 2, the RxJS asynchronous observables are first-class citizens and much of the core toolkit has been configured to rely upon them. Nonetheless, it is still valuable to be able to have conversion between them, especially since they have similar duties.

 For more on RxJS Observables, refer to `Chapter 5`, *ReactiveX Observables*, which covers them in depth.

 The code, links, and a live example of this are available at `http://ngcookbook.herokuapp.com/0905/`.

Getting ready

You'll begin with the following simplistic application:

```
[app/article.component.ts]

import {Component} from '@angular/core';
```

```
import {Http} from '@angular/http';

@Component({
  selector: 'article',
  template: `
    <p></p>
  `
})
export class ArticleComponent {
  constructor(private http:Http) {
    // For demo purposes, have this plunk request itself to
    // avoid cross origin errors
    console.log(
      http.get('//run.plnkr.co/plunks/TBtcNDRelAOHDVpIuWw1'));
  }
}

// Observable {...}
```

Suppose your goal was to convert this HTTP call to use promises instead.

How to do it...

For the purposes of this recipe, you don't really need to understand any details about the `http` service or RxJS asynchronous observables. All that you need to know is that any method exposed by the `http` service will return an observable. Happily, the RxJS implementation can expose a `.toPromise()` method that converts the observable into its equivalent Promise object:

```
[app/article.component.ts]

import {Component} from '@angular/core';
import {Http} from '@angular/http';
import 'rxjs/Rx';

@Component({
  selector: 'article',
  template: `
    <p></p>
  `
})
export class ArticleComponent {
  constructor(private http:Http) {
    // For demo purposes, have this plunk request itself to
    // avoid cross origin errors
    console.log(
```

```
        http.get('//run.plnkr.co/plunks/TBtcNDRelAOHDVpIuWw1')
        .toPromise());
    }
}

// ZoneAwarePromise {...}
```

How it works...

The HTTP service, by default, returns an observable; however, without the imported Rx module, this will throw an error, saying it cannot find the toPromise() method.

The Rx module confers to an observable the ability to convert itself into a promise object. Angular 2 is intentionally not utilizing the Observable spec with all the RxJS operators to allow you to specify exactly which ones you want. Because the operators exist as separate modules, this leads to a smaller payload sent to the browser.

Once the .toPromise() method is invoked, the object is created to a ZoneAwarePromise instance.

 This sounds gnarly, but really, it's just wrapping the Promise implementation as zone.js so that the Angular zone is aware of any actions the Promise could cause that it should be aware of. For your purposes, this can be treated as a regular Promise.

See also

- *Understanding and implementing basic Promises* gives an extensive rundown of how and why to use Promises
- *Converting a Promise into an Observable* gives you an example of how RxJS can be used to convert between these two powerful types

5

ReactiveX Observables

This chapter will cover the following recipes:

- Basic utilization of Observables with HTTP
- Implementing a Publish-Subscribe model using Subjects
- Creating an Observable Authentication Service using BehaviorSubjects
- Building a generalized Publish-Subscribe service to replace $broadcast, $emit, and $on
- Using QueryLists and Observables to follow the changes in ViewChildren
- Building a fully featured AutoComplete with Observables

Introduction

Before you get into the meat of Angular 2 Observables, it is important to first understand the problem you are trying to solve.

A frequently encountered scenario in software is where you are expecting some entity to broadcast that something happened; let's call this an "event" (distinct from a browser event). You would like to hook into this entity and attach behavior to it whenever an event occurs. You would also like to be able to detach from this entity when you no longer care about the events it is broadcasting.

There is more nuance and additional complexity to Observables that this chapter will cover, but this concept of events underscores the fundamental pattern that is useful to you as the developer.

The Observer Pattern

The Observer Pattern isn't a library or framework. It is just a software design pattern upon which ReactiveX Observables are built. Many languages and libraries implement this pattern, and ReactiveX is just one of these implementations; however, ReactiveX is the one that Angular 2 has formally incorporated into itself.

The Observer Pattern describes the relationship between `subject`, which was described as the "entity" earlier, and its observers. The `subject` is aware of any `observers` that are watching it. When an event is emitted, the `subject` is able to pass this event to each `observer` via methods that are provided when the `observer` begins to subscribe it.

ReactiveX and RxJS

The ReactiveX library is implemented in numerous languages, including Python, Java, and Ruby. RxJS, the JavaScript implementation of the ReactiveX library, is the dependency that Angular 2 utilizes to incorporate Observables into native framework behavior. Similar to Promises, you can create a standalone Observable instance through direct instantiation, but many Angular 2 methods and services will also utilize an Observable interface by default.

Observables in Angular 2

Angular 2 integrates Observables in a wide variety of ways. If you are new to them, you may initially feel odd using them. However, it is important you recognize that Observables provide a superior software development pattern.

Along with the bulk RxJS module `rxjs/Rx`, you are also provided with the stripped down Observable module `rxjs/Observable`. This minimal module allows individual pieces of non-essential behavior to be imported as required in order to reduce module bloat. For example, when using this lightweight Observable module, using `operators` or other such ReactiveX conventions necessitates that you explicitly incorporate these modules, in order to extend the available Observable interface.

Observables and Promises

Both Observables and Promises offer solutions to asynchronous constructs, but Observables are more robust, extensible, and useful. Although Promises are available by default in the ES6 specification, you will quickly realize that they become brittle when you attempt to apply them outside the realm of basic application behavior.

The ReactiveX library offers powerful tooling to which Promises cannot compare. Observables are composable, allowing you to transform and combine them into new Observables. They also encapsulate the concept of a continuous stream of events-a paradigm that is encountered in client-side programming extremely frequently and that Promises do not translate well to.

Basic utilization of Observables with HTTP

In Angular 2, the `Http` module now by default utilizes the `Observable` pattern to wrap `XMLHttpRequest`. For developers that are familiar with the pattern, it readily translates to the asynchronous nature of requests to remote resources. For developers that are newer to the pattern, learning the ins and outs of `Http Observables` is a good way to wrap your head around this new paradigm.

> The code, links, and a live example related to this are available at
> `http://ngcookbook.herokuapp.com/4121`.

Getting ready

For the purpose of this example, you'll just serve a static JSON file to the application. However note that this would be no different if you were sending requests to a dynamic API endpoint.

Begin by creating a skeleton component, including all the necessary modules for making HTTP requests:

```
[app/article.component.ts]

import {Component} from '@angular/core';
import {Http} from '@angular/http';
@Component({
  selector: 'article',
```

```
    template: `
      <h1>{{title}}</h1>
      <p>{{author}}</p>
      `
  })
  export class ArticleComponent {
    title:string;
    body:string;
    constructor (private http: Http) {
    }
  }
```

For this example, assume there is a JSON file inside the static directory named
`article.json`:

```
[article.json]

{
  "title": "Orthopedic Doctors Ask City for More Sidewalk Cracks",
  "author": "Jake Hsu"
}
```

How to do it...

Since you have already injected the `Http` service, you can begin by defining the get request:

```
[app/article.component.ts]

import {Component} from '@angular/core';
import {Http} from '@angular/http';
@Component({
  selector: 'article',
  template: `
    <h1>{{title}}</h1>
    <p>{{author}}</p>
    `
})
export class ArticleComponent {
  title:string;
  body:string;
  constructor (private http_: Http) {
    http_.get('static/article.json');
  }
}
```

This creates an `Observable` instance, but you still need to add instructions on how to handle the raw string of the response.

 At this point, you will notice that this does not actually fire a browser GET request. This is covered in this recipe's *There's more* section.

Since you know the request will return JSON, you can utilize the `json()` method that a `Response` would expose. This can be done inside the `map()` method. However, the `Observable` does not expose the `map()` method by default, so you must import it from the `rxjs` module:

```
[app/article.component.ts]

import {Component} from '@angular/core';
import {Http} from '@angular/http';
import 'rxjs/add/operator/map';

@Component({
  selector: 'article',
  template: `
    <h1>{{title}}</h1>
    <p>{{author}}</p>
  `
})
export class ArticleComponent {
  title:string;
  author:string;
  constructor (private http_: Http) {
    http_.get('static/article.json')
        .map(response => response.json());
  }
}
```

So far so good, but you're still not done. The preceding code will create the `Observable` instance, but you still have to subscribe to it in order to handle any data it would emit. This can be accomplished with the `subscribe()` method, which allows you to attach the callback and error handling methods of `observer`:

```
[app/article.component.ts]

import {Component} from '@angular/core';
import {Http} from '@angular/http';
import 'rxjs/add/operator/map';
```

```
@Component({
  selector: 'article',
  template: `
    <h1>{{title}}</h1>
    <p>{{author}}</p>
  `
})
export class ArticleComponent {
  title:string;
  author:string;
  constructor (private http_: Http) {
    http_.get('static/article.json')
      .map(response => response.json())
      .subscribe(
        article => {
          this.title = article.title;
          this.author = article.author;
        },
        error => console.error(error));
  }
}
```

With all of this, the GET request will return the JSON file, and the response data will be parsed and its data interpolated into the DOM by the component.

How it works...

The previous section gave a good high-level overview of what was happening, but it is useful to break things down more carefully to understand what each individual step accomplishes.

Observable<Response>

The Http service class exposes the methods get(), post(), put(), and so on—all the HTTP verbs that you would expect. Each of these will return Observable<Response>, which will emit a Response instance when the request is returned:

```
console.log(http_.get('static/article.json'));
// Observable { ... }
```

> It sounds obvious, but Observables are observed by an observer. The observer will wait for Observable to emit objects, which in this example takes the form of Response.

The RxJS map() operator

The `Response` instance exposes a `json()` method, which converts the returned serialized payload string into its corresponding in-memory object representation. You would like to be able to pass a regular object to the `observer` handler, so the ideal tool here is a wedge method that still gives you an `Observable` in the end:

```
console.log(http_.get('static/article.json')
  .map(response => response.json()));
// Observable {source: Observable, operator: MapOperator, ...}
```

Recall that the canonical form of `Observables` is a stream of events. In this case, we know there will only ever be one event, which is the HTTP response. Nonetheless, all the normal operators that would be used on a stream of events can just as easily be used on this single-event `Observable`.

In the same way that `Array.map()` can be used to transform each instance in the array, `Observable.map()` allows you to transform each event emitted from `Observable`. More specifically, it creates another `Observable` that emits the modified event passed from the initial observable.

Subscribe

`Observable` instances expose a `subscribe()` method that accepts an `onNext` handler, an `onError` handler, and an `onCompleted` handler as arguments. These handlers correspond to the events in the life cycle of the `Observable` when it emits `Response` instances. The parameter for the `onNext` method is whatever is emitted from the `Observable`. In this case, the emitted data is the returned value from `map()`, so it will be the parsed object that has returned after invoking `json()` on the `Response` instance.

All these methods are optional, but in this example, the `onNext` and `onError` methods are useful.

 Together, these methods when provided to `subscribe()` constitute what is identified as the `observer`.

```
http_.get('static/article.json')
  .map(respose => respose.json())
  .subscribe(
    article => {
      this.title = article.title;
```

```
        this.body = article.body;
    },
    error => console.error(error));
```

With all of this together, the browser will fetch the JSON and parse it, and the subscriber will pass its data to the respective component members.

There's more…

When constructing this recipe piece by piece, if you are watching your browser's network requests as you assemble it, you will notice that the actual GET request is not fired until the `subscribe()` method is invoked. This is because the type `Observable` you are using is "cold".

Hot and cold Observables

The "cold" designation means that the `Observable` does not begin to emit until an `observer` begins to subscribe to it. This is different from a "hot" `Observable`, which will emit items even if there are no `observers` subscribed to it. Since this means that events that occur before an `observer` is attached are lost, HTTP `Observables` demand a cold designation.

The `onNext` method is termed "emission" since there is associated data that is being emitted. The `onCompleted` and `onError` methods are termed "notifications," as they represent something of significance, but they do not have an associated event that would be considered part of the stream.

See also

- *Implementing a Publish-Subscribe model using Subjects* shows you how to configure input and output for RxJS Observables
- *Building a fully featured AutoComplete with Observables* gives you a broad tour of some of the utilities offered to you as part of the RxJS library

Implementing a Publish-Subscribe model using Subjects

Angular 2 will often provide you with an `Observable` interface to attach to for free, but it is important to know how they are created, configured, and used. More specifically, it is valuable for you to know how to take `Observables` and apply them to real scenarios that will be encountered in the client.

 The code, links, and a live example of this are available at
`http://ngcookbook.herokuapp.com/4839/`.

Getting ready

Suppose you started with the following skeleton application:

```
[app/click-observer.component.ts]

import {Component} from '@angular/core';

@Component({
  selector: 'click-observer',
  template: `
   <button>
     Emit event!
   </button>
   <p *ngFor="let click of clicks; let i = index">
     {{i}}: {{click}}
   </p>
   `
})
export class ClickObserverComponent {
  clicks:Array<Event> = [];
}
```

Your goal is to convert this so that all the button click events are logged in to the repeated field.

How to do it...

Accomplishing this with a component member method and using it in the `click` event binding in the template is possible, but this doesn't capture the real value of `Observables`. You want to be able to expose an `Observable` on `ClickObserverComponent`. This will allow any other part of your application to subscribe to these `click` events and handle them in its own way.

Instead, you would like to be able to funnel the `click` events from the button into the `Observable`. With a regular `Observable` instance, this isn't possible since it is only acting as the *Subscribe* part of the Publish-Subscribe model. To accomplish the *Publish* aspect, you must use a `Subject` instance:

```
[app/click-observer.component.ts]

import {Component} from '@angular/core';
import {Subject} from 'rxjs/Subject';

@Component({
  selector: 'click-observer',
  template: `
   <button>
     Emit event!
   </button>
   <p *ngFor="let click of clicks; let i = index">
     {{i}}: {{click}}
   </p>
   `
})
export class ClickObserverComponent {
  clickEmitter:Subject<Event> = new Subject();
  clicks:Array<Event> = [];
}
```

ReactiveX `Subjects` act as both the `Observable` and the `Observer`. Therefore, it exposes both the `subscribe()` method, used for the Subscribe behavior, and the `next()` method, used for the Publish behavior.

 In this example, the `next()` method is useful because you want to explicitly specify when an emission should occur and what that emission should contain. There are lots of ways of instantiating `Observables` in order to implicitly generate emissions, such as (but certainly not limited to) `Observable.range()`. In these cases, `Observable` understands how its input behaves, and thus it does not need direction as to when emissions occur and what they should contain.

In this case, you can pass the event directly to `next()` in the template click handler definition. With this, all that is left is to populate the array by directing the emissions into it:

```
[app/click-observer.component.ts]

import {Component} from '@angular/core';
import {Subject} from 'rxjs/Subject';

@Component({
  selector: 'click-observer',
  template: `
   <button (click)="clickEmitter.next($event)">
     Emit event!
   </button>
   <p *ngFor="let click of clicks; let i = index">
     {{i}}: {{click}}
   </p>
   `
})
export class ClickObserverComponent {
  clickEmitter:Subject<Event> = new Subject();
  clicks:Array<Event> = [];

  constructor() {
   this.clickEmitter
     .subscribe(clickEvent => this.clicks.push(clickEvent));
  }
}
```

That's all! With this, you should see click events populate in the browser with each successive button click.

How it works...

ReactiveX `Observables` and `Observers` are distinct, but their behavior is mutually compatible in such a way that their union, `Subject`, can act as either one of them. In this example, the `Subject` is used as the interface to feed in `Event` objects as the Publish modality as well as to handle the result that would come out as the Subscribe modality.

There's more...

The way this is constructed might feel a bit strange to you. The component is exposing the `Subject` instance as the point where your application will attach observer handlers.

However, you want to prevent other parts of the application from adding additional events, which is still possible should they choose to use the `next()` method. What's more, the `Subject` instance is referenced directly inside the template and exposing it there may feel a bit odd. Therefore, it is desirable, and certainly good software practice, to only expose the `Observable` component of the `Subject`.

To do this, you must import the `Observable` module and utilize the `Subject` instance's member method, namely `asObservable()`. This method will create a new `Observable` instance that will effectively pipe the observed emissions from the `Subject` into the new `Observable`, which will be exposed as a public component member:

```
[app/article.component.ts]

import {Component} from '@angular/core';
import {Observable} from 'rxjs/Observable';
import {Subject} from 'rxjs/Subject';

@Component({
  selector: 'click-observer',
  template: `
   <button (click)="publish($event)">
     Emit event!
   </button>
   <p *ngFor="let click of clicks; let i = index">
     {{i}}: {{click}}
   </p>
   `
})
export class ClickObserverComponent {
  clickEmitter: Observable<Event>;
  private clickSubject_: Subject<Event> = new Subject();
  clicks:Array<Event> = [];

  constructor() {
   this.clickEmitter = this.clickSubject_.asObservable();
   this.clickEmitter.subscribe(clickEvent =>
     this.clicks.push(clickEvent));
  }

  publish(e:Event):void {
   this.clickSubject_.next(e);
  }
}
```

Now even though only this component is referencing `clickEmitter`, every component that uses `clickEmitter` will not need or be able to touch the source, `Subject`.

Native RxJS implementation

This has all been a great example, but this is such a common pattern in that the RxJS library already provides a built-in way of implementing it. The Observable class exposes a static method fromEvent(), which takes in an element that is expected to generate events and the event type to listen to.

However, you need a reference to the actual element, which you currently do not have. For the present implementation, the Angular 2 ViewChild faculties will give you a very nice reference to the button, which will then be passed to the fromEvent() method once the template has been rendered:

```
[app/click-observer.component.ts]

import {Component, ViewChild, ngAfterViewInit}
  from '@angular/core';
import {Observable} from 'rxjs/Observable';
import 'rxjs/add/observable/fromEvent';

@Component({
  selector: 'click-observer',
  template: `
   <button #btn>
     Emit event!
   </button>
   <p *ngFor="let click of clicks; let i = index">
     {{i}}: {{click}}
   </p>
  `
})
export class ClickObserverComponent implements AfterViewInit {
  @ViewChild('btn') btn;
  clickEmitter:Observable<Event>;
  clicks:Array<Event> = [];

  ngAfterViewInit() {
    this.clickEmitter = Observable.fromEvent(
        this.btn.nativeElement, 'click');
    this.clickEmitter.subscribe(clickEvent =>
        this.clicks.push(clickEvent));
  }
}
```

With all of this, the component should still behave identically.

See also

- *Basic utilization of Observables with HTTP* demonstrates the basics of how to use an observable interface
- *Creating an Observable authentication service using BehaviorSubjects* instructs you on how to reactively manage the state in your application
- *Building a fully featured AutoComplete with Observables* gives you a broad tour of some of the utilities offered to you as part of the RxJS library

Creating an Observable authentication service using BehaviorSubjects

One of the most obvious and useful cases of the Observer Pattern is the one in which a single entity in your application unidirectionally communicates information to a field of listeners on the outside. These listeners would like to be able to attach and detach freely from the single broadcasting entity. A good initial example of this is the login/logout component.

 The code, links, and a live example of this are available at `http://ngcookbook.herokuapp.com/6957/`.

Getting ready

Suppose you have the following skeleton application:

```
[app/login.component.ts]

import {Component} from '@angular/core';

@Component({
  selector: 'login',
  template: `
    <button *ngIf="!loggedIn"
            (click)="loggedIn=true">
      Login
    </button>
    <button *ngIf="loggedIn"
```

```
                (click)="loggedIn=false">
      Logout
    </button>
    `
})
export class LoginComponent {
  loggedIn:boolean = false;
}
```

As it presently exists, this component will allow you to toggle between the login/logout button, but there is no concept of shared application state, and other components cannot utilize the login state that this component would track.

You would like to introduce this state to a shared service that is operated using the Observer Pattern.

How to do it...

Begin by creating an empty service and injecting it into this component:

```
[app/authentication.service.ts]

import {Injectable} from '@angular/core';

@Injectable()
export class AuthService {
  private authState_: AuthState;
}

export const enum AuthState {
    LoggedIn,
    LoggedOut
}
```

Notice that you are using a TypeScript `const enum` to keep track of the user's authentication state.

If you're new to ES6 and TypeScript, these keywords may feel a bit bizarre to you. The `const` keyword is from the ES6 specification, signifying that this value is read only once declared. In vanilla ES6, this will throw an error, usually `SyntaxError`, at runtime. With TypeScript compilation though, `const` will be caught at compile time.

The `enum` keyword is an offering of TypeScript. It is not dissimilar to a regular object literal, but note that the `enum` members do not have values.

Throughout the application, you will reference these via
`AuthState.LoggedIn` and `AuthState.LoggedOut`. If you reference the
compiled JavaScript that TypeScript generates, you will see that these are
actually assigned integer values. But for the purposes of building large
applications, this allows us to develop a centralized repository of possible
`AuthState` values without worrying about their actual values.

Injecting the authentication service

As the skeleton service currently exists, you are going to instantiate a `Subject` that will
emit `AuthState`, but there is no way available currently to interact with it. You will set this
up in a bit. First, you must inject this service into your component:

```
[app/app.module.ts]

import {NgModule} from '@angular/core';
import {BrowserModule} from '@angular/platform-browser';
import {LoginComponent} from './login.component';
import {AuthService} from './authentication.service';

@NgModule({
  imports: [
    BrowserModule
  ],
  declarations: [
    LoginComponent
  ],
  providers: [
    AuthService
  ],
  bootstrap: [
    LoginComponent
  ]
})
export class AppModule {}
```

This is all well and good, but the service is still unusable as is.

 Note that the path you import your `AuthService` from may vary
depending on where it lies in your file tree.

Adding BehaviorSubject to the authentication service

The core of this service is to maintain a global application state. It should expose itself to the rest of the application by letting other parts say to the service, "Let me know whenever the state changes. Also, I'd like to know what the state is right now." The perfect tool for this task is BehaviorSubject.

 RxJS Subjects also have several subclasses, and BehaviorSubject is one of them. Fundamentally, it follows all the rhythms of Subjects, but the main difference is that it will emit its current state to any observer that begins to listen to it, as if that event is entirely new. In cases like this, where you want to keep track of the state, this is extremely useful.

Add a private BehaviorSubject (initialized to the LoggedOut state) and a public Observable to AuthService:

```
[app/authentication.service.ts]

import {Injectable} from '@angular/core';
import {BehaviorSubject} from 'rxjs/BehaviorSubject';
import {Observable} from 'rxjs/Observable';

@Injectable()
export class AuthService {
  private authManager_:BehaviorSubject<AuthState>
    = new BehaviorSubject(AuthState.LoggedOut);
  private authState_:AuthState;
  authChange:Observable<AuthState>;

  constructor() {
    this.authChange = this.authManager_.asObservable();
  }
}

export const enum AuthState {
  LoggedIn,
  LoggedOut
}
```

Adding API methods to the authentication service

Recall that you do not want to expose the BehaviorSubject instance to outside actors. Instead, you would like to offer only its Observable component, which you can openly subscribe to. Furthermore, you would like to allow outside actors to set the authentication state, but only indirectly. This can be accomplished with the following methods:

```
[app/authentication.service.ts]

import {Injectable} from '@angular/core';
import {BehaviorSubject} from 'rxjs/BehaviorSubject';
import {Observable} from 'rxjs/Observable';

@Injectable()
export class AuthService {
  private authManager_:BehaviorSubject<AuthState>
    = new BehaviorSubject(AuthState.LoggedOut);
  private authState_:AuthState;
  authChange:Observable<AuthState>;

  constructor() {
    this.authChange = this.authManager_.asObservable();
  }
  login():void {
    this.setAuthState_(AuthState.LoggedIn);
  }
  logout():void {
    this.setAuthState_(AuthState.LoggedOut);
  }
  emitAuthState():void {
    this.authManager_.next(this.authState_);
  }
  private setAuthState_(newAuthState:AuthState):void {
    this.authState_ = newAuthState;
    this.emitAuthState();
  }
}

export const enum AuthState {
    LoggedIn,
    LoggedOut
}
```

Outstanding! With all of this, outside actors will be able to subscribe to authChange Observable and will indirectly control the state via login() and logout().

Note that the `Observable` component of `BehaviorSubject` is named `authChange`. Naming the different components of the elements in the Observer Pattern can be tricky. This naming convention was selected to represent what an event emitted from the `Observable` actually meant. Quite literally, `authChange` is the answer to the question, "What event am I observing?". Therefore, it makes good semantic sense that your component subscribes to `authChanges` when the authentication state changes.

Wiring the service methods into the component

`LoginComponent` does not yet utilize the service, so add in its newly created methods:

```
[app/login.component.ts]

import {Component} from '@angular/core';
import {AuthService, AuthState} from './authentication.service';

@Component({
  selector: 'login',
  template: `
    <button *ngIf="!loggedIn"
            (click)="login()">
      Login
    </button>
    <button *ngIf="loggedIn"
            (click)="logout()">
      Logout
    </button>
  `
})
export class LoginComponent {
  loggedIn:boolean;

  constructor(private authService_:AuthService) {
    authService_.authChange.subscribe(
      newAuthState =>
        this.loggedIn = (newAuthState === AuthState.LoggedIn));
  }

  login():void {
    this.authService_.login();
  }

  logout():void {
```

```
        this.authService_.logout();
    }
}
```

With all of this in place, you should be able to see your login/logout buttons function well. This means you have correctly incorporated `Observable` into your component.

This recipe is a good example of conventions you're required to maintain when using public/private. Note that the injected service is declared as a private member and wrapped with public component member methods. Anything that another part of the application calls or anything that is used inside the template should be a public member.

How it works...

Central to this implementation is that each component that is listening to `Observable` has an idempotent handling of events that are emitted. Each time a new component is connected to `Observable`, it instructs the service to emit whatever the current state is, using `emitAuthState()`. Necessarily, all components don't behave any differently if they see the same state emitted multiple times in a row; they will only alter their behavior if they see a change in the state.

Notice how you have totally encapsulated the authentication state inside the authentication service, and at the same time, have exposed and utilized a reactive API for the entire application to build upon.

There's more...

Two critical components of hooking into services such as these are the setup and teardown processes. A fastidious developer will have noticed that even if an instance of `LoginComponent` is destroyed, the subscription to `Observable` will still persist. This, of course, is extremely undesirable!

Fortunately, the `subscribe()` method of `Observables` returns an instance of Subscription, which exposes an `unsubscribe()` method. You can therefore capture this instance upon the invocation of `subscribe()` and then invoke it when the component is being torn down.

Similar to listener teardown in Angular 1, you must invoke the unsubscribe method when the component instance is being destroyed. Happily, the Angular 2 life cycle provides you with such a method, `ngOnDestroy`, in which you can invoke `unsubscribe()`:

```
[app/login.component.ts]

import {Component, ngOnDestroy} from '@angular/core';
import {AuthService, AuthState} from './authentication.service';
import {Subscription} from 'rxjs/Subscription';

@Component({
  selector: 'login',
  template: `
    <button *ngIf="!loggedIn"
            (click)="login()">
      Login
    </button>
    <button *ngIf="loggedIn"
            (click)="logout()">
      Logout
    </button>
  `
})
export class LoginComponent implements OnDestroy {
  loggedIn:boolean;
  private authChangeSubscription_: Subscription;

  constructor(private authService_:AuthService) {
    this.authChangeSubscription_ =
      authService_.authChange.subscribe(
        newAuthState =>
          this.loggedIn = (newAuthState === AuthState.LoggedIn));
  }

  login():void {
    this.authService_.login();
  }
  logout():void {
    this.authService_.logout();
  }
  ngOnDestroy() {
    this.authChangeSubscription_.unsubscribe();
  }
}
```

Now your application is safe from memory leaks should any instance of this component ever be destroyed in the lifetime of your application.

See also

- *Basic utilization of Observables with HTTP* demonstrates the basics of how to use an observable interface
- *Implementing a Publish-Subscribe model using Subjects* shows you how to configure input and output for RxJS Observables
- *Building a generalized Publish-Subscribe service to replace $broadcast, $emit, and $on* assembles a robust PubSub model for connecting application components with channels
- *Building a fully featured AutoComplete with Observables* gives you a broad tour of some of the utilities offered to you as part of the RxJS library

Building a generalized Publish-Subscribe service to replace $broadcast, $emit, and $on

In Angular 1, the `$emit` and `$broadcast` behaviors were indeed very useful tools. They gave you the ability to send custom events upwards and downwards through the scope tree to any listeners that might be waiting for such an event. This pushed the developer towards a very useful pattern: the ability for many components to be able to transmit events to and from a central source. However, using `$emit` and `$broadcast` for such a purpose was grossly inappropriate; they had the effect of feeding the event through huge numbers of scopes only to reach the single intended target.

In the previous edition of this book, the corresponding recipe demonstrated how to build a Publish-Subscribe service that used the `$emit` and `$rootScope` injection. The version in this recipe, although different in a handful of ways, achieves similar results in a substantially cleaner and more elegant fashion.

It is preferable to create a single entity that can serve as a generic throughway for events to pass from publishers to their subscribers.

The code, links, and a live example of this are available at `http://ngcookbook.herokuapp.com/2417/`.

Getting ready

Begin with a skeleton service injected into a component:

```
[app/node.component.ts]

import {Component, Input} from '@angular/core';
import {PubSubService} from './publish-subscribe.service';

@Component({
  selector: 'node',
  template: `
    <p>Heard {{count}} of {{subscribeChannel}}</p>
    <button (click)="send()">Send {{publishChannel}}</button>
  `
})
export class NodeComponent {
  @Input() publishChannel:string;
  @Input() subscribeChannel:string;
  count:number = 0;

  constructor(private pubSubService_:PubSubService) {}
  send() {}
}
[app/publish-subscribe.service.ts]

import {Injectable} from '@angular/core';

@Injectable()
export class PubSubService {
  constructor() {}

  publish() {}

  subscribe() {}
}
```

How to do it...

The groundwork for this implementation should be pretty obvious. The service is going to host a single `Subject` instance that is going to funnel events of any type into the service and out through the observers of the `Subject`.

First, implement the following so that `subscribe()` and `publish()` actually do work when you involve the `Subject` instance:

```
[app/publish-subscribe.service.ts]

import {Injectable} from '@angular/core';
import {Subject} from 'rxjs/Subject';
import {Observable} from 'rxjs/Observable';
import {Observer} from 'rxjs/Observer';
import {Subscriber} from 'rxjs/Subscriber;

@Injectable()
export class PubSubService {
  private publishSubscribeSubject_:Subject<any> = new Subject();
  emitter_:Observable<any>;

  constructor() {
    this.emitter_ = this.publishSubscribeSubject_.asObservable();
  }

  publish(event:any):void {
    this.publishSubscribeSubject_.next(event);
  }

  subscribe(handler:NextObserver<any>):Subscriber {
    return this.emitter_.subscribe(handler);
  }
}
```

This is terrific for an initial implementation, but yields a problem: every event published to this service will be broadcasted to all the subscribers.

Introducing channel abstraction

It is possible and in fact quite easy to restrict publish and subscribe in such a way that they will only pay attention to the channel they specify. First, modify publish() to nest the event inside the emitted object:

```
[app/publish-subscribe.service.ts]

import {Injectable} from '@angular/core';
import {Subject} from 'rxjs/Subject';
import {Observable} from 'rxjs/Observable';
import {Observer} from 'rxjs/Observer';
import {Subscriber} from 'rxjs/Subscriber;
@Injectable()
export class PubSubService {
  private publishSubscribeSubject_:Subject<any> = new Subject();
  emitter_:Observable<any>;
```

```
  constructor() {
    this.emitter_ = this.publishSubscribeSubject_.asObservable();
  }

  publish(channel:string, event:any):void {
    this.publishSubscribeSubject_.next({
      channel: channel,
      event: event
    });
  }

  subscribe(handler:NextObserver<any>):Subscriber {
    return this.emitter_.subscribe(handler);
  }
}
```

With this, you are now able to utilize some `Observable` behavior to restrict which events the subscription is paying attention to.

`Observable` emissions can have `filter()` and `map()` applied to them. `filter()` will return a new `Observable` instance that only emits whichever emissions evaluate as true in its `filter` function. `map()` returns a new `Observable` instance that transforms all emissions into a new value.

```
[app/publish-subscribe.service.ts]

import {Injectable} from '@angular/core';
import {Subject} from 'rxjs/Subject';
import {Observable} from 'rxjs/Observable';
import {Observer} from 'rxjs/Observer';
import {Subscriber} from 'rxjs/Subscriber;
import 'rxjs/add/operator/filter';
import 'rxjs/add/operator/map';

@Injectable()
export class PubSubService {
  private publishSubscribeSubject_:Subject<any> = new Subject();
  emitter_:Observable<any>;

  constructor() {
    this.emitter_ = this.publishSubscribeSubject_.asObservable();
  }

  publish(channel:string, event:any):void {
    this.publishSubscribeSubject_.next({
      channel: channel,
      event: event
```

```
      });
    }

  subscribe(channel:string, handler:((value:any) => void)):Subscriber {
    return this.emitter_
      .filter(emission => emission.channel === channel)
      .map(emission => emission.event)
      .subscribe(handler);
  }
}
```

Hooking components into the service

The service is complete, but the component doesn't yet have the ability to use it. Use the injected service to link the component to the channels specified by its input strings:

```
[app/node.component.ts]

import {Component, Input} from '@angular/core';
import {PubSubService} from './publish-subscribe.service';

@Component({
  selector: 'node',
  template: `
    <p>Heard {{count}} of {{subscribeChannel}}</p>
    <button (click)="send()">Send {{publishChannel}}</button>
  `
})
export class NodeComponent {
  @Input() publishChannel:string;
  @Input() subscribeChannel:string;
  count:number = 0;

  constructor(private pubSubService_:PubSubService) {}

  send() {
    this.pubSubService_
      .publish(this.publishChannel, {});
  }

  ngAfterViewInit() {
    this.pubSubService_
      .subscribe(this.subscribeChannel,
                 event => ++this.count);
  }
}
```

The `publish()` method has an empty object literal as its second argument. This is the payload for the published message, which isn't used in this recipe. If you want to send data along with a message, this is where it would go.

With all of this, test your application with the following:

```
[app/root.component.ts]

import {Component} from '@angular/core';

@Component({
  selector: 'root',
  template: `
    <node subscribeChannel="foo"
          publishChannel="bar">
    </node>
    <node subscribeChannel="bar"
          publishChannel="foo">
    </node>
  `
})
export class RootComponent {}
```

You will see that channel publishing and subscribing is happening as you would expect.

Unsubscribing from channels

Of course, you want to avoid memory leaks wherever possible. This requires that you explicitly complete the cleanup process when your component instance is destroyed:

```
[app/node.component.ts]

import {Component, Input, OnDestroy} from '@angular/core';
import {PubSubService} from './publish-subscribe.service';
import {Subscription} from 'rxjs/Subscription';

@Component({
  selector: 'node',
  template: `
    <p>Heard {{count}} of {{subscribeChannel}}</p>
    <button (click)="send()">Send {{publishChannel}}</button>
  `
})
export class NodeComponent implements OnDestroy {
  @Input() publishChannel:string;
```

```
@Input() subscribeChannel:string;
count:number = 0;
private pubSubServiceSubscription_:Subscription;

constructor(private pubSubService_:PubSubService) {}

send() {
  this.pubSubService_
    .publish(this.publishChannel, {});
}

ngAfterViewInit() {
  this.pubSubService_
    .subscribe(this.subscribeChannel,
               event => ++this.count);
}

ngOnDestroy() {
  this.pubSubServiceSubscription_.unsubscribe();
}
}
```

How it works...

Each time `publish()` is invoked, the provided event is wrapped by the provided channel and submitted to a central `Subject`, which is private inside the service. At the same time, the fact that each invocation of `subscribe()` wants to listen to a different channel presents a problem. This is because an `Observable` does not draw distinctions regarding what is being emitted without explicit direction.

You are able to utilize the `filter()` and `map()` operators to establish a customized view of the emissions of `Subject` and use this view in the application of the `Observer` handler. Each time `subscribe()` is invoked, it creates a new `Observable` instance; however, these are all merely points of indirection from the one true `Observable`, which is owned by the private instance hidden inside the service.

There's more...

It's important to understand why this service is not built in a different way.

An important feature of `Observables` is their ability to be composed. That is, several `Observable` instances independently emitting events can be combined into one `Observable` instance, which will emit all the events from a combined source. This can be accomplished in several different ways, including `flatMap()` or `merge()`. This ability is what is being referred to when ReactiveX Observables are described as "composable."

Therefore, a developer might see this composition ability and think it would be suitable for a Publish-Subscribe entity. The entity would accept `Observable` instances from the publishers. They would be combined to create a single `Observable` instance, and subscribers would attach `Observable` to this combination. What could possibly go wrong?

Considerations of an Observable's composition and manipulation

One primary concern is that the composed `Observable` that the subscribers are being attached to will change constantly. As is the case with `map()` and `filter()`, any modulation performed on an `Observable` instance, including composition, will return a new `Observable` instance. This new instance would become the `Observable` that subscribers would attach to, and therein lies the problem.

Let's examine this problem step by step:

1. PubSub service emits events from Observable *A*.
2. Node *X* subscribes to the service and receives events from Observable *A*.
3. Some other part of the application adds Observable *B* to the PubSub service.
4. The PubSub service composes Observable *A* and Observable *B* into Observable *AB*.
5. Node *Y* subscribes to the service and receives events from Observable *AB*.

Note that in this case, Node *X* would still receive events from only Observable *A* since that is the Observable instance where it invoked `subscribe()`.

Certainly, there are steps that can be taken to mitigate this problem, such as having an additional level of indirection between the subscribe `Observable` and the composed `Observable`. However, a wise engineer will step back at this point and take stock of the situation. Publish-Subscribe is supposed to be a relatively "dumb" protocol, meaning that it shouldn't be delegated too much responsibility around managing the events it has been passed with—messages in and messages out, with no real concern for what is contained as long as they get there. One could make a very strong argument that introducing `Observables` in the Publish side greatly overcomplicates things.

In the case of this recipe, you have developed an elegant and simple version of a Publish-Subscribe module, and it feels right to delegate complexity outside of it. In the case of entities wanting to use Publish with `Observables`, a solution might be to just pipe the `Observable` emissions into the service's `publish()` method.

See also

- *Basic utilization of Observables with HTTP* demonstrates the basics of how to use an observable interface
- *Implementing a Publish-Subscribe model using Subjects* shows you how to configure input and output for RxJS Observables
- *Creating an Observable authentication service using BehaviorSubjects* instructs you on how to reactively manage the state in your application
- *Building a fully featured AutoComplete with Observables* gives you a broad tour of some of the utilities offered to you as part of the RxJS library

Using QueryLists and Observables to follow changes in ViewChildren

One very useful piece of behavior in components is the ability to track changes to the collections of children in the view. In many ways, this is quite a nebulous subject, as the number of ways in which view collections can be altered is numerous and subtle. Thankfully, Angular 2 provides a solid foundation for tracking these changes.

 The code, links, and a live example of this are available at `http://ngcookbook.herokuapp.com/4112/`.

Getting ready

Suppose you begin with the following skeleton application:

```
[app/inner.component.ts]

import {Component, Input} from '@angular/core';
```

```
@Component({
  selector: 'inner',
  template: `<p>{{val}}`
})
export class InnerComponent {
  @Input() val:number;
}
[app/outer.component.ts]

import {Component} from '@angular/core';

@Component({
  selector: 'outer',
  template: `
    <button (click)="add()">Moar</button>
    <button (click)="remove()">Less</button>
    <button (click)="shuffle()">Shuffle</button>
    <inner *ngFor="let i of list"
            val="{{i}}">
    </inner>

  `
})
export class OuterComponent {
  list:Array<number> = [];

  add():void {
    this.list.push(this.list.length)
  }

  remove():void {
    this.list.pop();
  }

  shuffle():void {
    // simple assignment shuffle
    this.list = this.list.sort(() => (4*Math.random()>2)?1:-1);
  }
}
```

As is, this is a very simple list manager that gives you the ability to add, remove, and shuffle a list interpolated as `InnerComponent` instances. You want the ability to track when this list undergoes changes and keep references to the component instances that correspond to the view collection.

How to do it...

Begin by using `ViewChildren` to collect the `InnerComponent` instances into a single `QueryList`:

```
[app/outer.component.ts]

import {Component, ViewChildren, QueryList} from '@angular/core';
import {InnerComponent} from './inner.component';

@Component({
  selector: 'outer',
  template: `
    <button (click)="add()">Moar</button>
    <button (click)="remove()">Less</button>
    <button (click)="shuffle()">Shuffle</button>
    <inner *ngFor="let i of list"
           val="{{i}}">
    </inner>
  `
})
export class OuterComponent {
  @ViewChildren(InnerComponent) innerComponents:
    QueryList<InnerComponent>;
  list:Array<number> = [];

  add():void {
    this.list.push(this.list.length)
  }

  remove():void {
    this.list.pop();
  }

  shuffle():void {
    // simple assignment shuffle
    this.list = this.list.sort(() => (4*Math.random()>2)?1:-1);
  }
}
```

Easy! Now, once the view of `OuterComponent` is initialized, you will be able to use `this.innerComponents` to reference `QueryList`.

Dealing with QueryLists

`QueryLists` are strange birds in Angular 2, but like many other facets of the framework, they are just a convention that you will have to learn. In this case, they are an immutable and iterable collection that exposes a handful of methods to inspect what they contain and when these contents are altered.

In this case, the two instance properties you care about are `last` and `changes`. `last`, as you might expect, will return the last instance of `QueryList`—in this case, an instance of `InnerComponent` if `QueryList` is not empty. `changes` will return an `Observable` that will emit `QueryList` whenever a change occurs inside it. In the case of a collection of `InnerComponent` instances, the addition, removal, and shuffling options will all be registered as changes.

Using these properties, you can very easily set up `OuterComponent` to keep track of what the value of the last `InnerComponent` instance is:

```
import {Component, ViewChildren, QueryList} from '@angular/core';
import {InnerComponent} from './inner.component';

@Component({
  selector: 'app-outer',
  template: `
    <button (click)="add()">Moar</button>
    <button (click)="remove()">Less</button>
    <button (click)="shuffle()">Shuffle</button>
    <app-inner *ngFor="let i of list"
               val="{{i}}">
    </app-inner>
    <p>Value of last: {{lastVal}}</p>
  `
})
export class OuterComponent {
  @ViewChildren(InnerComponent) innerComponents:
    QueryList<InnerComponent>;
  list: Array<number> = [];
  lastVal: number;

  constructor() {}

  add() {
    this.list.push(this.list.length)
  }

  remove() {
    this.list.pop();
```

```
  }

  shuffle() {
    this.list = this.list.sort(() => (4*Math.random()>2)?1:-1);
  }

  ngAfterViewInit() {
    this.innerComponents.changes
      .subscribe(e => this.lastVal = (e.last || {}).val);
  }
}
```

With all of this, you should be able to find that `lastVal` will stay up to date with any changes you would trigger in the `InnerComponent` collection.

Correcting the expression changed error

If you run the application as is, you will notice that an error is thrown after you click on the **Moar** button the first time:

```
Expression has changed after it was checked
```

This is an error you will most likely see frequently in Angular 2. The meaning is simple: since you are, by default, operating in development mode, Angular will check twice to see that any bound values do not change after all of the change detection logic has been resolved. In the case of this recipe, the emission by `QueryList` modifies `lastVal`, which Angular does not expect. Thus, you'll need to explicitly inform the framework that the value is expected to change again. This can be accomplished by injecting `ChangeDetectorRef`, which allows you to trigger a change detection cycle once the value is changed:

```
import {Component, ViewChildren, QueryList, ngAfterViewInit,
  ChangeDetectorRef} from '@angular/core';
import {InnerComponent} from './inner.component';

@Component({
  selector: 'outer',
  template: `
    <button (click)="add()">Moar</button>
    <button (click)="remove()">Less</button>
    <button (click)="shuffle()">Shuffle</button>
    <inner *ngFor="let i of list"
           val="{{i}}">
    </inner>
    <p>Value of last: {{lastVal}}</p>
```

```
})
export class OuterComponent implements AfterViewInit {
  @ViewChildren(InnerComponent) innerComponents:
    QueryList<InnerComponent>;
  list:Array<number> = [];
  lastVal:number;

  constructor(private changeDetectorRef_:ChangeDetectorRef) {}

  add():void {
    this.list.push(this.list.length)
  }

  remove():void {
    this.list.pop();
  }

  shuffle():void {
    // simple assignment shuffle
    this.list = this.list.sort(() => (4*Math.random()>2)?1:-1);
  }
  ngAfterViewInit() {
    this.innerComponents.changes
      .subscribe(innerComponents => {
        this.lastVal = (innerComponents.last || {}).val;
        this.changeDetectorRef_.detectChanges();
      });
  }
}
```

At this point, everything should work correctly with no errors.

How it works...

Once the OuterComponent view is initialized, you will be able to interact with QueryList that is obtained using ViewChildren. Each time the collection that QueryList wraps is modified, the Observable exposed by its changes property will emit QueryList, signaling that something has changed.

Hate the player, not the game

Importantly, `Observable<QueryList>` does not track changes in the array of numbers. It tracks the generated collection of `InnerComponents`. The `ngFor` structural directive is responsible for generating the list of `InnerComponent` instances in the view. It is this collection that `QueryList` is concerned with, not the original array.

This is a good thing! `ViewChildren` should only be concerned with the components as they have been rendered inside the view, not the data that caused them to be rendered in such a fashion.

One important consideration of this is that upon each emission, it is entirely possible that `QueryList` will be empty. As shown above, since the `Observer` of the `QueryList.changes` `Observable` tries to reference a property of `last`, it is necessary to have a fallback object literal in the event that `last` returns `undefined`.

See also

- *Basic Utilization of Observables with HTTP* demonstrates the basics of how to use an observable interface
- *Building a fully featured AutoComplete with Observables* gives you a broad tour of some of the utilities offered to you as part of the RxJS library

Building a fully featured AutoComplete with Observables

RxJS Observables afford you a lot of firepower, and it would be a shame to miss out on them. A huge library of transformations and utilities are baked right in that allow you to elegantly architect complex portions of your application in a reactive fashion.

In this recipe, you'll take a naïve autocomplete form and build a robust set of features to enhance behavior and performance.

 The code, links, and a live example of this are available at
`http://ngcookbook.herokuapp.com/8629/`.

Getting ready

Begin with the following application:

```
[app/app.module.ts]

import {NgModule} from '@angular/core';
import {BrowserModule} from '@angular/platform-browser';
import {SearchComponent} from './search.component';
import {APIService} from './api.service';
import {HttpModule} from '@angular/http';

@NgModule({
  imports: [
    BrowserModule,
    HttpModule
  ],
  declarations: [
    SearchComponent
  ],
  providers: [
    APIService
  ],
  bootstrap: [
    SearchComponent
  ]
})
export class AppModule {}
[app/search.component.ts]

import {Component} from '@angular/core';
import {APIService} from './api.service';

@Component({
  selector: 'search',
  template: `
    <input #queryField (keyup)="search(queryField.value)">
    <p *ngFor="let result of results">{{result}}</p>
  `
})
export class SearchComponent {
  results:Array<string> = [];
  constructor(private apiService_:APIService) {}
  search(query:string):void {
    this.apiService_
      .search(query)
      .subscribe(result => this.results.push(result));
  }
```

```
}

[app/api.service.ts]

import {Injectable} from '@angular/core';
import {Http} from '@angular/http';
import {Observable} from 'rxjs/Rx';

@Injectable()
export class APIService {
  constructor(private http_:Http) {}
  search(query:string):Observable<string> {
    return this.http_
      .get('static/response.json')
      .map(r => r.json()['prefix'] + query)
      // Below is just a clever way of randomly
      // delaying the response between 0 to 1000ms
      .concatMap(
        x => Observable.of(x).delay(Math.random()*1000));
  }
}
```

Your objective is to dramatically enhance this using RxJS.

How to do it...

As is, this application is listening for keyup events in the search input, performing an HTTP request to a static JSON file and adding the response to a list of results.

Using the FormControl valueChanges Observable

Angular 2 has observable behavior already available to you in a number of places. One of them is inside ReactiveFormsModule, which allows you to use an Observable that is attached to a form input. Convert this input to use FormControl, which exposes a valueChanges Observable:

```
[app/app.module.ts]

import {NgModule} from '@angular/core';
import {BrowserModule} from '@angular/platform-browser';
import {SearchComponent} from './search.component';
import {APIService} from './api.service';
import {HttpModule} from '@angular/http';
import {ReactiveFormsModule} from '@angular/forms';
```

```
@NgModule({
  imports: [
    BrowserModule,
    HttpModule,
    ReactiveFormsModule
  ],
  declarations: [
    SearchComponent
  ],
  providers: [
    APIService
  ],
  bootstrap: [
    SearchComponent
  ]
})
export class AppModule {}

[app/search.component.ts]

import {Component} from '@angular/core';
import {APIService} from './api.service';
import {FormControl} from '@angular/forms';

@Component({
  selector: 'search',
  template: `
    <input [formControl]="queryField">
    <p *ngFor="let result of results">{{result}}</p>
  `
})
export class SearchComponent {
  results:Array<string> = [];
  queryField:FormControl = new FormControl();
  constructor(private apiService_:APIService) {
    this.queryField.valueChanges
      .subscribe(query => this.apiService_
        .search(query)
        .subscribe(result => this.results.push(result)));
  }
}
```

Debouncing the input

Each time the input value changes, Angular will dutifully fire off a request and handle the response as soon as it is ready. In the case where the user is querying a very long term, such as supercalifragilisticexpialidocious, it may be necessary for you to only send off a single request once you think they're done with typing, as opposed to 34 requests, one for each time the input changes.

RxJS Observables have this built in. debounceTime(delay) will create a new Observable that will only pass along the latest value when there haven't been any other values for <delay> ms. This should be added to the valueChanges Observable since this is the source that you wish to debounce. 200 ms will be suitable for your purposes:

```
[app/search.component.ts]

import {Component} from '@angular/core';
import {APIService} from './api.service';
import {FormControl} from '@angular/forms';

@Component({
  selector: 'search',
  template: `
    <input [formControl]="queryField">
    <p *ngFor="let result of results">{{result}}</p>
  `
})
export class SearchComponent {
  results:Array<string> = [];
  queryField:FormControl = new FormControl();
  constructor(private apiService_:APIService) {
    this.queryField.valueChanges
      .debounceTime(200)
      .subscribe(query => this.apiService_
        .search(query)
        .subscribe(result => this.results.push(result)));
  }
}
```

The origin of the term **debounce** comes from the world of circuits. Mechanical buttons or switches utilize metal contacts to open and close circuit connections. When the metal contacts are closed, they will bang together and rebound before being settled, causing bounce. This bounce is problematic in the circuit, as it will often register as a repeat toggling of the switch or button—obviously buggy behavior. The workaround for this is to find a way to ignore the expected bounce noise—debouncing! This can be accomplished by either ignoring the bounce noise or introducing a delay before reading the value, both of which can be done with hardware or software.

Ignoring serial duplicates

Since you are reading input from a textbox, it is very possible that the user will type one character, then type another character and press backspace. From the perspective of the `Observable`, since it is now debounced by a delay period, it is entirely possible that the user input will be interpreted in such a way that the debounced output will emit two identical values sequentially. RxJS offers excellent protection against this, `distinctUntilChanged()`, which will discard an emission that will be a duplicate of its immediate predecessor:

```
[app/search.component.ts]

import {Component} from '@angular/core';
import {APIService} from './api.service';
import {FormControl} from '@angular/forms';

@Component({
  selector: 'search',
  template: `
    <input [formControl]="queryField">
    <p *ngFor="let result of results">{{result}}</p>
  `
})
export class SearchComponent {
  results:Array<string> = [];
  queryField:FormControl = new FormControl();
  constructor(private apiService_:APIService) {
    this.queryField.valueChanges
      .debounceTime(200)
      .distinctUntilChanged()
      .subscribe(query => this.apiService_
        .search(query)
        .subscribe(result => this.results.push(result)));
```

```
      }
  }
```

Flattening Observables

You have chained quite a few RxJS methods up to this point, and seeing nested `subscribe()` invocations might feel a bit funny to you. It should make sense since the `valueChanges Observable` handler is invoking a service method, which returns a separate `Observable`. In TypeScript, this is effectively represented as `Observable<Observable<string>>`. Gross!

Since you only really care about the emitted strings coming from the service method, it would be much easier to just combine all the emitted strings coming out of each returned `Observable` into a single `Observable`. Fortunately, RxJS makes this easy with `flatMap`, which flattens all the emissions from the inner Observables into a single outer `Observable`. In TypeScript, using `flatMap` would convert this into `Observable<string>`, which is exactly what you need:

```
[app/search.component.ts]

import {Component} from '@angular/core';
import {APIService} from './api.service';
import {FormControl} from '@angular/forms';

@Component({
  selector: 'search',
  template: `
    <input [formControl]="queryField">
    <p *ngFor="let result of results">{{result}}</p>
  `
})
export class SearchComponent {
  results:Array<string> = [];
  queryField:FormControl = new FormControl();
  constructor(private apiService_:APIService) {
    this.queryField.valueChanges
      .debounceTime(200)
      .distinctUntilChanged()
      .flatMap(query => this.apiService_.search(query))
      .subscribe(result => this.results.push(result));
  }
}
```

Handling unordered responses

When testing input now, you will surely notice that the delay intentionally introduced inside the API service will cause the responses to be returned out of order. This is a pretty effective simulation of network latency, so you'll need a good way of handling this.

Ideally, you would like to be able to throw out Observables that are in flight once you have a more recent query to execute. For example, consider that you've typed g and then o. Now once the second query for go is returned and if the first query for g hasn't returned yet, you'd like to just throw it out and forget about it since the response is now irrelevant.

RxJS also makes this very easy with switchMap. This does the same things as flatMap, but it will unsubscribe from any in-flight Observables that have not emitted any values yet:

```
[app/search.component.ts]

import {Component} from '@angular/core';
import {APIService} from './api.service';
import {FormControl} from '@angular/forms';

@Component({
  selector: 'search',
  template: `
    <input [formControl]="queryField">
    <p *ngFor="let result of results">{{result}}</p>
  `
})
export class SearchComponent {
  results:Array<string> = [];
  queryField:FormControl = new FormControl();
  constructor(private apiService_:APIService) {
    this.queryField.valueChanges
      .debounceTime(200)
      .distinctUntilChanged()
      .switchMap(query => this.apiService_.search(query))
      .subscribe(result => this.results.push(result));
  }
}
```

Your AutoComplete input should now be debounced and it should ignore redundant requests and return in-order results.

How it works...

There are a lot of moving pieces going on in this recipe, but the core theme remains the same: RxJS Observables expose many methods that can pipe the output from one observable into an entirely different observable. It can also combine multiple observables into a single observable, as well as introduce state-dependent operations into a stream of the input. At the end of this recipe, the power of reactive programming should be obvious.

See also

- *Basic Utilization of Observables with HTTP* demonstrates the basics of how to use an observable interface
- *Implementing a Publish-Subscribe model using Subjects* shows you how to configure input and output for RxJS Observables
- *Creating an Observable authentication service using BehaviorSubjects* instructs you on how to reactively manage the state in your application
- *Building a generalized Publish-Subscribe service to replace $broadcast, $emit, and $on* assembles a robust PubSub model for connecting application components with channels

6
The Component Router

This chapter will cover the following recipes:

- Setting up an application to support simple routes
- Navigating with routerLinks
- Navigating with the Router service
- Selecting LocationStrategy for Path Construction
- Building stateful RouterLink behavior with RouterLinkActive
- Implementing nested views with route parameters and child routes
- Working with Matrix URL parameters and routing arrays
- Adding route authentication controls with route guards

Introduction

Few features of Angular 2 should be anticipated more than the Component Router. This new routing implementation affords you a dazzling array of features that were missing or severely lacking in Angular 1.

Angular 2 implements matrix parameters; this is an entirely new syntax for URL structures. Originally proposed by Tim Berners-Lee in 1996, this semicolon-based syntax gives you the ability to robustly associate parameters not just with a single URL, but with different levels in that URL. Your application can now introduce an additional dimension of application state in the URLs.

Additionally, Component Router gives you a method of elegantly nesting views within each other as well as a simple way of defining routes and links to these component hierarchies. For you, this means your applications can truly take maximal advantage of defining an application as an independent module.

Finally, Component Router fully embraces integration with Observable structures and provides you with some beautiful ways of navigating and controlling navigation within your application.

Setting up an application to support simple routes

Central to the behavior of single-page applications is the ability to perform navigation without a formal browser page reload. Angular 2 is well-equipped to work around the default browser page reload behavior and allow you to define a routing structure within it, which will make it look and feel like actual page navigation.

 The code, links, and a live example of this are available at
`http://ngcookbook.herokuapp.com/6214.`

Getting ready

Suppose you have the following function defined globally:

```
function visit(uri) {
  // For this recipe, you don't care about the state or title
  window.history.pushState(null, null, uri);
}
```

The purpose of this is to merely allow you to navigate inside the browser from JavaScript using the HTML5 History API.

How to do it...

In order for Angular to simulate page navigation inside the browser, there are several steps you must take to create a navigable single-page application.

Setting the base URL

The first step in configuring your application is to specify the base URL. This instructs the browser what network requests performed with a relative URL should begin with.

Anytime the page makes a request using a relative URL, when generating the network request, it will use the current domain and then append the relative URL. For relative URLs, a prepended "/" means it will always use the root directory. If the forward slash is unavailable, the relative path will prepend whatever is specified as the base href. Any URL behavior, including requesting static resources, anchor links, and the history API, will exhibit this behavior.

 `<base>` is not a part of Angular but rather a default HTML5 element.

Here are some examples of this:

```
[Example 1]
// <base href="/">
// initial page location: foo.com

visit('bar');
// new page location: foo.com/bar

visit('bar');
// new page location: foo.com/bar
// The browser recognizes that this is a relative path
// with no prepended / and so it will visit the page at the
// same "depth" as before.

visit('bar/');
// new page location: foo.com/bar/
// Same as before, but the trailing slash will be important once
// you invoke this again.

visit('bar/');
// new page location: foo.com/bar/bar/
// The browser recognizes that the URL ends with a /, and so
// visiting a relative path is treated as a navigation into a
// subpath

visit('/qux');
// new page location: foo.com/qux
// With a / prepended to the URL, the browser recognizes that it
```

```
// should navigate from the root domain

[Example 2]
// <base href="xyz/">
// initial page location: foo.com

visit('bar');
// new page location: foo.com/xyz/bar
// Base URL is prepended to the relative URL

visit('bar');
// new page location: foo.com/xyz/bar
// As was the case before, the local path is treated the same
// by the browser

visit('/qux');
// new page location: foo.com/qux
// Note that in this case, you specified a relative path
// originating from the root domain, so the base href is ignored
```

Defining routes

Next, you need to define what your application's routes are. For the purpose of this recipe, it is more important to understand the setup of routing than how to define and navigate between routes. So, for now, you will just define a single catchall route.

As you might suspect, route views in Angular 2 are defined as components. Each route path is represented at the very least by the string that the browser's location will match against and the component that it will map to. This can be done with an object implementing the `Routes` interface, which is an array of route definitions.

It makes sense that the route definitions should happen very early in the application initialization, so you'll do it inside the top-level module definition.

First, create your view component that this route will map to:

```
[app/default.component.ts]

import {Component} from '@angular/core';

@Component({
  template: 'Default component!'
})
export class DefaultComponent {}
```

Next, wherever your application module is defined, import RouterModule and the Routes interface, namely DefaultComponent, and define a catchall route inside the Routes array:

```
[app/app.module.ts]
import {NgModule} from '@angular/core';
import {BrowserModule} from '@angular/platform-browser';
import {RouterModule, Routes} from '@angular/router';
import {RootComponent} from './root.component';
import {DefaultComponent} from './default.component';

const appRoutes:Routes = [
  {path: '**', component: DefaultComponent}
];

@NgModule({
  imports: [
    BrowserModule
  ],
  declarations: [
    DefaultComponent,
    RootComponent
  ],
  bootstrap: [
    RootComponent
  ]
})
export class AppModule {}
```

Providing routes to the application

You've defined the routes in an object, but your application still is not aware that they exist. You can do this with the forRoot method defined in RouterModule. This function does all the dirty work of installing your routes in the application as well as passing along a number of routing providers for use elsewhere in the application:

```
[app/app.module.ts]

import {NgModule} from '@angular/core';
import {BrowserModule} from '@angular/platform-browser';
import {RouterModule, Routes} from '@angular/router';
import {RootComponent} from './root.component';
import {DefaultComponent} from './default.component';

const appRoutes:Routes = [
  {path: '**', component: DefaultComponent}
];
```

```
@NgModule({
  imports: [
    BrowserModule,
    RouterModule.forRoot(appRoutes)
  ],
  declarations: [
    DefaultComponent,
    RootComponent
  ],
  bootstrap: [
    RootComponent
  ]
})
export class AppModule {}
```

With this, your application is fully configured to understand the route you have defined.

Rendering route components with RouterOutlet

The component needs a place to be rendered, and in Angular 2, this takes the form of a
RouterOutlet tag. This directive will be targeted by the component attached to the active
route, and the component will be rendered inside it. To keep things simple, in this recipe,
you can use the directive inside the root application component:

```
[app/app.component.ts]

import {Component} from '@angular/core';

@Component({
  selector: 'root',
  template: `
    <h1>Root component</h1>
    <router-outlet></router-outlet>
  `
})
export class RootComponent {}
```

That's all! Your application now has a single route defined that will render
DefaultComponent inside RootComponent.

How it works...

This recipe doesn't show a very complicated example of routing, since every possible route that you can visit will lead you to the same component.

Nonetheless, it demonstrates several fundamental principles of Angular routing:

- In its most basic form, a route is comprised of a string path (matched against the browser path) and the component that should be rendered when this route is active.
- Routes are installed via `RouterModule`. In this example, since there is only one module, you can do this once using `forRoot()`. However, keep in mind that you can break your routing structure into pieces and between different `NgModules`.
- Navigating to a route will cause a component to be rendered inside a different component-more specifically, wherever the `<router-outlet>` tag exists. There are many ways in which this can be configured and made more complex, but for the purpose of this simple module, you don't need to worry about these different ways.

There's more...

Angular 2 applications will not raise issues when operating with no form of routing. If your application does not need to understand and manage the page URL, then feel free to totally discard the routing files and modules from your application.

Initial page load

The flow you are hoping your users would go through is as follows:

1. The user visits `http://www.foo.com/`.
2. The server matches the empty route to `index.html`.
3. The page loads, requesting static files.
4. The Angular static files are loaded and application is bootstrapped.
5. The user clicks on the links and navigates around the site.
6. Since Angular is wholly managing the navigation and routing, everything works as expected.

This is the ideal case. Consider a different case:

1. The user has already visited `http://www.foo.com/` before and bookmarked it.
2. The user enters `foo.com/bar` in their URL bar and navigates to it from there directly.
3. The server sees the request path as `/bar` and tries to handle the request.

Depending on how your server is configured, this might cause problems for you. This is because the last time the user visited `foo.com/bar`, no request for that resource reached the server because Angular was only emulating a real navigation event.

This scenario is discussed elsewhere in this chapter, but keep in mind that without a correctly configured server, the user in the second case might see a 404 page error instead of your application.

See also

- *Navigating with routerLinks* demonstrates how to navigate around Angular applications
- *Navigating with the Router service* uses an Angular service to navigate around an application
- *Building stateful RouterLink behavior with RouterLinkActive* shows how to integrate application behavior with a URL state

Navigating with routerLinks

Navigating around a single page application is a fundamental task, and Angular offers you a built-in directive, `routerLink`, to accomplish this.

 The code, links, and a live example of this are available at `http://ngcookbook.herokuapp.com/9983/`.

Getting ready

Begin with the application setup assembled in the *Setting up an application to support simple routes* recipe.

Your goal is to add an additional route to this application accompanied by a component; also, you want to be able to navigate between them using links.

How to do it...

To begin, create another component, `ArticleComponent`, and an associated route:

```
[app/article/article.component.ts]

import {Component} from '@angular/core';

@Component({
  template: 'Article component!'
})
export class ArticleComponent {}
```

Next, install an article route accompanied by this new component:

```
[app/app.module.ts]

import {NgModule} from '@angular/core';
import {BrowserModule} from '@angular/platform-browser';
import {RouterModule, Routes} from '@angular/router';
import {RootComponent} from './root.component';
import {DefaultComponent} from './default.component';
import {ArticleComponent} from './article.component';

const appRoutes:Routes = [
  {path: 'article', component: ArticleComponent},
  {path: '**', component: DefaultComponent}
];

@NgModule({
  imports: [
    BrowserModule,
    RouterModule.forRoot(appRoutes)
  ],
  declarations: [
    DefaultComponent,
    ArticleComponent,
    RootComponent
```

```
  ],
  bootstrap: [
    RootComponent
  ]
})
export class AppModule {}
```

With the routes defined, you can now build a rudimentary navbar comprised of routerLinks. The markup surrounding the `<router-outlet>` tag will remain irrespective of the route, so the root app component seems like a suitable place for the nav links.

The routerLink directive is available as part of RouterModule, so you can go straight to adding some anchor tags:

```
[app/root.component.ts]

import {Component} from '@angular/core';

@Component({
  selector: 'root',
  template: `
    <h1>Root component</h1>
    <a [routerLink]="''">Default</a>
    <a [routerLink]="'article'">Article</a>
    <router-outlet></router-outlet>
  `
})
export class RootComponent {}
```

In this case, since the routes are simple and static, binding routerLink to a string is allowed. routerLink also accepts the array notation:

```
[app/root.component.ts]

import {Component} from '@angular/core';

@Component({
  selector: 'root',
  template: `
    <h1>Root component</h1>
    <a [routerLink]="['']">Default</a>
    <a [routerLink]="['article']">Article</a>
    <router-outlet></router-outlet>
  `
})
export class RootComponent {}
```

For the purpose of this recipe, the array notation doesn't add anything. However, when developing more complicated URL structures, the array notation becomes useful, as it allows you to generate links in a piecewise fashion.

How it works...

At a high level, this is no different than the behavior of a vanilla `href` attribute. After all, the routes behave in the same way and are structured similarly. The important difference here is that using a `routerLink` directive instead of `href` allows you to move around your application the Angular way, without ever having the anchor tag click interpreted by the browser as a non-Angular navigation event.

There's more...

Of course, the `routerLink` directive is also superior as it is more extensible as a tool for navigating. Since it is an HTML attribute after all, there's no reason `routerLink` can't be attached to, for example, a button instead:

```
[app/root.component.ts]

import {Component} from '@angular/core';

@Component({
  selector: 'root',
  template: `
    <h1>Root component</h1>
    <button [routerLink]="['']">Default</button>
    <button [routerLink]="['article']">Article</button>
    <router-outlet></router-outlet>
  `
})
export class RootComponent {}
```

What's more, you'll also note that the array notation allows the dynamic generation of links via all of the tremendous data binding that Angular affords you:

```
[app/root.component.ts]

import {Component} from '@angular/core';

@Component({
  selector: 'root',
```

```
  template: `
    <h1>Root component</h1>
    <a [routerLink]="[defaultPath]">Default</a>
    <a [routerLink]="[articlePath]">Article</a>
    <router-outlet></router-outlet>
    `
})
export class RootComponent {
  defaultPath:string = '';
  articlePath:string = 'article';
}
```

As the URL structure gets ever more advanced, it will be easy to see how a clever application of data binding could make for some very elegant dynamic link generation.

Route order considerations

The ordering of routes inside the `Routes` definition specifies the descending priority of each of them. In this recipe's example, suppose you were to reverse the order of the routes:

```
[app/app.module.ts]

import {NgModule} from '@angular/core';
import {BrowserModule} from '@angular/platform-browser';
import {RouterModule, Routes} from '@angular/router';
import {RootComponent} from './root.component';
import {DefaultComponent} from './default.component';
import {ArticleComponent} from './article.component';

const appRoutes:Routes = [
  {path: '**', component: DefaultComponent},
  {path: 'article', component: ArticleComponent}
];

@NgModule({
  imports: [
    BrowserModule,
    RouterModule.forRoot(appRoutes)
  ],
  declarations: [
    DefaultComponent,
    ArticleComponent,
    RootComponent
  ],
  bootstrap: [
    RootComponent
  ]
```

```
})
export class AppModule {}
```

When experimenting, you will find that the browser's URL changes correctly with the various `routerLink` interactions, but both routes will use `DefaultComponent` as the rendered view. This is simply because all the routes match the `**` catchall, and Angular doesn't bother to traverse the routes any further once it has a matching route. Keep this in mind when authoring large route tables.

See also

- *Setting up an application to support simple routes* shows you the basics of Angular routing
- *Navigating with the Router service* uses an Angular service to navigate around an application
- *Building stateful RouterLink behavior with RouterLinkActive* shows how to integrate application behavior with a URL state
- *Implementing nested views with route parameters and child routes* gives an example of how to configure Angular URLs to support nesting and data passing
- *Working with matrix URL parameters and routing arrays* demonstrates Angular's built-in matrix URL support

Navigating with the Router service

The companion to using `routerLink` inside the template to navigate is doing it from inside JavaScript. Angular exposes the `navigate()` method from inside a service, which allows you to accomplish exactly this.

 The code, links, and a live example of this are available at `http://ngcookbook.herokuapp.com/8004/`.

Getting ready

Begin with the application that exists at the end of the *How to do it...* section of the *Navigating with routerLinks* recipe.

Your goal is to add an additional route accompanied by a component to this application; also, you wish to be able to navigate between them using links.

How to do it...

Instead of using `routerLink`, which is the most sensible choice in this situation, you can also trigger a navigation using the `Router` service. First, add `nav` buttons and attach some empty click handlers to them:

```
[app/root.component.ts]

import {Component} from '@angular/core';

@Component({
  selector: 'root',
  template: `
    <h1>Root component</h1>
    <button (click)="visitDefault()">Default</button>
    <button (click)="visitArticle()">Article</button>
    <router-outlet></router-outlet>
  `
})
export class RootComponent {
  visitDefault():void {}
  visitArticle():void {}
}
```

Next, import the `Router` service and use its `navigate()` method to change the page location:

```
[app/root.component.ts]

import {Component} from '@angular/core';
import {Router} from '@angular/router';

@Component({
  selector: 'root',
  template: `
    <h1>Root component</h1>
    <button (click)="visitDefault()">Default</button>
```

```
    <button (click)="visitArticle()">Article</button>
    <router-outlet></router-outlet>
    `
})
export class RootComponent {
  constructor(private router:Router) {}
  visitDefault():void {
    this.router.navigate(['']);
  }
  visitArticle():void {
    this.router.navigate(['article']);
  }
}
```

With this addition, you should be able to navigate around your application in the same way you did before.

How it works...

The Router service exposes an API with which you can control your application's navigation behavior, among many other things. Its navigate() method accepts an array-structured route, which operates identically to the Arrays bound to routerLink.

There's more...

Obviously, this is an utter antipattern for building applications that are designed to scale. In this scenario, routerLink is a much more succinct and effective choice for building a simple navbar. Nevertheless, the Router service is an equally effective tool for traversing an Angular application's route structure.

See also

- *Navigating with routerLinks* demonstrates how to navigate around Angular applications
- *Building stateful RouterLink behavior with RouterLinkActive* shows how to integrate application behavior with a URL state
- *Working with matrix URL parameters and routing arrays* demonstrates Angular's built-in matrix URL support

- *Adding route authentication controls with route guards* details the entire process of configuring protected routes in your application

Selecting a LocationStrategy for path construction

A simple but important choice for your application is which type of `LocationStrategy` you want to make use of. The following two URLs are equivalent when their respective `LocationStrategy` is selected:

- `PathLocationStrategy: foo.com/bar`
- `HashLocationStrategy: foo.com/#/bar`

The code, links, and a live example of this are available at `http://ngcookbook.herokuapp.com/1355/`.

How to do it...

Angular 2 will default to `PathLocationStrategy`. Should you want to select `HashLocationStrategy`, it can be imported from the `@angular/common` module. Once imported, it can be listed as a provider inside an object literal:

```
[app/app.module.ts]

import {NgModule} from '@angular/core';
import {BrowserModule} from '@angular/platform-browser';
import {RouterModule, Routes} from '@angular/router';
import {RootComponent} from './root.component';
import {DefaultComponent} from './default.component';
import {ArticleComponent} from './article.component';
import {LocationStrategy, HashLocationStrategy}
  from '@angular/common';


const appRoutes:Routes = [
  {path: 'article', component: ArticleComponent},
  {path: '**', component: DefaultComponent},
];
```

```
@NgModule({
  imports: [
    BrowserModule,
    RouterModule.forRoot(appRoutes)
  ],
  declarations: [
    DefaultComponent,
    ArticleComponent,
    RootComponent
  ],
  providers: [
    {provide: LocationStrategy, useClass: HashLocationStrategy}
  ],
  bootstrap: [
    RootComponent
  ]
})
export class AppModule {}
```

With this addition, your application will transition to prefix #/ to all application-defined URLs. This will occur in transparence with the rest of your application, which can use its routing definitions normally without having to worry about prefixing #/.

There's more...

There are tradeoffs for each of these strategies. As the Angular documentation notes, once you choose one, it is inadvisable to switch to the other since bookmarks, SEO, and user history will all be coupled to the URL strategy utilized during that visit.

PathLocationStrategy:

- Here, the URLs appear normal to the end user
- The server must be configured to handle page loads from any application path
- This allows the hybrid server-side rendering of routes for improved performance

HashLocationStrategy:

- Here, the URLs may look funny to the end user.
- No server configuration is required if the root domain serves index.html. This is a good option if you only want to serve static files (for example, an Amazon AWS-based site).
- It cannot be easily intermixed with hybrid server-side rendering.

Configuring your application server for PathLocationStrategy

Angular is smart enough to recognize the browser state and manage it accordingly once bootstrapping occurs. However, bootstrapping requires an initial load of the static compiled JS assets, which will bootstrap Angular once the browser loads them. When the user initially visits a root domain, such as foo.com, the server is normally configured to respond with `index.html`, which will in turn request the static assets at render time. So, Angular will work!

However, in cases where the user initially visits a non-root path, such as foo.com/bar, the browser will send a request to the server at foo.com/bar. If you aren't careful when setting up your server, a common mistake you may commit is having only the root foo.com path return `index.html`.

In order for `PathLocationStrategy` to work correctly in all cases, you must configure your web server to set up a catchall route for all the requests that have paths intended for the single-page application's route in the client, and to invariably return `index.html`. In other words, visiting `foo.com`, `foo.com/bar`, or `foo.com/bar/baz` as the first page in the browser will all return the same thing: `index.html`. Once you do this, postbootstrap Angular will examine the current browser path and recognize which path it is on and what view needs to be displayed.

Building stateful route behavior with RouterLinkActive

It is often the case when building applications that you will want to build features that would involve which page the application is currently on. When this is a one-time inspection, it isn't a problem, as both Angular and default browser APIs allow you to easily inspect the current page.

Things get a bit stickier when you want the state of the page to reflect the state of the URL, for example, if you want to visually indicate which link corresponds to the current page. A from-scratch implementation of this would require some sort of state machine that would know when navigation events occur and what and how to modify at each given route.

Fortunately, Angular 2 gives you some excellent tools to do this right out of the box.

The code, links, and a live example of this are all available at `http://ngcookbook.herokuapp.com/3308/`.

Getting ready

Begin with the Array and anchor-tag-based implementation shown in the *Navigating with routerLinks* recipe.

Your goal is to use `RouterLinkActive` to introduce some simple stateful route behavior.

How to do it...

`RouterLinkActive` allows you to conditionally apply classes when the current route matches the corresponding `routerLink` on the same element. Proceed directly to adding it as an attribute directive to each link as well as a matching CSS class:

```
[app/root.component.ts]

import {Component} from '@angular/core';

@Component({
  selector: 'root',
  template: `
    <h1>Root component</h1>
    <a [routerLink]="['']"
       [routerLinkActive]="'active-navlink'">Default</a>
    <a [routerLink]="['article']"
       [routerLinkActive]="'active-navlink'">Article</a>
    <router-outlet></router-outlet>
  `,
  styles: [`
    .active-navlink {
      color: red;
      text-transform: uppercase;
    }
  `]
})
export class RootComponent {}
```

This is all you need for links to become active! You will notice that Angular will conditionally apply the `active-navlink` class based on the current route.

However, when testing this, you will notice that the `/article` route makes both the links appear active. This is due to the fact that by default, Angular marks all `routerLinks` that match the current route as active.

 This behavior is useful in cases where you may want to show a hierarchy of links as active for example, at route `/user/123/detail`, it could make sense that the separate links `/user`, `/user/123`, and `/user/123/detail` are all shown as active.

However, in the case of this recipe, this behavior is not useful to you, and Angular has another router directive, `routerLinkActiveOptions`, which binds to an options object. The exact property inside the options object is useful in this case; it controls whether the active state should only be applied in cases of an exact match:

```
[app/root.component.ts]

import {Component} from '@angular/core';
import {Router} from '@angular/router';

@Component({
  selector: 'root',
  template: `
    <h1>Root component</h1>
    <a [routerLink]="['']"
       [routerLinkActive]="'active-navlink'"
       [routerLinkActiveOptions]="{exact:true}">Default</a>
    <a [routerLink]="['article']"
       [routerLinkActive]="'active-navlink'"
       [routerLinkActiveOptions]="{exact:true}">Article</a>
    <router-outlet></router-outlet>
  `,
  styles: [`
    .active-navlink {
      color: red;
      text-transform: uppercase;
    }
  `]
})
export class RootComponent {}
```

Now you will find that each link will only be active at its respective route.

How it works...

The `routerLinkActive` implementation subscribes to navigation change events that Angular emits from the `Router` service. When it sees a `NavigationEnd` event, it performs an update of all the attached HTML tags, which includes adding and stripping applicable "active" CSS classes that the element is bound to via the directive.

There's more...

If you need to bind `routerLinkActive` to a dynamic value, the preceding syntax will allow you to do exactly that. For example, you can bind to a

component

member and

modify

it elsewhere, and Angular will handle everything for you. However, if this is not required, Angular will handle `routerLinkActive` without the data binding brackets. In this case, the value of the directive no longer needs to be an Angular expression, so you can remove the nested quotes.

The following is behaviorally identical:

```
[app/root.component.ts]

import {Component} from '@angular/core';
import {Router} from '@angular/router';

@Component({
  selector: 'root',
  template: `
    <h1>Root component</h1>
    <a [routerLink]="['']"
       routerLinkActive="active-navlink"
       [routerLinkActiveOptions]="{exact:true}">
       Default</a>
    <a [routerLink]="['article']"
       routerLinkActive="active-navlink"
       [routerLinkActiveOptions]="{exact:true}">
```

```
        Article</a>
      <router-outlet></router-outlet>
    `,
  styles: [`
    .active-navlink {
      color: red;
      text-transform: uppercase;
    }
  `]
})
export class RootComponent {}
```

See also

- *Setting up an application to support simple routes* shows you the basics of Angular routing
- *Navigating with routerLinks* demonstrates how to navigate around Angular applications
- *Building stateful RouterLink behavior with RouterLinkActive* shows how to integrate application behavior with a URL state
- *Implementing nested views with route parameters and child routes* gives an example of how to configure Angular URLs to support nesting and data passing
- *Adding route authentication controls with route guards* details the entire process of configuring protected routes in your application

Implementing nested views with route parameters and child routes

Angular 2's component router offers you the necessary concept of child routes. As you might expect, this brings the concept of recursively defined views to the table, which affords you an incredibly useful and elegant way of building your application.

 The code, links, and a live example of this are available at
http://ngcookbook.herokuapp.com/7892/.

Getting ready

Begin with the Array and anchor-tag-based implementation shown in *Navigating with routerLinks* recipe.

Your goal is to extend this simple application to include /article, which will be the list view, and /article/:id, which will be the detail view.

How to do it…

First, modify the route structure for this simple application by extending the /article path to include its subpaths: / and /:id. Routes are defined hierarchically, and each route can have child routes using the children property.

Adding a routing target to the parent component

First, you must modify the existing ArticleComponent so that it can contain child views. As you might expect, the child view is rendered in exactly the same way as it is done from the root component, using RouterOutlet:

```
[app/article.component.ts]

import {Component} from '@angular/core';

@Component({
  template: `
    <h2>Article</h2>
    <router-outlet></router-outlet>
  `
})
export class ArticleComponent {}
```

This won't do anything yet, but adding RouterOutlet describes to Angular how route component hierarchies should be rendered.

Defining nested child views

In this recipe, you would like to have the parent ArticleComponent contain a child view, either ArticleListComponent or ArticleDetailComponent. For the simplicity of this recipe, you can just define your list of articles as an array of integers.

Define the skeleton of these two components as follows:

```
[app/article-list.component.ts]

import {Component} from '@angular/core';

@Component({
  template: `
    <h3>Article List</h3>
  `
})
export class ArticleListComponent {
  articleIds:Array<number> = [1,2,3,4,5];
}
[app/article-detail.component.ts]

import {Component} from '@angular/core';

@Component({
  template: `
    <h3>Article Detail</h3>
    <p>Showing article {{articleId}}</p>
  `
})
export class ArticleDetailComponent {
  articleId:number;
}
```

Defining the child routes

At this point, nothing in the application yet points to either of these child routes, so you'll need to define them now.

The `children` property of a route should just be another `Route`, which should represent the nested routes that are appended to the parent route.

 In this way, you are defining a sort of routing "tree," where each route entry can have many child routes defined recursively. This will be discussed in greater detail later in this chapter.

Furthermore, you should also use the URL parameter notation to declare `:articleId` as a variable in the route. This allows you to pass values inside the route and then retrieve these values inside the component that is rendered.

Add these route definitions now:

```
[app/app.module.ts]

import {NgModule} from '@angular/core';
import {BrowserModule} from '@angular/platform-browser';
import {RouterModule, Routes} from '@angular/router';
import {RootComponent} from './root.component';
import {DefaultComponent} from './default.component';
import {ArticleComponent} from './article.component';
import {ArticleListComponent} from './article-list.component';
import {ArticleDetailComponent} from './article-detail.component';

const appRoutes:Routes = [
  {path: 'article', component: ArticleComponent,
    children: [
      {path: '', component: ArticleListComponent},
      {path: ':articleId', component: ArticleDetailComponent}
    ]
  },
  {path: '**', component: DefaultComponent},
];

@NgModule({
  imports: [
    BrowserModule,
    RouterModule.forRoot(appRoutes)
  ],
  declarations: [
    DefaultComponent,
    ArticleComponent,
    ArticleListComponent,
    ArticleDetailComponent,
    RootComponent
  ],
  bootstrap: [
    RootComponent
  ]
})
export class AppModule {}
```

You'll note that `ArticleListComponent` is keyed by an empty string. This should make sense, as each of these routes are joined to their parent routes to create the full route. If you were to join each route in this tree with its ancestral path to get the full route, the route definition you've just created would have the following three entries:

```
/article    => ArticleComponent
                ArticleListComponent
```

```
/article/4 => ArticleComponent
                 ArticleDetailComponent<articleId=4>
/**        => DefaultComponent
```

 Note that in this case, the number of actual routes corresponds to the number of leaves of the URL tree since the article parent route will also map to the child article's + " route. Depending on how you configure your route structure, the leaf/route parity will not always be the case.

Defining child view links

With the routes being mapped to the child components, you can flesh out the child views. Starting with ArticleList, create a repeater to generate the links to each of the child views:

```
[app/article-list.component.ts]

import {Component} from '@angular/core';

@Component({
  template: `
    <h3>Article List</h3>
    <p *ngFor="let articleId of articleIds">
      <a [routerLink]="articleId">
        Article {{articleId}}
      </a>
    </p>
    `
})
export class ArticleListComponent {
  articleIds:Array<number> = [1,2,3,4,5];
}
```

 Note that routerLink is linking to the relative path of the detail view. Since the current path for this view is /article, a relative routerLink of 4 will navigate the application to /article/4 upon a click.

These links should work, but when you click on them, they will take you to the detail view that cannot display articleId from the route since you have not extracted it yet.

Inside ArticleDetailComponent, create a link that will take the user back to the article/ route. Since routes behave like directories, you can just use a relative path that will take the user up one level:

```
[app/article-detail.component.ts]

import {Component} from '@angular/core';

@Component({
  template: `
    <h3>Article Detail</h3>
    <p>Showing article {{articleId}}</p>
    <a [routerLink]="'../'">Back up</a>
  `
})
export class ArticleDetailComponent {
  articleId:number;
}
```

Extracting route parameters

A crucial difference between Angular 1 and 2 is the reliance on `Observable` constructs. In the context of routing, Angular 2 wields `Observables` to encapsulate that routing occurs as a sequence of events and that values are produced at different states in these events and will be ready eventually.

More concretely, route params in Angular 2 are not exposed directly, but rather through an `Observable` inside `ActivatedRoute`. You can set `Observer` on its `params` Observable to extract the route params once they are available.

Inject the `ActivatedRoute` interface and use the params Observable to extract `articleId` and assign it to the `ArticleDetailComponent` instance member:

```
[app/article-detail/article-detail.component.ts]

import {Component} from '@angular/core';
import {ActivatedRoute} from '@angular/router';

@Component({
  template: `
    <h3>Article Detail</h3>
    <p>Showing article {{articleId}}</p>
    <a [routerLink]="'../'">Back up</a>
  `
})
export class ArticleDetailComponent {
  articleId:number;
  constructor(private activatedRoute_: ActivatedRoute) {
    activatedRoute_.params
      .subscribe(params => this.articleId = params['articleId']);
```

```
        }
    }
```

With this, you should be able to see the `articleId` parameter interpolated into `ArticleDetailComponent`.

How it works...

In this application, you have nested components, `AppComponent` and `ArticleComponent`, both of which contain `RouterOutlet`. Angular is able to take the routing hierarchy you defined and apply it to the component hierarchy that it maps to. More specifically, for every `Route` you define in your routing hierarchy, there should be an equal number of `RouterOutlets` in which they can render.

There's more...

To some, it will feel strange to need to extract the route params from an `Observable` interface. If this solution feels a bit clunky to you, there are ways of tidying it up.

Refactoring with async pipes

Recall that Angular has the ability to interpolate `Observable` data directly into the template as it becomes ready. Especially since you should only ever expect the param `Observable` to emit once, you can use it to insert `articleId` into the template without explicitly setting an `Observer`:

```
[app/article-detail.component.ts]

import {Component} from '@angular/core';
import {ActivatedRoute } from '@angular/router';

@Component({
  template: `
    <h3>Article Detail</h3>
    <p>Showing article
       {{(activatedRoute.params | async).articleId}}</p>
    <a [routerLink]="'../'">Back up</a>
  `
})
export class ArticleDetailComponent {
  constructor(activatedRoute: ActivatedRoute) {}
```

```
}
```

Even though this works perfectly well, using a private reference to an injected service directly into the template may feel a bit funny to you. A superior strategy is to grab a reference to the public `Observable` interface you need and interpolate that instead:

```
[app/article-detail.component.ts]

import {Component} from '@angular/core';
import {Observable} from 'rxjs/Observable';
import {ActivatedRoute, Params} from '@angular/router';

@Component({
  template: `
    <h3>Article Detail</h3>
    <p>Showing article {{(params | async).articleId}}</p>
    <a [routerLink]="'../'">Back up</a>
  `
})
export class ArticleDetailComponent {
  params:Observable<Params>;
  constructor(private activatedRoute_: ActivatedRoute) {
    this.params = activatedRoute_.params;
  }
}
```

See also

- *Navigating with routerLinks* demonstrates how to navigate around Angular applications
- *Navigating with the Router service* uses an Angular service to navigate around an application
- *Building stateful RouterLink behavior with RouterLinkActive* shows how to integrate application behavior with a URL state
- *Working with matrix URL parameters and routing arrays* demonstrates Angular's built-in matrix URL support
- *Adding route authentication controls with route guards* details the entire process of configuring protected routes in your application

Working with matrix URL parameters and

routing arrays

Angular 2 introduces native support for an awesome feature that seems to be frequently overlooked: matrix URL parameters. Essentially, these allow you to attach an arbitrary amount of data inside a URL to any routing level in Angular, and giving you the ability to read that data out as a regular URL parameter.

> The code, links, and a live example of this are available at
> `http://ngcookbook.herokuapp.com/4553/`.

Getting ready

Begin with the code created at the end of the *How to do it...* section in *Implementing nested views with route parameters and child routes*.

Your goal is to pass arbitrary data to both the `ArticleList` and `ArticleDetail` levels of this application via only the URL.

How to do it...

`routerLink` arrays are processed serially, so any string that will become part of the URL that is followed by an object will have that object converted into matrix URL parameters. It will be easier to understand this by example, so begin by passing in some dummy data to the `ArticleList` view from `routerLink`:

```
[app/root.component.ts]

import {Component} from '@angular/core';

@Component({
  selector: 'root',
  template: `
    <h1>Root component</h1>
    <a [routerLink]="['']">
      Default</a>
    <a [routerLink]="['article', {listData: 'foo'}]">
      Article</a>
    <router-outlet></router-outlet>
  `
})
```

```
export class RootComponent {}
```

Now, if you click on this link, you will see your browser navigate to the following path while still successfully rendering the `ArticleList` view:

```
/article;listData=foo
```

To access this data, simply extract it from the `ActivatedRoute` params:

```
[app/article-list.component.ts]

import {Component} from '@angular/core';
import {ActivatedRoute} from '@angular/router';

@Component({
  template: `
    <h3>Article List</h3>
    <p *ngFor="let articleId of articleIds">
      <a [routerLink]="[articleId]">
        Article {{articleId}}
      </a>
    </p>
  `
})
export class ArticleListComponent {
  articleIds:Array<number> = [1,2,3,4,5];
  constructor(private activatedRoute_:ActivatedRoute) {
    activatedRoute_.params
      .subscribe(params => {
        console.log('List params:');
        console.log(window.location.href)
        console.log(params);
      });
  }
}
```

When the view is loaded, you'll see the following:

```
List params:
/article;listData=foo
Object {listData: "foo"}
```

Awesome! Do the same for the detail view:

```
[app/article-list.component.ts]

import {Component} from '@angular/core';
import {ActivatedRoute} from '@angular/router';
```

```
@Component({
  template: `
    <h3>Article List</h3>
    <p *ngFor="let articleId of articleIds">
      <a [routerLink]="[articleId, {detailData: 'bar'}]">
        Article {{articleId}}
      </a>
    </p>
  `
})
export class ArticleListComponent {
  articleIds:Array<number> = [1,2,3,4,5];
  constructor(private activatedRoute_:ActivatedRoute) {
    activatedRoute_.params
      .subscribe(params => {
        console.log('List params:');
        console.log(window.location.href)
        console.log(params);
      });
  }
}
```

Add the same amount of logging to the detail view:

```
[app/article-detail.component.ts]

import {Component} from '@angular/core';
import {ActivatedRoute} from '@angular/router';

@Component({
  template: `
    <h3>Article Detail</h3>
    <p>Showing article {{articleId}}</p>
    <a [routerLink]="'../'">Back up</a>
  `
})
export class ArticleDetailComponent {
  articleId:number;
  constructor(private activatedRoute_:ActivatedRoute) {
    activatedRoute_.params
      .subscribe(params => {
        console.log('Detail params:');
        console.log(window.location.href)
        console.log(params);
        this.articleId = params['articleId']
      });
  }
}
```

When you visit a detail page, you'll see the following logged:

```
Detail params:
/article;listData=foo/1;detailData=bar
Object {articleId: "1", detailData: "foo"}
```

Very interesting! Not only is Angular able to associate different matrix parameters with different routing levels, but it has combined both the expected `articleId` parameter and the unexpected `detailData` parameter into the same `Observable` emission.

How it works...

Angular is able to seamlessly convert from a routing array containing a matrix param object to a serialized URL containing the matrix params, then back into a deserialized JavaScript object containing the parameter data. This allows you to store arbitrary data inside URLs at different levels, without having to cram it all into a query string at the end.

There's more...

Notice that when you click on Back up in the detail view, the `listData` URL param is preserved. Angular will dutifully maintain the state as you navigate throughout the application, so using matrix parameters can be a very effective way of storing stateful data that survives navigation or page reloads.

See also

- *Navigating with routerLinks* demonstrates how to navigate around Angular applications
- *Navigating with the Router service* uses an Angular service to navigate around an application
- *Building stateful RouterLink behavior with RouterLinkActive* shows how to integrate application behavior with a URL state
- *Implementing nested views with route parameters and child routes* gives an example of how to configure Angular URLs to support nesting and data passing

Adding route authentication controls with route guards

The nature of single-page applications wholly controlling the process of routing affords them the ability to control each stage of the process. For you, this means that you can intercept route changes as they happen and make decisions about where the user should go.

 The code, links, and a live example of this are available at
`http://ngcookbook.herokuapp.com/6135/`.

Getting ready

In this recipe, you'll build a simple pseudo-authenticated application from scratch.

You goal is to protect users from certain views when they are not authenticated, and at the same time, implement a sensible login/logout flow.

How to do it...

Begin by defining two initial views with routes in your application. One will be a Default view, which will be visible to everybody, and one will be a Profile view, which will be only visible to authenticated users:

```
[app/app.module.ts]

import {NgModule} from '@angular/core';
import {BrowserModule} from '@angular/platform-browser';
import {RouterModule, Routes} from '@angular/router';
import {RootComponent} from './root.component';
import {DefaultComponent} from './default.component';
import {ProfileComponent} from './profile.component';

const appRoutes:Routes = [
  {path: 'profile', component: ProfileComponent},
  {path: '**', component: DefaultComponent}
];

@NgModule({
  imports: [
    BrowserModule,
```

```
      RouterModule.forRoot(appRoutes)
    ],
    declarations: [
      DefaultComponent,
      ProfileComponent,
      RootComponent
    ],
    bootstrap: [
      RootComponent
    ]
})
export class AppModule {}

[app/default.component.ts]

import {Component} from '@angular/core';

@Component({
  template: `
    <h2>Default view!</h2>
    `
})
export class DefaultComponent {}
[app/profile.component.ts]

import {Component} from '@angular/core';

@Component({
  template: `
    <h2>Profile view</h2>
    Username: <input>
    <button>Update</button>
    `
})
export class ProfileComponent {}
```

Obviously, this does not do anything yet.

Implementing the Auth service

As done in the `Observables` chapter, you will implement a service that will maintain the state entirely within a `BehaviorSubject`.

Recall that a `BehaviorSubject` will rebroadcast its last emitted value whenever an `Observer` is subscribed to it. This means it requires setting the initial state, but for an authentication service this is easy; it can just start in the unauthenticated state.

For the purpose of this recipe, let's assume that a username of `null` means the user is not authenticated and any other string value means they are authenticated:

```
[app/auth.service.ts]

import {Injectable} from '@angular/core';
import {BehaviorSubject} from 'rxjs/BehaviorSubject';
import {Observable} from 'rxjs/Observable';

@Injectable()
export class AuthService {
  private authSubject_:BehaviorSubject<any> =
    new BehaviorSubject(null);
  usernameEmitter:Observable<string>;

  constructor() {
    this.usernameEmitter = this.authSubject_.asObservable();
    this.logout();
  }

  login(username:string):void {
    this.setAuthState_(username);
  }

  logout():void {
    this.setAuthState_(null);
  }

  private setAuthState_(username:string):void {
    this.authSubject_.next(username);
  }
}
```

Note that nowhere are we storing the username as a string. The state of the authentication lives entirely within `BehaviorSubject`.

Wiring up the profile view

Next, make this service available to the entire application and wire up the profile view:

```
[app/app.module.ts]
```

```
import {NgModule} from '@angular/core';
import {BrowserModule} from '@angular/platform-browser';
import {RouterModule, Routes} from '@angular/router';
import {RootComponent} from './root.component';
import {DefaultComponent} from './default.component';
import {ProfileComponent} from './profile.component';
import {AuthService} from './auth.service';

const appRoutes:Routes = [
  {path: 'profile', component: ProfileComponent},
  {path: '**', component: DefaultComponent}
];

@NgModule({
  imports: [
    BrowserModule,
    RouterModule.forRoot(appRoutes)
  ],
  declarations: [
    DefaultComponent,
    ProfileComponent,
    RootComponent
  ],
  providers: [
    AuthService
  ],
  bootstrap: [
    RootComponent
  ]
})
export class AppModule {}
[app/profile.component.ts]

import {Component} from '@angular/core';
import {AuthService} from './auth.service';
import {Observable} from 'rxjs/Observable';

@Component({
  template: `
    <h2>Profile view</h2>
    Username: <input #un value="{{username | async}}">
    <button (click)=update(un.value)>Update</button>
  `
})
export class ProfileComponent {
  username:Observable<string>;

  constructor(private authService_:AuthService) {
```

[251]

```
      this.username = authService_.usernameEmitter;
   }

   update(username:string):void {
     this.authService_.login(username);
   }
}
```

It's very handy to use the `async` pipe when interpolating values. Recall that when you invoke `subscribe()` on a service `Observable` from inside an instantiated view component, you must invoke `unsubscribe()` on the `Subscription` when the component is destroyed; otherwise, your application will have a leaked listener. Making the `Observable` available to the view saves you this trouble!

With the profile view wired up, add links and interpolate the username into the root app view in a navbar, to give yourself the ability to navigate around. You don't have to revisit the file; just add all the links you'll need in this recipe now:

```
[app/root.component.ts]

import {Component} from '@angular/core';
import {Router} from '@angular/router';
import {AuthService} from './auth.service';
import {Observable} from 'rxjs/Observable';

@Component({
  selector: 'root',
  template: `
    <h3 *ngIf="!!(username | async)">
      Hello, {{username | async}}.
    </h3>
    <a [routerLink]="['']">Default</a>
    <a [routerLink]="['profile']">Profile</a>
    <a *ngIf="!!(username | async)"
       [routerLink]="['login']">Login</a>
    <a *ngIf="!!(username | async)"
       [routerLink]="['logout']">Logout</a>
    <router-outlet></router-outlet>
  `
})
export class RootComponent {
  username:Observable<string>;

  constructor(private authService_:AuthService) {
    this.username = authService_.usernameEmitter;
  }
```

```
}
```

For consistency, here you are using the `async` pipe to make the component definition simpler. However, since you have four instances in the template referencing the same `Observable`, it might be better down the road to instead set one subscriber to `Observable`, bind it to a string member in `RootComponent`, and interpolate this instead. Angular's data binding makes this easy for you, but you would still need to deregister the subscriber when this is destroyed. However, since it is the application's root component, you shouldn't really expect this to happen.

Restricting route access with route guards

So far so good, but you will notice that the profile view is allowing the user to effectively log in willy-nilly. You would instead like to restrict access to this view and only allow the user to visit it when they are already authenticated.

Angular gives you the ability to execute code, inspect the route, and redirect it as necessary before the navigation occurs using a Route Guard.

Guard is a bit of a misleading term here. You should think of this feature as a route shim that lets you add logic that executes before Angular actually goes to the new route. It can indeed "Guard" a route from an unauthenticated user, but it can also just as easily conditionally redirect, save the current URL, or perform other tasks.

Since the Route Guard needs to have the `@Injectable` decorator, it makes good sense to treat it as a service type.

Start off with the skeleton `AuthGuardService` defined inside a new file for route guards:

```
[app/route-guards.service.ts]

import {Injectable} from '@angular/core';
import {CanActivate} from '@angular/router';


@Injectable()
export class AuthGuardService implements CanActivate {
  constructor() {}

  canActivate() {
    // This method is invoked during route changes if this
```

```
    // class is listed in the Routes
  }
}
```

Before having this do anything, import the module and add it to `Routes`:

```
[app/app.module.ts]

import {NgModule} from '@angular/core';
import {BrowserModule} from '@angular/platform-browser';
import {RouterModule, Routes} from '@angular/router';
import {RootComponent} from './root.component';
import {DefaultComponent} from './default.component';
import {ProfileComponent} from './profile.component';
import {AuthService} from './auth.service';
import {AuthGuardService} from './route-guards.service';

const appRoutes:Routes = [
  {
    path: 'profile',
    component: ProfileComponent,
    canActivate: [AuthGuardService]
  },
  {
    path: '**',
    component: DefaultComponent
  }
];

@NgModule({
  imports: [
    BrowserModule,
    RouterModule.forRoot(appRoutes)
  ],
  declarations: [
    DefaultComponent,
    ProfileComponent,
    RootComponent
  ],
  providers: [
    AuthService,
    AuthGuardService
  ],
  bootstrap: [
    RootComponent
  ]
})
export class AppModule {}
```

Now, each time the application matches a route to a profile and tries to navigate there, the canActivate method defined inside AuthGuardService will be called. The return value of true means the navigation can occur; the return value of false means the navigation is cancelled.

 canActivate can either return a boolean or an Observable<boolean>. Be aware, should you return Observable, the application will dutifully wait for the Observable to emit a value and complete it before navigating.

Since the application's authentication state lives inside BehaviorSubject, all this method needs to do is subscribe, check the username, and navigate if it is not null. It suits this to return Observable<boolean>:

```
[app/route-guards.service.ts]

import {Injectable} from '@angular/core';
import {CanActivate, Router} from '@angular/router';
import {AuthService} from './auth.service';
import {Observable} from 'rxjs/Observable';

@Injectable()
export class AuthGuardService implements CanActivate {
  constructor(private authService_:AuthService,
    private router_:Router) {}

  canActivate():Observable<boolean> {
    return this.authService_.usernameEmitter.map(username => {
      if (!username) {
        this.router_.navigate(['login']);
      } else {
        return true;
      }
    });
  }
}
```

Once you implement this, you will notice that the navigation will never occur, even though the service is emitting the username correctly. This is because the recipient of the return value of canActivate isn't just waiting for an Observable emission; it is waiting for the Observable to *complete*. Since you just want to peek at the username value inside BehaviorSubject, you can just return a new Observable that returns one value and then is completed using take():

```
[app/route-guards.service.ts]
```

```
import {Injectable} from '@angular/core';
import {CanActivate, Router} from '@angular/router';
import {AuthService} from './auth.service';
import {Observable} from 'rxjs/Observable';
import 'rxjs/add/operator/take';

@Injectable()
export class AuthGuardService implements CanActivate {
  constructor(private authService_:AuthService,
    private router_:Router) {}

  canActivate():Observable<Boolean> {
    return this.authService_.usernameEmitter.map(username => {
      if (!username) {
        this.router_.navigate(['login']);
      } else {
        return true;
      }
    }).take(1);
  }
}
```

Superb! However, this application still lacks a method to formally log in and log out.

Adding login behavior

Since the login page will need its own view, it should get its own route and component.
Once the user logs in, there is no need to keep them on the login page, so you want to
redirect them to the default view once they are done.

First, create the login component and its corresponding view:

```
[app/login.component.ts]

import {Component} from '@angular/core';
import {Router} from '@angular/router';
import {AuthService} from './auth.service';

@Component({
  template: `
    <h2>Login view</h2>
    <input #un>
    <button (click)="login(un.value)">Login</button>
  `
})
export class LoginComponent {
  constructor(private authService_:AuthService,
```

```
      private router_:Router) { }

  login(newUsername:string):void {
    this.authService_.login(newUsername);
    this.authService_.usernameEmitter
      .subscribe(username => {
        if (!!username) {
          this.router_.navigate(['']);
        }
      });
  }
}
[app/app.module.ts]

import {NgModule} from '@angular/core';
import {BrowserModule} from '@angular/platform-browser';
import {RouterModule, Routes} from '@angular/router';
import {RootComponent} from './root.component';
import {DefaultComponent} from './default.component';
import {ProfileComponent} from './profile.component';
import {LoginComponent} from './login.component';
import {AuthService} from './auth.service';
import {AuthGuardService} from './route-guards.service';

const appRoutes:Routes = [
  {
    path: 'login',
    component: LoginComponent
  },
  {
    path: 'profile',
    component: ProfileComponent,
    canActivate: [AuthGuardService]
  },
  {
    path: '**',
    component: DefaultComponent
  }
];

@NgModule({
  imports: [
    BrowserModule,
    RouterModule.forRoot(appRoutes)
  ],
  declarations: [
    LoginComponent,
    DefaultComponent,
```

```
      ProfileComponent,
      RootComponent
   ],
   providers: [
      AuthService,
      AuthGuardService
   ],
   bootstrap: [
      RootComponent
   ]
})
export class AppModule {}
```

You should now be able to log in. This is all well and good, but you will notice that with this implemented, updating the username in the profile view will navigate to the default view, exhibiting the same behavior defined in the login component. This is because the subscriber is still listening to `AuthService` Observable. You need to add in an OnDestroy method to correctly tear down the login view:

```
[app/login.component.ts]

import {Component, ngOnDestroy} from '@angular/core';
import {Router} from '@angular/router';
import {AuthService} from './auth.service';
import {Subscription} from 'rxjs/Subscription';

@Component({
  template: `
    <h2>Login view</h2>
    <input #un>
    <button (click)="login(un.value)">Login</button>
  `
})
export class LoginComponent implements OnDestroy {
  private usernameSubscription_:Subscription;
  constructor(private authService_:AuthService,
    private router_:Router) { }

  login(newUsername:string):void {
    this.authService_.login(newUsername);
    this.usernameSubscription_ = this.authService_
      .usernameEmitter
      .subscribe(username => {
        if (!!username) {
          this.router_.navigate(['']);
        }
      });
```

```
    }
  ngOnDestroy() {
    // Only invoke unsubscribe() if this exists
    this.usernameSubscription_ &&
      this.usernameSubscription_.unsubscribe();
  }
}
```

Adding the logout behavior

Finally, you want to add a way for users to log out. This can be accomplished in a number of ways, but a good implementation will be able to delegate the logout behavior to its associated methods without introducing too much boilerplate code.

Ideally, you would like for the application to just be able to navigate to the logout route and let Angular handle the rest. This, too, can be accomplished with `canActivate`. First, define a new Route Guard:

```
[app/route-guards.service.ts]

import {Injectable} from '@angular/core';
import {CanActivate, Router} from '@angular/router';
import {AuthService} from './auth.service';
import {Observable} from 'rxjs/Observable';
import 'rxjs/add/operator/take';


@Injectable()
export class AuthGuardService implements CanActivate {
  constructor(private authService_:AuthService,
    private router_:Router) {}

  canActivate():Observable<boolean> {
    return this.authService_.usernameEmitter.map(username => {
      if (!username) {
        this.router_.navigate(['login']);
      } else {
        return true;
      }
    }).take(1);
  }
}

@Injectable()
export class LogoutGuardService implements CanActivate {
  constructor(private authService_:AuthService,
```

```
      private router_:Router) {}

   canActivate():boolean {
     this.authService_.logout();
     this.router_.navigate(['']);
     return true;
   }
 }
```

This behavior should be pretty self-explanatory.

 Your `canActivate` method must match the signature defined in the `CanActivate` interface, so even though it will always navigate to a new view, you should add a return value to please the compiler and to handle any cases where the preceding code should fall through.

Next, add the logout component and the route. The logout component will never be rendered, but the route definition requires that it is mapped to a valid component. So `LogoutComponent` will consist of a dummy class:

```
[app/logout.component.ts]

import {Component} from '@angular/core';

@Component({
  template: ''
})
export class LogoutComponent{}
[app/app.module.ts]

import {NgModule} from '@angular/core';
import {BrowserModule} from '@angular/platform-browser';
import {RouterModule, Routes} from '@angular/router';
import {RootComponent} from './root.component';
import {DefaultComponent} from './default.component';
import {ProfileComponent} from './profile.component';
import {LoginComponent} from './login.component';
import {LogoutComponent} from './logout.component';
import {AuthService} from './auth.service';
import {AuthGuardService, LogoutGuardService}
  from './route-guards.service';

const appRoutes:Routes = [
  {
    path: 'login',
    component: LoginComponent
  },
```

```
    {
      path: 'logout',
      component: LogoutComponent,
      canActivate: [LogoutGuardService]
    },
    {
      path: 'profile',
      component: ProfileComponent,
      canActivate: [AuthGuardService]
    },
    {
      path: '**',
      component: DefaultComponent
    }
];

@NgModule({
  imports: [
    BrowserModule,
    RouterModule.forRoot(appRoutes)
  ],
  declarations: [
    LoginComponent,
    LogoutComponent,
    DefaultComponent,
    ProfileComponent,
    RootComponent
  ],
  providers: [
    AuthService,
    AuthGuardService,
    LogoutGuardService
  ],
  bootstrap: [
    RootComponent
  ]
})
export class AppModule {}
```

With this, you should have a fully functional login/logout behavior process.

How it works...

The core of this implementation is built around Observables and Route Guards. Observables allow your `AuthService` module to maintain the state and expose it simultaneously through `BehaviorSubject`, and Route Guards allow you to conditionally navigate and redirect at your application's discretion.

There's more...

Application security is a broad and involved subject. The recipe shown here involves how to smoothly move your user around the application, but it is by no means a rigorous security model.

The actual authentication

You should always assume the client can manipulate its own execution environment. In this example, even if you protect the login/logout methods on `AuthService` as well as you can, it will be easy for the user to gain access to these methods and authenticate themselves.

User interfaces, which Angular applications squarely fall into, are not meant to be secure. Security responsibilities fall on the server side of the client/server model since the user does not control that execution environment. In an actual application, the `login()` method here would make a network request get some sort of a token from the server. Two very popular implementations, JSON Web Tokens and Cookie auth, do this in different ways, but they are essentially variations of the same theme. Angular or the browser will store and send these tokens, but ultimately the server should act as the gatekeeper of secure information.

Secure data and views

Any secure information you might send to the client should be behind server-based authentication. For many developers, this is an obvious fact, especially when dealing with an API. However, Angular also requests templates and static files from the server, and some of these you might not want to serve to the wrong people. In this case, you will need to configure your server to authenticate requests for these static files before you serve them to the client.

See also

- *Navigating with the Router service* uses an Angular service to navigate around an application
- *Building stateful RouterLink behavior with RouterLinkActive* shows how to integrate application behavior with a URL state
- *Implementing nested views with route parameters and child routes* gives an example of how to configure Angular URLs to support nesting and data passing
- *Working with matrix URL parameters and routing arrays* demonstrates Angular's built-in matrix URL support

7
Services, Dependency Injection, and NgModule

This chapter will cover the following recipes:

- Injecting a simple service into a component
- Controlling service instance creation and injection with NgModule
- Service injection aliasing with useClass and useExisting
- Injecting a value as a service with useValue and OpaqueTokens
- Building a provider-configured service with useFactory

Introduction

Angular 1 gave you a hodgepodge of different service types. Many of them had a great deal of overlap. Many of them were confusing. And all of them were singletons.

Angular 2 has totally thrown away this concept. In its place, there is a shiny new dependency injection system that is far more extensible and sensible than its predecessor. It allows you to have atomic and non-atomic service types, aliasing, factories, and all kinds of incredibly useful tools for use in your application.

If you are looking to use services much in the same way as earlier, you will find that your understanding of service types will easily carry over to the new system. But for developers who want more out of their applications, the new world of dependency injection is incredibly powerful and obviously built for applications that can scale.

Injecting a simple service into a component

The most common use case will be for a component to directly inject a service into itself. Although the rhythms of defining service types and using dependency injection remain mostly the same, it's important to get a good hold of the fundamentals of Angular 2's dependency injection schema, as it differs in several important ways.

 The code, links, and a live example of this are available at
`http://ngcookbook.herokuapp.com/4263.`

Getting ready

Suppose you had the following skeleton application:

```
[app/root.component.ts]

import {Component} from '@angular/core';

@Component({
  selector: 'root',
  template: `
    <h1>root component!</h1>
    <button (click)="fillArticle()">Show article</button>
    <h2>{{title}}</h2>
  `
})
export class RootComponent {
  title:string;
  constructor() {}
  fillArticle() {}
}
```

Your objective is to implement a service that can be injected into this component and return an article title to fill the template.

How to do it...

As you might expect, services in Angular 2 are represented as classes. Similar to components, services are designated as such with an @Injectable decorator. Create this service in its own file:

```
[app/article.service.ts]

import {Injectable} from '@angular/core';

@Injectable()
export class ArticleService {
  private title_:string = `
    CFO Yodels Quarterly Earnings Call, Stock Skyrockets
  `
}
```

This service has a private title that you need to transfer to the component, but first you must make the service itself available to the component. This can be done by importing the service, then listing it in the providers property of the application module:

```
[app/app.module.ts]

import {NgModule} from '@angular/core';
import {BrowserModule} from '@angular/platform-browser';
import {RootComponent} from './root.component';
import {ArticleService} from './article.service';

@NgModule({
  imports: [
    BrowserModule
  ],
  declarations: [
    RootComponent
  ],
  providers: [
    ArticleService
  ],
  bootstrap: [
    RootComponent
  ]
})
export class AppModule {}
```

Now that the service can be provided, inject it into the component:

```
[app/root.component.ts]
import {Component} from '@angular/core';
import {ArticleService} from './article.service';

@Component({
  selector: 'root',
  template: `
    <h1>root component!</h1>
    <button (click)="fillArticle()">Show article</button>
    <h2>{{title}}</h2>
  `
})
export class RootComponent {
  title:string;

  constructor(private articleService_:ArticleService) {}

  fillArticle() {}
}
```

This new code will create a new instance of `ArticleService` when `RootComponent` is instantiated, and then inject it into the constructor. Anything injected into a component will be available as a component instance member, which you can use to connect a service method to a component method:

```
[app/article.service.ts]

import {Injectable} from '@angular/core';

@Injectable()
export class ArticleService {
  private title_:string = `
    CFO Yodels Quarterly Earnings Call, Stock Skyrockets
  `;
  getTitle() {
    return this.title_;
  }
}
[app/root.component.ts]

import {Component} from '@angular/core';
import {ArticleService} from './article.service';

@Component({
  selector: 'root',
  template: `
```

```
    <h1>root component!</h1>
    <button (click)="fillArticle()">Show article</button>
    <h2>{{title}}</h2>
    `
})
export class RootComponent {
  title:string;

  constructor(private articleService_:ArticleService) {}

  fillArticle():void {
    this.title = this.articleService_.getTitle();
  }
}
```

How it works...

Without the decorator, the service you have just built is rather plain in composition. With the @Injectable() decoration, the class is designated to the Angular framework as one that will be injected elsewhere.

Designation as an injectable has a number of considerations that are importantly distinct from just being passed in parametrically. When is the injected class instantiated? How is it linked to the component instance? How are global and local instances controlled? These are all discussed in the more advanced recipes in this chapter.

Designation as an injectable service is only one piece of the puzzle. The component needs to be informed of the existence of the service. You must first import the service class into the component module, but this alone is not sufficient. Recall that the syntax used to inject a service was simply a way to list it as a constructor parameter. Behind the scenes, Angular is smart enough to recognize that these component arguments are to be injected, but it requires the final piece to connect the imported module to its place as an injected resource.

This final piece takes the form of the providers property of the NgModule definition. For the purpose of this recipe, it isn't important that you know the details of the property. In short, this array designates the articleService constructor parameter as an injectable and identifies that ArticleService should be injected into the constructor.

There's more…

It's important to acknowledge here how the TypeScript decorators help the dependency injection setup. Decorators do not modify an instance of a class; rather, they modify the class definition. The NgModule containing the providers list will be initialized prior to any instance of the actual component being instantiated. Thus, Angular will be aware of all the services that you might want to inject into the constructor.

See also

- *Controlling service instance creation and injection with NgModule* gives a broad overview of how Angular 2 architects provider hierarchies using modules

Controlling service instance creation and injection with NgModule

In a stark departure from Angular 1.x, Angular 2 features a hierarchical injection scheme. This has a substantial number of implications, and one of the more prominent one is the ability to control when, and how many, services are created.

 The code, links, and a live example of this are available at `http://ngcookbook.herokuapp.com/2102/`.

Getting ready

Suppose you begin with the following simple application:

```
[app/root.component.ts]

import {Component} from '@angular/core';

@Component({
  selector: 'root',
  template: `
    <h1>root component!</h1>
    <article></article>
```

```
    <article></article>
    `
})
export class RootComponent {}
[app/article.component.ts]

import {Component} from '@angular/core';

@Component({
  selector: 'article',
  template: `
    <p>Article component!</p>
    `
})
export class ArticleComponent {}
[app/article.service.ts]

import {Injectable} from '@angular/core';

@Injectable()
export class ArticleService {
  constructor() {
    console.log('ArticleService constructor!');
  }
}
[app/app.module.ts]

import {NgModule} from '@angular/core';
import {BrowserModule} from '@angular/platform-browser';
import {RootComponent} from './root.component';
import {ArticleComponent} from './article.component;

@NgModule({
  imports: [
    BrowserModule,
  ],
  declarations: [
    RootComponent,
    ArticleComponent
  ],
  bootstrap: [
    RootComponent
  ]
})
export class AppModule {}
```

Your objective is to inject a single instance of `ArticleService` into the two child components. In this recipe, `console.log` inside the `ArticleService` constructor allows you to see when one is instantiated.

How to do it...

Begin by importing the service into `AppModule`, then providing it with the following:

```
[app/app.module.ts]

import {NgModule} from '@angular/core';
import {BrowserModule} from '@angular/platform-browser';
import {RootComponent} from './root.component';
import {ArticleComponent} from './article.component;
import {ArticleService} from './article.service;


@NgModule({
  imports: [
    BrowserModule,
  ],
  declarations: [
    RootComponent,
    ArticleComponent
  ],
  providers: [
    ArticleService
  ]
  bootstrap: [
    RootComponent
  ]
})
export class AppModule {}
```

Since `ArticleService` is provided in the same module where `ArticleComponent` is declared, you are now able to inject `ArticleService` into the child `ArticleComponent` instances:

```
[app/article/article.component.ts]

import {Component} from '@angular/core';
import {ArticleService} from './article.service';

@Component({
  selector: 'article',
  template: `
```

```
      <p>Article component!</p>
      `
})
export class ArticleComponent {
  constructor(private articleService_:ArticleService) {}
}
```

With this, you will find that the same service instance is injected into both the child components as the `ArticleService` constructor, namely `console.log`, is only executed once.

Splitting up the root module

As the application grows, it will make less and less sense to cram everything into the same top-level module. Instead, it would be ideal for you to break apart modules into chunks that make sense. In the case of this recipe, it would be preferable to provide `ArticleService` to the application pieces that are actually going to inject it.

Define a new `ArticleModule` and move the relevant module imports into that file instead:

```
[app/article.module.ts]

import {NgModule} from '@angular/core';
import {ArticleComponent} from './article.component';
import {ArticleService} from './article.service';

@NgModule({
  declarations: [
    ArticleComponent
  ],
  providers: [
    ArticleService
  ],
  bootstrap: [
    ArticleComponent
  ]
})
export class ArticleModule {}
```

Then, import this entire module into `AppModule` instead:

```
[app/app.module.ts]

import {NgModule} from '@angular/core';
import {BrowserModule} from '@angular/platform-browser';
import {RootComponent} from './root.component';
```

```
import {ArticleModule} from './article.module';

@NgModule({
  imports: [
    BrowserModule,
    ArticleModule
  ],
  declarations: [
    RootComponent
  ],
  bootstrap: [
    RootComponent
  ]
})
export class AppModule {}
```

If you stop here, you'll find that there are no errors, but `AppModule` isn't able to render `ArticleComponent`. This is because Angular modules, like other module systems, need to explicitly define what is being exported to other modules:

```
[app/article.module.ts]

import {NgModule} from '@angular/core';
import {ArticleComponent} from './article.component';
import {ArticleService} from './article.service';

@NgModule({
  declarations: [
    ArticleComponent
  ],
  providers: [
    ArticleService
  ],
  bootstrap: [
    ArticleComponent
  ],
  exports: [
    ArticleComponent
  ]
})
export class ArticleModule {}
```

With this, you will still see that `ArticleService` is instantiated once.

How it works...

Angular 2's dependency injection takes advantage of its hierarchy structure when providing and injecting services. From where a service is injected, Angular will instantiate a service wherever it is provided. Inside a module definition, this will only ever happen once.

In this case, you provided `ArticleService` to both `AppModule` and `ArticleModule`. Even though the service is injected twice (once for each `ArticleComponent`), Angular uses the `providers` declaration to decide when to create the service.

There's more...

At this point, a curious developer should have lots of questions about how exactly this injection schema behaves. There are numerous different configuration flavors that can be useful to the developer, and these configurations only require a minor code adjustment from the preceding result.

Injecting different service instances into different components

As you might anticipate from the preceding explanation, you can reconfigure this application to inject a different `ArticleService` instance into each child, two in total. This can be done by migrating the `providers` declaration out of the module definition and into the `ArticleComponent` definition:

```
[app/article.module.ts]

import {NgModule} from '@angular/core';
import {ArticleComponent} from './article.component';

@NgModule({
  declarations: [
    ArticleComponent
  ],
  bootstrap: [
    ArticleComponent
  ],
  exports: [
    ArticleComponent
  ]
})
export class ArticleModule {}
```

```
[app/article.component.ts]

import {Component} from '@angular/core';
import {ArticleService} from './article.service';

@Component({
  selector: 'article',
  template: `
    <p>Article component!</p>
  `,
  providers: [
    ArticleService
  ]
})
export class ArticleComponent {
  constructor(private articleService_:ArticleService) {}
}
```

You can verify that two instances are being created by observing the two `console.log` statements called from the `ArticleService` constructor.

Service instantiation

The location of the providers also means that service instance instantiation is bound to the lifetime of the component. For this application, this means that whenever a component is created, if a service is provided inside that component definition, a new service instance will be created.

For example, if you were to toggle the existence of a child component with `ArticleService` provided inside it, it will create a new `ArticleService` every time `ArticleComponent` is constructed:

```
[app/root.component.ts]

import {Component} from '@angular/core';

@Component({
  selector: 'root',
  template: `
    <h1>root component!</h1>
    <button (click)="toggle=!toggle">Toggle</button>
    <article></article>
    <article *ngIf="toggle"></article>
  `
})
export class RootComponent {}
```

You can verify that new instances are being created each time `ngIf` evaluates to `true` by observing additional `console.log` statements called from the `ArticleService` constructor.

See also

- *Injecting a simple service into a component* walks you through the basics of Angular 2's dependency injection schema
- *Service injection aliasing with useClass and useExisting* demonstrates how to intercept dependency injection provider requests

Service injection aliasing with useClass and useExisting

As your application becomes more complex, you may come to a situation where you would like to use your services in a polymorphic style. More specifically, some places in your application may want to request Service A, but a configuration somewhere in your application will actually give it Service B. This recipe will demonstrate one way in which this can be useful, but this behavior allows your application to be more extensible in multiple ways.

 The code, links, and a live example of this are available at `http://ngcookbook.herokuapp.com/1109/`.

Getting ready

Suppose you begin with the following skeleton application.

Dual services

You begin with two services, `ArticleService` and `EditorArticleService`, and their shared interface, `ArticleSourceInterface`. `EditorArticleService` inherits from `ArticleService`:

```
[app/article-source.interface.ts]

export interface ArticleSourceInterface {
  getArticle():Article
}

export interface Article {
  title:string,
  body:string,
  // ? denotes an optional property
  notes?:string
}
[app/article.service.ts]

import {Injectable} from '@angular/core';
import {Article, ArticleSourceInterface}
  from './article-source.interface';

@Injectable()
export class ArticleService implements ArticleSourceInterface {
  private title_:string =
    "Researchers Determine Ham Sandwich Not Turing Complete";
  private body_:string =
    "Computer science community remains skeptical";

  getArticle():Article {
    return {
      title: this.title_,
      body: this.body_
    };
  }
}
[app/editor-article.service.ts]

import {Injectable} from '@angular/core';
import {ArticleService} from './article.service';
import {Article, ArticleSourceInterface}
  from './article-source.interface';

@Injectable()
export class EditorArticleService extends ArticleService
```

```
  implements ArticleSourceInterface {
private notes_:string = "Swing and a miss!";

  constructor() {
    super();
  }

  getArticle():Article {
    // Combine objects and return the joined object
    return Object.assign(
      {},
      super.getArticle(),
      {
        notes: this.notes_
      });
  }
}
```

A unified component

Your objective is to be able to use the following component so that both these services can be injected into the following component:

```
[app/article.component.ts]

import {Component} from '@angular/core';
import {ArticleService} from './article.service';
import {Article} from './article-source.interface';

@Component({
  selector: 'article',
  template: `
    <h2>{{article.title}}</h2>
    <p>{{article.body}}</p>
    <p *ngIf="article.notes">
      <i>Notes: {{article.notes}}</i>
    </p>
  `
})
export class ArticleComponent {
  article:Article;
  constructor(private articleService_:ArticleService) {
    this.article = articleService.getArticle();
  }
}
```

How to do it...

When listing providers, Angular 2 allows you to declare an aliased reference that specifies what service should actually be provided when one of the certain types is requested. Since Angular 2 injection will follow the component tree upwards to find the provider, one way to declare this alias is by wrapping the component with a parent component that will specify this alias:

```
[app/default-view.component.ts]

import {Component} from '@angular/core';
import {ArticleService} from './article.service';

@Component({
  selector: 'default-view',
  template: `
    <h3>Default view</h3>
    <ng-content></ng-content>
  `,
  providers: [ArticleService]
})
export class DefaultViewComponent {}
[app/editor-view.component.ts]

import {Component } from '@angular/core';
import {ArticleService} from './article.service';
import {EditorArticleService} from './editor-article.service';

@Component({
  selector: 'editor-view',
  template: `
    <h3>Editor view</h3>
    <ng-content></ng-content>
  `,
  providers: [
    {provide: ArticleService, useClass: EditorArticleService}
  ]
})
export class EditorViewComponent {}
```

 Note that both these classes are acting as passthrough components. Other than adding a header (which is merely for learning the purpose of instruction in this recipe), these classes are only specifying a provider and are unconcerned with their content.

With the wrapper classes defined, you can now add them to the application module, then use them to create two instances of `ArticleComponent`:

```
[app/app.module.ts]

import {NgModule} from '@angular/core';
import {BrowserModule} from '@angular/platform-browser';
import {RootComponent} from './root.component';
import {ArticleComponent} from './article.component';
import {DefaultViewComponent} from './default-view.component';
import {EditorViewComponent} from './editor-view.component';
import {ArticleComponent} from './article.component';
import {ArticleService} from './article.service';
import {EditorArticleService} from './editor-article.service';

@NgModule({
  imports: [
    BrowserModule
  ],
  declarations: [
    RootComponent,
    ArticleComponent,
    DefaultViewComponent,
    EditorViewComponent
  ],
  bootstrap: [
    RootComponent
  ]
})
export class AppModule {}
[app/root.component.ts]

import {Component} from '@angular/core';

@Component({
  selector: 'root',
  template: `
    <default-view>
      <article></article>
    </default-view>
    <hr />
    <editor-view>
      <article></article>
    </editor-view>
  `
})
export class RootComponent {}
```

With this, you should now see that the editor version of `ArticleComponent` gets the notes, but the default version does not.

How it works...

In Angular 1, the service type that was supposed to be injected was identified from a function parameter by doing a direct match of the parameter symbol. `function(Article)` would inject the `Article` service, `function (User)` the `User` service, and so on. This led to nastiness, such as the minification-proofing of constructors by providing an array of strings to match against `['Article', function(Article) {}]`.

This is no longer the case. When a provider is registered, the `useClass` option utilizes the two-part dependency injection matching scheme in Angular 2. The first part is the provider token, which is the parameter type of the service being injected. In this case, `private articleService_:ArticleService` uses the `ArticleService` token to request that an instance be injected. Angular 2 takes this and matches this token against the declared `providers` in the component hierarchy. When a token is matched, Angular 2 will use the second part, the `provider` itself, to inject an instance of the service.

In reality, `providers: [ArticleService]` is a shorthand for `providers: [{provide: ArticleService, useClass: ArticleService}]`. The shorthand is useful since you will almost always be requesting the service class that would match the injected class. However, in this recipe, you are configuring Angular 2 to recognize an `ArticleService` token and so use the `EditorArticleService` provider.

There's more...

An attentive developer will have realized by this point that the utility of `useClass` is limited in the sense that it does not allow you to independently control where the actual service is provided. In other words, the place where you intercept the provider definition with `useClass` is also the place where the replacement class will be provided.

In this example, `useClass` is suitable since you are perfectly happy to provide `EditorArticleService` in the same place where you are specifying that it should be used to replace `ArticleService`. However, it is not difficult to imagine a scenario in which you would like to specify the replacement service type but have it injected higher up in the component tree. This, after all, would allow you to reuse instances of a service instead of having to create a new one for each `useClass` declaration.

For this purpose, you can use `useExisting`. It requires you to explicitly provide the service type separately, but it will reuse the provided instance instead of creating a new one. For the application you just created, you can now reconfigure it with `useExisting`, and provide both the services at the `RootComponent` level.

To demonstrate that your reasoning about the service behavior is correct, double the number of `Article` components, and add a log statement to the constructor of `ArticleService` to ensure you are only creating one of each service:

```
[app/root.component.ts]

import {Component} from '@angular/core';

@Component({
  selector: 'root',
  template: `
    <default-view>
      <article></article>
    </default-view>
    <editor-view>
      <article></article>
    </editor-view>
    <default-view>
      <article></article>
    </default-view>
    <editor-view>
      <article></article>
    </editor-view>
  `
})
export class RootComponent {}
[app/article.service.ts]

import {Injectable} from '@angular/core';
import {Article, ArticleSourceInterface} from './article-source.interface';

@Injectable()
export class ArticleService implements ArticleSourceInterface {
  private title_:string =
    "Researchers Determine Ham Sandwich Not Turing Complete";
  private body_:string =
    "Computer science community remains skeptical";

  constructor() {
    console.log('Instantiated ArticleService!');
  }
```

```
  getArticle():Article {
    return {
      title: this.title_,
      body: this.body_
    };
  }
}
[app/editor-view.component.ts]

import {Component} from '@angular/core';
import {ArticleService} from './article.service';
import {EditorArticleService} from './editor-article.service';

@Component({
  selector: 'editor-view',
  template: `
    <h3>Editor view</h3>
    <ng-content></ng-content>
  `,
  providers: [
    {provide: ArticleService, useExisting: EditorArticleService}
  ]
})
export class EditorViewComponent {}
[app/default-view.component.ts]

import {Component} from '@angular/core';
import {ArticleService} from './article.service';

@Component({
  selector: 'default-view',
  template: `
    <h3>Default view</h3>
    <ng-content></ng-content>
  `
  // providers removed
})
export class DefaultViewComponent {}
```

In this configuration, with `useClass`, you will see that one instance of `ArticleService` and two instances of `EditorArticleService` are created. When replaced with `useExisting`, you will find that only one instance of each is created.

Thus, in this reconfigured version of the recipe, your application is doing the following:

- At the `RootComponent` level, it is providing `EditorArticleService`
- At the `EditorViewComponent` level, it is redirecting `ArticleService` injection tokens to `EditorArticleService`
- At the `ArticleComponent` level, it is injecting `ArticleService` using the `ArticleService` token

Refactoring with directive providers

If this implementation seems clunky and verbose to you, you are certainly on to something. The intermediate components are performing their jobs quite well, but aren't really doing anything other than shimming in an intermediate provider's declaration. Instead of wrapping in a component, you can migrate the provider's statement into a directive and do away with both the view components:

```
[app/root.component.ts]

import {Component} from '@angular/core';
import {ArticleComponent} from './ article.component';
import {ArticleService} from './article.service';
import {EditorArticleService} from './editor-article.service';

@Component({
  selector: 'root',
  template: `
    <article></article>
    <article editor-view></article>
    <article></article>
    <article editor-view></article>
  `
})
export class RootComponent {}
[app/editor-view.directive.ts]

import {Directive } from '@angular/core';
import {ArticleService} from './article.service';
import {EditorArticleService} from './editor-article.service';

@Directive({
```

```
    selector: '[editor-view]',
    providers: [
      {provide: ArticleService, useExisting: EditorArticleService}
    ]
})
export class EditorViewDirective {}
[app/app.module.ts]

import {NgModule} from '@angular/core';
import {BrowserModule} from '@angular/platform-browser';
import {RootComponent} from './root.component';
import {ArticleComponent} from './article.component';
import {DefaultViewComponent} from './default-view.component';
import {EditorViewDirective} from './editor-view.directive';
import {ArticleComponent} from './article.component';
import {ArticleService} from './article.service';
import {EditorArticleService} from './editor-article.service';

@NgModule({
  imports: [
    BrowserModule
  ],
  declarations: [
    RootComponent,
    ArticleComponent,
    DefaultViewComponent,
    EditorViewDirective
  ],
  providers: [
    ArticleService,
    EditorArticleService
  ],
  bootstrap: [
    RootComponent
  ]
})
export class AppModule {}
```

Your application should work just the same!

See also

- *Injecting a simple service into a component* walks you through the basics of Angular 2's dependency injection schema
- *Controlling service instance creation and injection with NgModule* gives a broad overview of how Angular 2 architects provider hierarchies using modules
- *Injecting a value as a service with useValue and OpaqueTokens* shows how you can use dependency-injected tokens to inject generic objects
- *Building a provider-configured service with useFactory* details the process of setting up a service factory to create configurable service definitions

Injecting a value as a service with useValue and OpaqueTokens

In Angular 1, there was a broad selection of service types you could use in your application. A subset of these types allowed you to inject a static value instead of a service instance, and this useful ability is continued in Angular 2.

 The code, links, and a live example of this are available at
`http://ngcookbook.herokuapp.com/3032/`.

Getting ready

Begin with the following simple application:

```
[app/app.module.ts]

import {NgModule} from '@angular/core';
import {BrowserModule} from '@angular/platform-browser';
import {RootComponent} from './root.component';
import {ArticleComponent} from './article.component';

@NgModule({
  imports: [
    BrowserModule
  ],
  declarations: [
```

```
      RootComponent,
      ArticleComponent
    ],
    bootstrap: [
      RootComponent
    ]
})
export class AppModule {}
[app/root.component.ts]

import {Component} from '@angular/core';

@Component({
  selector: 'root',
  template: `
    <article></article>
  `
})
export class RootComponent {}
[app/article.component.ts]

import {Component} from '@angular/core';

@Component({
  selector: 'article',
  template: `
    <img src="{{logoUrl}}">
    <h2>Fool and His Money Reunited at Last</h2>
    <p>Author: Jake Hsu</p>
  `
})
export class ArticleComponent {}
```

How to do it...

Although a formal service class declaration and @Injectable decorator designation is no longer necessary for injecting a value, token/provider mapping is still needed. Since there is no longer a class available that can be used to type the injectable, something else will have to act as its replacement.

Angular 2 solves this problem with OpaqueToken. This module allows you to create a classless token that can be used to pair the injected value with the constructor argument. This can be used alongside the useValue provide option, which simply directly provides whatever its contents are as injected values.

Define a token using a unique string in its constructor:

```
[app/logo-url.token.ts]

import {OpaqueToken} from '@angular/core';

export const LOGO_URL = new OpaqueToken('logo.url');
```

Incorporate this token into the application module definition as you normally would. However, you must specify what it will actually point to when it is injected. In this case, it should resolve to an image URL string:

```
[app/app.module.ts]

import {NgModule} from '@angular/core';
import {BrowserModule} from '@angular/platform-browser';
import {RootComponent} from './root.component';
import {ArticleComponent} from './article.component';
import {LOGO_URL} from './logo-url.token';

@NgModule({
  imports: [
    BrowserModule
  ],
  declarations: [
    RootComponent,
    ArticleComponent
  ],
  providers: [
    {provide: LOGO_URL, useValue:
      'https://angular.io/resources/images/logos/standard/logo-nav.png'}
  ],
  bootstrap: [
    RootComponent
  ]
})
export class AppModule {}
```

Finally, you'll be able to inject this into a component. However, since you're injecting something that wasn't defined with the `@Injectable()` decoration, you'll need to use `@Inject()` inside the constructor to tell Angular that it should be provided, using dependency injection. Furthermore, the injection will not attach itself to the component's `this`, so you'll need to do this manually as well:

```
[app/article.component.ts]

import {Component, Inject} from '@angular/core';
```

```
import {LOGO_URL} from './logo-url.token';

@Component({
  selector: 'article',
  template: `
    <img src="{{logoUrl}}">
    <h2>Fool and His Money Reunited at Last</h2>
    <p>Author: Jake Hsu</p>
  `
})
export class ArticleComponent {
  logoUrl:string;
  constructor(@Inject(LOGO_URL) private logoUrl_) {
    this.logoUrl = logoUrl_;
  }
}
```

With this, you should be able to see the image rendered in your browser!

How it works...

OpaqueToken allows you to use non-class types inside Angular 2's class-centric provider schema. It generates a simple class instance that essentially is just a wrapper for the custom string you provided. This class is what the dependency injection framework will use when attempting to map injection tokens to provider declarations. This gives you the ability to more widely utilize dependency injection throughout your application since you can now feed any type of value wherever a service type can be injected.

There's more...

One other way in which injecting values is useful is that it gives you the ability to stub out services. Suppose you wanted to define a default stub service that should be overridden with an explicit provider to enable useful behavior. In such a case, you can imagine a default article entity that could be differently configured via a directive while reusing the same component:

```
[app/root.component.ts]

import {Component} from '@angular/core';

@Component({
  selector: 'root',
  template: `
```

```
    <article></article>
    <article editor-view></article>
  `
})
export class RootComponent {}


[app/editor-article.service.ts]


import {Injectable} from '@angular/core';

export const MockEditorArticleService = {
  getArticle: () => ({
    title: "Mock title",
    body: "Mock body"
  })
};


@Injectable()
export class EditorArticleService {
  private title_:string =
    "Prominent Vegan Embroiled in Scrambled Eggs Scandal";
  private body_:string =
    "Tofu Farming Alliance retracted their endorsement.";

  getArticle() {
    return {
      title: this.title_,
      body: this.body_
    };
  }
}
[app/editor-view.directive.ts]


import {Directive} from '@angular/core';
import {EditorArticleService} from './editor-article.service';

@Directive({
  selector: '[editor-view]',
  providers: [EditorArticleService]
})
export class EditorViewDirective {}
[app/article.component.ts]


import {Component, Inject} from '@angular/core';
import {EditorArticleService} from './editor-article.service';

@Component({
  selector: 'article',
```

[291]

```
  template: `
    <h2>{{title}}</h2>
    <p>{{body}}</p>
    `
})
export class ArticleComponent {
  title:string;
  body:string;
  constructor(private editorArticleService_:EditorArticleService) {
    let article = editorArticleService_.getArticle();
    this.title = article.title;
    this.body = article.body;
  }
}
```

With this, your `ArticleComponent`, as defined in the preceding code, would use the mock service when the directive is not attached and the actual service when it is attached.

See also

- *Controlling service instance creation and injection with NgModule* gives a broad overview of how Angular 2 architects provider hierarchies using modules
- *Service injection aliasing with useClass and useExisting* demonstrates how to intercept dependency injection provider requests
- *Building a provider-configured service with useFactory* details the process of setting up a service factory to create configurable service definitions

Building a provider-configured service with useFactory

One further extension of dependency injection in Angular 2 is the ability to use factories when defining your provider hierarchy. A provider factory allows you to accept input, perform arbitrary operations to configure the provider, and return that provider instance for injection.

 The code, links, and a live example of this are available at
`http://ngcookbook.herokuapp.com/0049/`.

Getting ready

Begin again with the dual service and article component setup shown in *Service injection aliasing with useClass and useExisting*, earlier in the chapter.

How to do it...

Provider factories in Angular 2 are exactly as you might imagine they would be: functions that return a provider. The factory can be specified in a separate file and referenced with the `useFactory provide` option.

Begin by combining the two services into a single service, which will be configured with a method call:

```
[app/article.service.ts]

import {Injectable} from '@angular/core';

@Injectable()
export class ArticleService {
  private title_:string =
    "Flying Spaghetti Monster Sighted";
  private body_:string =
    "Adherents insist we are missing the point";
  private notes_:string = "Spot on!";
  private editorEnabled_:boolean = false;

  getArticle():Object {
    var article = {
      title: this.title_,
      body: this.body_
    };
    if (this.editorEnabled_) {
      Object.assign(article, article, {
        notes: this.notes_
      });
    }
    return article;
  }

  enableEditor():void {
    this.editorEnabled_ = true;
  }
}
```

Defining the factory

Your objective is to configure this service to have `enableEditor()` invoked based on a `boolean` flag. With provider factories, this is possible. Define the factory in its own file:

```
[app/article.factory.ts]

import {ArticleService} from './article.service';

export function articleFactory(enableEditor?:boolean):ArticleService {
  return (articleService:ArticleService) => {
    if (enableEditor) {
      articleService.enableEditor();
    }
    return articleService;
  }
}
```

Injecting OpaqueToken

Splendid! Next, you'll need to reconfigure `ArticleComponent` to inject a token rather than the desired service:

```
[app/article.token.ts]

import {OpaqueToken} from '@angular/core';

export const ArticleToken = new OpaqueToken('app.article');
[app/article.component.ts]

import {Component, Inject} from '@angular/core';
import {ArticleToken} from './article.token';

@Component({
  selector: 'article',
  template: `
    <h2>{{article.title}}</h2>
    <p>{{article.body}}</p>
    <p *ngIf="article.notes">
      <i>Notes: {{article.notes}}</i>
    </p>
  `
})
export class ArticleComponent {
  article:Object;
  constructor(@Inject(ArticleToken) private articleService_) {
```

```
        this.article = articleService_.getArticle();
    }
}
```

Creating provider directives with useFactory

Finally, you'll need to define the directives that specify how to use this factory and incorporate them into the application:

```
[app/default-view.directive.ts]

import {Directive} from '@angular/core';
import {ArticleService} from './article.service';
import {articleFactory} from './article.factory';
import {ArticleToken} from './article.token';

@Directive({
  selector: '[default-view]',
  providers: [
    {provide: ArticleToken,
      useFactory: articleFactory(),
      deps: [ArticleService]
    }
  ]
})
export class DefaultViewDirective {}
[app/editor-view.directive.ts]

import {Directive} from '@angular/core';
import {ArticleService} from './article.service';
import {articleFactory} from './article.factory';
import {ArticleToken} from './article.token';

@Directive({
  selector: '[editor-view]',
  providers: [
    {
      provide: ArticleToken,
      useFactory: articleFactory(true),
      deps: [ArticleService]
    }
  ]
})
export class EditorViewDirective {}
[app/root.component.ts]

import {Component} from '@angular/core';
```

```
@Component({
  selector: 'root',
  template: `
    <article default-view></article>
    <article editor-view></article>
  `
})
export class RootComponent {}
```

With this, you should be able to see both the versions of `ArticleComponent`.

How it works...

The article component is redefined to use a token instead of a service injection. With the token, Angular will walk up the component tree to find where that token is provided. The directives declare that the token is mapped to a provider factory, which is a method invoked to return the actual provider.

`useFactory` is the property that maps to the factory function. `deps` is the property that maps to the service dependencies that the factory has.

There's more...

An important distinction at this point is to recognize that all these factory configurations are happening before any components are instantiated. The class decoration that defines the providers will invoke the factory function on setup.

See also

- *Controlling service instance creation and injection with NgModule* gives a broad overview of how Angular 2 architects provider hierarchies using modules
- *Service injection aliasing with useClass and useExisting* demonstrates how to intercept dependency injection provider requests
- *Injecting a value as a service with useValue and OpaqueTokens* show how you can use dependency injected tokens to inject generic objects

8
Application Organization and Management

This chapter will cover the following recipes:

- Composing package.json for a minimum viable Angular 2 application
- Configuring TypeScript for a minimum viable Angular 2 application
- Performing in-browser transpilation with SystemJS
- Composing application files for a minimum viable Angular 2 application
- Migrating the minimum viable Angular 2 application to Webpack bundling
- Incorporating shims and polyfills into Webpack
- HTML generation with html-webpack-plugin
- Setting up an application with Angular's CLI

Introduction

The Angular 2 project's ambitions goals involve the utilization of a different language with different syntax and constructs, as well as providing high efficiency and modularity. What this means for you is that the process of maintaining an Angular 2 application may be difficult.

The ultimate goal is to efficiently serve HTML, CSS, and JS to a web browser and to make it easy to develop the source components of these static files. How one arrives at this endpoint can be worked out in a number of different ways, and it would be an exercise in futility to write a chapter on all of them.

Instead, this chapter will provide a few opinionated ways of arranging your Angular 2 application in a way that it would reflect the most popular and effective strategies. It will also show you how to build and extend a minimum viable Angular 2 application. For some, this will seem a bit simple and rudimentary. However, the majority of Quickstart projects or code generation frameworks simply give you a repository and a few commands to run in order to get out of the door, and these commands run without telling you what they're doing or how they're doing it! In this chapter, you will learn how to build an Angular 2 application from the ground up along with the packages and tools that will help you do it and why these methods were selected.

Composing package.json for a minimum viable Angular 2 application

When thinking about a minimum viable Angular 2 application, the configuration files are as close to the metal of the runtime environment as you'll get. In this case, there are two configuration files that will control how npm and its installed packages will manage the files and the start-up processes: `package.json` and `tsconfig.json`.

Some part of this recipe may be a review for developers that are more experienced with npm and its faculties. However, it's important to understand how a very simple Angular 2 project configuration can be structured, so that you are able to wholly understand more complex configurations that are build upon its fundamentals.

 The code, links, and a live example of this are available at `http://ngcookbook.herokuapp.com/1332/`.

Getting ready

You'll need Node.js installed for this recipe to work; you'll also need an empty project directory. You should create these two skeleton configuration files in the root project directory:

```
[package.json]

{
  "name": "angular2-minimum-viable-application"
}
[tsconfig.json]
```

```
{
  "compilerOptions": {
  }
}
```

For a quick and easy way to ensure you have npm set up and ready to go, use the following:

npm --version

It should spit out a version number if everything is set up properly.

How to do it...

You'll start with package.json. The package.json file for a minimum viable application contains three sections:

- dependencies: This is a list of package targets that the production application directly depends upon
- devDependencies: This is a list of package targets that the local environment needs for various reasons, such as compilation, running tests, or linting
- scripts: These are custom-defined command-line utilities run through npm

package.json dependencies

First, you need to add in all the dependencies that your application will need. This includes Angular 2 core modules, which live inside the node_modules/@angular directory, as well as a handful of library dependencies:

- core-js is the polyfill for the ES6 syntax that the TypeScript compiler depends upon, such as Set, Promise, and Map.
- reflect-metadata is the polyfill for the Reflect Metadata API. This allows your TypeScript to use decorators that are not part of the standard TypeScript specification, such as @Component.
- rxjs is available for the ReactiveX JavaScript observables library. Angular 2 natively uses Observables, and this is a direct dependency of the framework.

- `SystemJS` is the dynamic module loader that this project needs for two purposes: to import and map all the source files, and to be able to resolve the ES6 `import/export` declarations.
- `zonejs` is the ZoneJS library that provides Angular 2 with the ability to use asynchronous execution contexts. This is a direct dependency of the framework.

This leaves you with the following:

```
[package.json]

{
  "name": "angular2-minimum-viable-application",
  "dependencies": {
    "@angular/common": "2.0.0",
    "@angular/compiler": "2.0.0",
    "@angular/core": "2.0.0",
    "@angular/platform-browser": "2.0.0",
    "@angular/platform-browser-dynamic": "2.0.0",
    "core-js": "^2.4.1",
    "reflect-metadata": "^0.1.3",
    "rxjs": "5.0.0-beta.12",
    "systemjs": "0.19.27",
    "zone.js": "^0.6.23"
  }
}
```

package.json devDependencies

Next, you need to specify the `devDependencies`.

> Here's an `npm` refresher: `devDependencies` are dependencies that are specific to a development environment. Build scripts can use this to differentiate between packages that need to be included in a production bundle and ones that don't.

- `lite-server` is the simple file server you'll use to test this application locally. This could be replaced by any number of simple file servers.
- `typescript` is the TypeScript compiler.
- `concurrently` is a simple command-line utility for running simultaneous commands from an `npm` script.

This leaves you with the following:

```
[package.json]

{
  "name": "angular2-minimum-viable-application",
  "dependencies": {
    "@angular/common": "2.0.0",
    "@angular/compiler": "2.0.0",
    "@angular/core": "2.0.0",
    "@angular/platform-browser": "2.0.0",
    "@angular/platform-browser-dynamic": "2.0.0",
    "core-js": "^2.4.1",
    "reflect-metadata": "^0.1.3",
    "rxjs": "5.0.0-beta.12",
    "systemjs": "0.19.27",
    "zone.js": "^0.6.23"
  },
  "devDependencies": {
    "concurrently": "^2.2.0",
    "lite-server": "^2.2.2",
    "typescript": "^2.0.2"
  }
}
```

package.json scripts

Finally, you need to create the scripts that you'll use to generate compiled files and run the development server:

```
[package.json]

{
  "name": "angular2-minimum-viable-application",
  "scripts": {
    "lite": "lite-server",
    "postinstall": "npm install -S @types/node @types/core-js",
    "start": "tsc && concurrently 'npm run tsc:w' 'npm run lite'",
    "tsc": "tsc",
    "tsc:w": "tsc -w"
  },
  "dependencies": {
    "@angular/common": "2.0.0",
    "@angular/compiler": "2.0.0",
    "@angular/core": "2.0.0",
    "@angular/platform-browser": "2.0.0",
    "@angular/platform-browser-dynamic": "2.0.0",
```

```
      "core-js": "^2.4.1",
      "reflect-metadata": "^0.1.3",
      "rxjs": "5.0.0-beta.12",
      "systemjs": "0.19.27",
      "zone.js": "^0.6.23"
    },
    "devDependencies": {
      "concurrently": "^2.2.0",
      "lite-server": "^2.2.2",
      "typescript": "^2.0.2"
    }
  }
}
```

Each of these scripts serves a purpose, but most you will not need to invoke manually. Here is a brief description of each of these scripts:

- `lite` starts off an instance of `lite-server`.
- `postinstall` is the hook definition that will run after `npm install` is completed. In this case, after `npm` has installed all the project dependencies, you want to install the declaration files for modules that do not have them. `npm` recognizes the pre- and post- prefixes for script strings. Anytime a script is run, `npm` will check for scripts with pre- and post- prefixing them and run them before and after the script, respectively. In this recipe, `prelite` would run before `lite`, and `postlite` would run after `lite` is run.
- `start` is the definition of the default value of `npm start`. This script runs the TypeScript compiler once to completion, then simultaneously invokes the TypeScript compiler watcher and starts up a development server. It is a reserved script keyword in `npm`, thus there is no need for `npm run start`, although that does work.
- `tsc` kicks off the TypeScript compiler. The TypeScript compiler reads its settings from the `tsconfig.json` that exists in the same directory.
- `tsc:w` sets a file watcher to recompile upon file changes.

See also

- *Composing package.json for a minimum viable Angular 2 application* describes how all the pieces work for the core node project file
- *Configuring TypeScript for a minimum viable Angular 2 application* talks about how to configure the compilation to support an Angular 2 project

- *Performing in-browser transpilation with SystemJS* demonstrates how SystemJS can be used to connect uncompiled static files together
- *Composing application files for a minimum viable Angular 2 Application* walks you through how to create an extremely simple Angular 2 app from scratch
- *Migrating the minimum viable Angular 2 application to Webpack bundling* describes how to integrate Webpack into your Angular application build process
- *Incorporating shims and polyfills into Webpack* gives you a handy way of managing Angular 2 polyfill dependencies
- *HTML generation with html-webpack-plugin* shows you how you can configure an npm package to add compiled files to your HTML automatically
- *Setting up an application with Angular CLI* gives a description of how to use the CLI, what it gives you, and what these individual pieces do

Configuring TypeScript for a minimum viable Angular 2 application

In order to use TypeScript alongside Angular 2, there are two major considerations: module interoperability and compilation. You'll need to handle both in order to take your application's .ts files, mix them with external library files, and output the files that would be compatible with your target device.

TypeScript comes ready as an npm package, but you will need to tell it how to interact with the files and modules you've written, and with files from other packages that you want to use in your modules.

 The code, links, and a live example of this are available at http://ngcookbook.herokuapp.com/1053/.

Getting ready

You should first complete the instructions mentioned in the preceding recipe. This will give you the framework necessary to define your TypeScript configuration.

How to do it...

To configure TypeScript, you'll need to add declaration files to incompatible modules and generate a configuration file that will specify how the compiler should work.

Declaration files

TypeScript declaration files exist to specify the shape of a library. These files can be identified by a `.d.ts` suffix. The majority of `npm` packages and other JavaScript libraries already include these files in a standardized location, so that TypeScript can locate them and learn about how the library should be interpreted. Libraries that don't include these need to be given the files, and fortunately the open source community already provides a lot of them.

Two libraries that this project uses don't have declaration files: `node` and `core-js`. As of TypeScript 2.0, you are able to natively install the declaration files for these libraries directly through `npm`. The `-S` flag is a shorthand for saving them to `package.json`:

```
npm install -S @types/node @types/core-js
```

A sensible place for this is inside the `postinstall` script.

tsconfig.json

The TypeScript compiler will look for the `tsconfig.json` file to determine how it should compile the TypeScript files in this directory. This configuration file isn't required, as TypeScript will fall back to the compiler defaults; however, you want to manage exactly how the `*.js` and `*.map.js` files are generated. Modify the `tsconfig.json` file to appear as follows:

```
[tsconfig.json]

{
  "compilerOptions": {
    "target": "es5",
    "module": "commonjs",
    "moduleResolution": "node",
    "emitDecoratorMetadata": true,
    "experimentalDecorators": true,
    "noImplicitAny": false
  }
}
```

The `compilerOptions` property, as you might expect, specifies the settings the compiler should use when the compiling process finds TypeScript files. In the absence of a files property, TypeScript will traverse the entire project directory structure searching for `*.ts` and `*.tsx` files.

All the `compilerOptions` properties can be specified equivalently as command-line flags, but doing so in `tsconfig.json` is a more organized way of going about your project.

- `target` specifies the ECMAScript version that the compiler should output. For broad browser compatibility, ES5 is a sensible default here. Recall that ECMAScript is the specification upon which JavaScript is built. The newest finished specification is ES6 (also called ES2015), but many browsers do not fully support this specification yet. The TypeScript compiler will compile ES6 constructs, such as `class` and `Promise`, to non-native implementations.

- `module` specifies how the output files will handle the modules in the output files. Since you cannot assume that browsers are able to handle ES6 modules, the TypeScript compiler will have to convert them into a module system that browsers are able to handle. CommonJS is a sensible choice here. The CommonJS module style involves defining all the exports in a single module as properties of a single "exports" object. The TypeScript compiler also supports AMD modules (`require.js` style), UMD modules, SystemJS modules, and of course, leaving the modules as their existing ES6 module style. It's out of the scope of this recipe to dive deep into modules.

- `moduleResolution` defines how module paths will be resolved. It's not critical that you understand the exact details of the resolution strategy, but the node setting will give you the proper output format.

- `emitDecoratorMetadata` and `experimentalDecorators` enable TypeScript to handle Angular 2's use of decorators. Recall the addition of the `reflect-metadata` library to support experimental decorators. These flags are the point where it is able to tie into the TypeScript compiler.

- `noImplicitAny` controls whether or not TypeScript files must be typed. When set to `true`, this will throw an error if there is any missed typing in your project. There is an ongoing discussion regarding whether or not this flag should be set, as forcing objects to be typed is obviously useful to prevent errors that may arise from ambiguity in codebases. If you'd like to see an example of the compiler throwing an error, set `noImplicitAny` to true and add `constructor (foo) {}` inside `AppComponent`. You should see the compiler complain about `foo` being untyped.

How it works...

Running the following command will start up the TypeScript compiler from the command line at the root level of your project directory:

```
npm run tsc
```

The compiler will look for tsconfig.json if it is there and fall back to its defaults otherwise. The settings within direct the compiler how to handle and validate the files, which is where everything you just set up comes into play.

The TypeScript compiler doesn't run the code or meaningfully understand what it does, but it can detect when different pieces of the application are trying to interact in a way that doesn't make sense. The .d.ts declaration file for a module gives TypeScript a way to inspect the interface that the module will make available for consumption when it is imported.

For example, suppose that auth is an external module that contains a User class. This would then be imported via the following:

```
import {User} from './auth';
```

By adding the declaration file to the imported module, TypeScript is able to check that the User class exists; it also behaves in the way you are attempting to in the local module. If it sees a mismatch, it will throw an error at compilation.

Compilation

Depending on your framework experience, this may be something you have or have not had experience with previously. Angular 2 (among many frameworks) operates under the notion that JavaScript, as it currently exists, is insufficient for writing good code. The definition of "good" here is subjective, but all frameworks that require compilation want to extend or modify JavaScript in some form or another.

However, all platforms that these applications need to run on—for your purposes, web browsers—only have a JavaScript execution environment that executes from uncompiled code. It isn't feasible for you to extend how the browser handles payloads or delivers a compiled binary, so the files that you send to the client must play by its rules.

TypeScript, by definition and design, is a strict superset of ES6, but these extensions can't be used natively in a browser. Even today, the majority of browsers still do not fully support ES6. Therefore, a sensible objective is to convert TypeScript into ES5.1, which is the ECMAScript standard that is supported on all modern browsers. How you arrive at this output can occur in one of two ways:

- Send the TypeScript to the client as is. There are in-browser compilation libraries that can perform a compilation on the client and execute the resulting ES5.1-compliant code as normal JavaScript. This method makes development easier since your backend doesn't need to do much other than serve the files; however, it defers computing to the client, which degrades performance and is therefore considered a bad practice for production applications.
- Compile the TypeScript into JavaScript before sending it to the client. The overwhelming majority of production applications will elect to handle their business this way. Especially since static files are often served from a CDN or static directory, it makes good sense to compile your descriptive TypeScript codebase into JavaScript files as part of a release and then serve those files to the client.

When you look at the compiled JavaScript that results from compiling TypeScript, it can appear awfully brutal and unreadable. Don't worry! The browser does not care how mangled the JavaScript files are as long as they can be executed.

With the compiler options you've specified in this recipe, the TypeScript compiler will output a `.js` file of the same name right next to its source, the `.ts` file.

There's more...

By no means is the TypeScript compiler limited to a one-off `.ts` file generation. If offers you a broad range of tooling functions for specifying exactly how your output files should appear.

Source map generation

The TypeScript compiler is also capable of generating source maps to go along with output files. If you're not familiar with them, the utility of source maps stems from the nature of compilation and minification: files being debugged in the browsers are not the files that you have written. What's more, when using a compiled TypeScript, the compiled files won't even be in the same language.

Source maps are indexes that pair with compiled files to describe how they originally appeared before they were compiled. More specifically, the .js.map files contain an encoding scheme that associates the compiled and/or minified tokens with their original name and structure in the uncompiled.ts file. Browsers that understand how to use source maps can reconstruct how the original file appeared and allow you to set breakpoints, step through, and inspect lexical constructs inside it as if it were the original.

Source maps can be specified with a special token added to the compiled file://# sourceMappingURL=/dist/example.js.map

If you want to generate source map files for the output, you can specify this in the configuration file as well by adding "sourceMap": true. By default, the .js.map files will be created in the same place as the output .js files; alternatively, you can direct the compiler to create the source maps inside the .js file itself.

> Even though extraneous map files won't affect the resultant application behavior, adding them inline may be undesirable if you don't want to bloat your .js payload size unnecessarily. This is because clients that don't want or need the map files can't decline to request them.

Single file compilation

Since TypeScript checks all the linked modules against their imports and exports, there's no reason you need to have all the compiled files exist as 1:1 mappings to their input files. TypeScript is perfectly happy to combine the compiled files into a single file if the output module format supports it. Specify the single file where you wish all the modules to be compiled with "outFile": "/dist/bundle.js".

> Certain output module formats, such as CommonJS, won't work as concatenated modules in a single file, so using them in conjunction with outFile will not work. As of the TypeScript 1.8 release, AMD and system output formats are supported.
>
> If you plan on using SystemJS, this compiler option can potentially help you, as System works with virtually any module format. If, however, you're using a CommonJS-based bundler, such as Webpack, it's best to delegate the file combination to the bundler.

See also

- *Composing package.json for a minimum viable Angular 2 application* describes how all the pieces work for the core node project file
- *Performing in-browser transpilation with SystemJS* demonstrates how SystemJS can be used to connect uncompiled static files together
- *Composing application files for a minimum viable Angular 2 application* walks you through how to create an extremely simple Angular 2 app from scratch
- *Migrating the minimum viable Angular 2 application to Webpack bundling* describes how to integrate Webpack into your Angular application build process

Performing in-browser transpilation with SystemJS

It can be often useful to be able to deliver TypeScript files directly to the browser and to defer the transpilation to JavaScript until then. While this method has performance drawbacks, it is extremely useful when prototyping and performing experimentations.

The code, links, and a live example of this are available at
`http://ngcookbook.herokuapp.com/2283/`.

Getting ready

Create an empty project directory and create the following `package.json` inside it:

```
[package.json]

{
  "scripts": {
    "lite-server": "lite-server"
  },
  "devDependencies": {
    "lite-server": "^2.2.2",
    "systemjs": "^0.19.38",
    "typescript": "^2.0.3"
  }
}
```

Running `npm install` should get you ready to write code.

How to do it...

The TypeScript `npm` package comes bundled with a transpiler. When combined with SystemJS as the designated transpilation utility, this allows you to serve TypeScript files to the client; SystemJS will transpile them into browser-compatible JavaScript.

First, create the `index.html` file. This file will import the two required JS libraries: `system.js` and `typescript.js`. Next, it specifies the typescript as the desired transpiler and imports the top-level `main.ts` file:

```
[index.html]

<html>
<head>
  <script src="node_modules/systemjs/dist/system.js">
  </script>
  <script src="node_modules/typescript/lib/typescript.js">
  </script>
  <script>
    System.config({
      transpiler: 'typescript'
    });
    System.import('main.ts');
  </script>
</head>
<body>
  <h1 id="text"></h1>
</body>
</html>
```

Next, create the top-level TypeScript file:

```
[main.ts]

import {article} from './article.ts';

document.getElementById('text')
  .innerHTML = article;
```

Finally, create the dependency TypeScript file:

```
[article.ts]

export const article = "Cool story, bro";
```

With this, you should be able to start a development server with `npm run lite-server` and see the TypeScript application running normally in your browser at `localhost:3000`.

How it works...

SystemJS is able to resolve module dependencies as well as apply the transpiler to the module before it reaches the browser. If you look at the transpiled files in a browser inspector, you can see the emitted files exist as vanilla JavaScript **IIFEs (instantaneously invoked function expressions)** as well as their coupled source maps. With these tools, it is possible to build a surprisingly complex application without any sort of backend file management.

There's more...

Unless you're experimenting or doing a rough project, doing transpilation in the browser isn't preferred. Any computation you can do on the server should be done whenever possible. Additionally, all the clients transpiling their own files all perform highly redundant operations since all of them transpile the same files.

See also

- *Composing package.json for a minimum viable Angular 2 application* describes how all the pieces work for the core node project file
- *Configuring TypeScript for a minimum viable Angular 2 application* talks about how to configure the compilation to support an Angular 2 project
- *Composing application files for a minimum viable Angular 2 application* walks you through how to create an extremely simple Angular 2 app from scratch
- *Migrating the minimum viable Angular 2 application to Webpack bundling* describes how to integrate Webpack into your Angular application build process
- *Incorporating shims and polyfills into webpack* gives you a handy way of managing Angular 2 polyfill dependencies
- *HTML generation with html-webpack-plugin* shows you how you can configure an npm package to add compiled files to your HTML automatically
- *Setting up an application with Angular CLI* gives a description of how to use the CLI, what it gives you, and what these individual pieces do

Composing application files for a minimum viable Angular 2 application

When approaching Angular 2 initially, it is useful to have an understanding of an application structure that is torn down to the bare metal. In the case of a minimum viable application, it will consist of a single component. Since this is a chapter on application organization, it isn't so much about what that component will look like, but rather how to take the TypeScript component definition and actually get it to render in a web page.

 The code, links, and a live example of this are available at `http://ngcookbook.herokuapp.com/6323/`.

Getting ready

This recipe assumes you have completed all the steps given in the *Composing configuration files for a minimum viable Angular 2 application* recipe. The npm module installation should succeed with no errors:

```
npm install
```

How to do it...

The simplest place to start is the core application component.

app.component.ts

Implement a component inside a new app/ directory as follows; there should be no surprises:

```
[app/app.component.ts]

import {Component} from '@angular/core';

@Component({
  selector: 'app-root',
  template: '<h1>AppComponent template!</h1>'
})
export class AppComponent {}
```

This is about as simple a component can possibly get. Once this is successfully rendered in the client, this component should just be a big line of text.

app.module.ts

Next, you need to define the NgModule that will be associated with this component. Create another file in the app/ directory, app.module.ts, and have it match the following:

```
[app/app.module.ts]

import {NgModule} from '@angular/core';
import {BrowserModule} from '@angular/platform-browser';
import {AppComponent} from './app.component';

@NgModule({
  imports: [BrowserModule],
  declarations: [AppComponent],
  bootstrap: [AppComponent]
})
export class AppModule {}
```

There's a bit more going on here:

- imports specifies the modules whose exported directives/pipes should be available to this module.

 Importing BrowserModule gives you access to core directives such as NgIf and also specifies the type of renderer, event management, and document type. If your application is rendering in a web browser, this module gives you the tools you need to do this.

- declarations specifies which directives/pipes are being exported by this module. In this case, AppComponent is the sole export.
- bootstrap specifies which components should be bootstrapped when this module is bootstrapped. More specifically, components listed here will be designated for rendering within this module. AppComponent needs to be bootstrapped and rendered somewhere, and this is where this specification will occur.

This completes the module definition. At this point, you have successfully linked the component to its module, but this module isn't being bootstrapped anywhere or even included.

main.ts

You'll change this next with `main.ts`, the top-level TypeScript file:

```
[app/main.ts]

import {platformBrowserDynamic}
  from '@angular/platform-browser-dynamic';
import {AppModule} from './app.module';

platformBrowserDynamic().bootstrapModule(AppModule);
```

This file defines the `NgModule` decorator that will be used for `AppComponent`. Inside it, you specify that the module must import `BrowserModule`.

Recall that Angular 2 is designed to be platform-independent. More specifically, it strives to allow you to write code that might not necessarily run on a conventional web browser. In this case, you are targeting a standard web browser, so importing `BrowserModule` from the `platformBrowser` target is the way in which you can inform the application of this. If you were targeting a separate platform, you would select a different platform to import into your root application component.

This `NgModule` declaration also specifies that `AppComponent` exists and should be bootstrapped.

Bootstrapping is how you kick off your Angular 2 application, but it has a very specific definition. Invoking `bootstrap()` tells Angular to mount the specified application component onto DOM elements identified by the component's selector. This kicks off the initial round of change detection and its side effects, which will complete the component initialization.

Since you've declared that this module will bootstrap `AppComponent` when it is bootstrapped, this module will in turn be the one bootstrapped from the top-level TypeScript file. Angular 2 pushes for this convention as a `main.ts` file:

```
[app/main.ts]

import {platformBrowserDynamic}
  from '@angular/platform-browser-dynamic';
import {AppModule} from './app.module';

platformBrowserDynamic().bootstrapModule(AppModule);
```

The `platformBrowserDynamic` method returns a platform object that exposes the `bootstrapModule` method. It configures your application to be bootstrapped with Angular 2's just-in-time (JIT) compiler.

 For now, the details of why you are specifying just-in-time compilation aren't important. It's enough to know that JIT compilation is a simpler version (as opposed to ahead-of-time compilation) in Angular 2's offerings.

index.html

Finally, you need to build an HTML file that is capable of bundling together all these compiled files and kicking off the application initialization. Begin with the following:

```
[index.html]

<html>
<head>
  <title>Angular 2 Minimum Viable Application</title>
  <script src="node_modules/zone.js/dist/zone.js">
  </script>
  <script src="node_modules/reflect-metadata/Reflect.js">
  </script>
  <script src="node_modules/systemjs/dist/system.src.js">
  </script>
</head>
<body>
  <app-root></app-root>
</body>
</html>
```

Most of this so far should be expected. ZoneJS and Reflect are Angular 2 dependencies. The module loader you'll use is SystemJS. `<app-root>` is the element that `AppComponent` will render inside.

Configuring SystemJS

Next, SystemJS needs to be configured to understand how to import module files and how to connect modules from being imported inside other modules. In other words, it needs to be given a file to begin with and a directory of mappings for dependencies of that main file. This can be accomplished with `System.config()` and `System.import()`, which are methods exposed on the global `System` object:

```
[index.html]

<html>
<head>
  <title>Angular 2 Minimum Viable Application</title>
  <script src="node_modules/zone.js/dist/zone.js">
  </script>
  <script src="node_modules/reflect-metadata/Reflect.js">
  </script>
  <script src="node_modules/systemjs/dist/system.src.js">
  </script>
  <script>
    System.config({
      paths: {
        'ng:': 'node_modules/@angular/'
      },
      map: {
        '@angular/core': 'ng:core/bundles/core.umd.js',
        '@angular/common': 'ng:common/bundles/common.umd.js',
        '@angular/compiler':
          'ng:compiler/bundles/compiler.umd.js',
        '@angular/platform-browser':
          'ng:platform-browser/bundles/platform-browser.umd.js',
        '@angular/platform-browser-dynamic':
          'ng:platform-browser-dynamic/bundles/platform-browser-
          dynamic.umd.js',
        'rxjs': 'node_modules/rxjs'
      },
      packages: {
        app: {
          main: './main.js'
        },
        rxjs: {
          defaultExtension: 'js'
        }
      }
    });
    System.import('app');
  </script>
```

```
</head>

<body>
  <app-root></app-root>
</body>
</html>
```

`System.config()` specifies how SystemJS should handle the files passed to it.

- The `paths` property specifies an alias to shorten the path's inside `map`. It acts as a simple find and replace function, so any found instances of `ng:` are replaced with `node_modules/@angular/`.

- The `map` property specifies how SystemJS should resolve the module imports that you have not explicitly defined. Here, this takes the form of five core Angular modules and the RxJS library.

- The `packages` property specifies the targets that will be imported by this property and the files they need to map to.

For example, the `app` property will be used when a module imports `app`, and inside SystemJS, this will map to `main.js`. Similarly, when a module requires an RxJS module, such as `Subject`, SystemJS will take the `rxjs/Subject` import path, recognize that `defaultExtension` is specified as `js`, map the module to its file representation `node_modules/rxjs/Subject.js`, and import it.

See also

- *Composing package.json for a minimum viable Angular 2 application* describes how all the pieces work for the core node project file
- *Configuring TypeScript for a minimum viable Angular 2 application* talks about how to configure compilation to support an Angular 2 project
- *Performing in-browser transpilation with SystemJS* demonstrates how SystemJS can be used to connect uncompiled static files together
- *Migrating the minimum viable Angular 2 application to Webpack bundling* describes how to integrate Webpack into your Angular application build process
- *Incorporating shims and polyfills into Webpack* gives you a handy way of managing Angular 2 polyfill dependencies

- *HTML generation with html-webpack-plugin* shows you how you can configure an npm package to add compiled files to your HTML automatically
- *Setting up an application with Angular CLI* gives a description of how to use the CLI, what it gives you, and what these individual pieces do

Migrating the minimum viable application to Webpack bundling

It is advantageous for many reasons to make it as easy and quick as possible for the client to load and run the code sent from your server. One of the easiest and most effective ways of doing this is by bundling lots of code into a single file. In nearly all cases, it is highly efficient for the browser to load a single file that contains all the dependencies required to bootstrap an application.

Webpack offers many useful tools and among them is the terrific JS bundler. This recipe demonstrates how you will be able to combine your entire application (including npm package dependencies) into a single JavaScript file that the browser will be served.

The code, links, and a live example of this are available at `http://ngcookbook.herokuapp.com/3310/`.

Getting ready

You should have completed all the steps given in the *Composing configuration files for a minimum viable Angular 2 application* and *Composing application files for a minimum viable Angular 2 application* recipes. `npm start` should start up the development server, and it should be visible at `localhost:3000`.

How to do it...

Begin by removing the application's dependency on `SystemJS`. `webpack` is able to resolve dependencies and bundle all your files into a single JS file. Begin by installing `webpack` with the global flag:

```
npm install webpack -g
```

webpack.config.js

`webpack` looks for a `webpack.config.js` file for instructions on how to behave. Create this now:

```
[webpack.config.js]

module.exports = {
  entry: "./app/main.js",
  output: {
    path: "./dist",
    filename: "bundle.js"
  }
};
```

Nothing exceptionally complicated is going on here. This tells `webpack` to select `main.js` as the top-level application file, resolve all its dependencies to the files that define them, and bundle them into a single `bundle.js` inside a `dist/` directory.

> At this point, you can check that this is working by invoking `webpack` from the command line, which will run the bundler. You should see `bundle.js` appear inside `dist/` with all the module dependencies inside it.

This is a good start, but this generated file still isn't being used anywhere. Next, you'll modify `index.html` to use the file:

```
[index.html]

<html>
<head>
  <title>Angular 2 Minimum Viable Application</title>
  <script src="node_modules/zone.js/dist/zone.js">
  </script>
  <script src="node_modules/reflect-metadata/Reflect.js">
  </script>
  <script src="dist/bundle.js">
  </script>
</head>
<body>
  <app-root></app-root>
</body>
</html>
```

Probably not what you were expecting at all! Since `bundle.js` is the application entry point and `SystemJS` is no longer needed to resolve any modules (because `webpack` is already doing this for you when bundling the files), you can remove the application's dependency on `SystemJS`.

Since this is the case, you can remove the System dependency from your `package.json` and add the `webpack` scripts and dependency:

```
[package.json]

{
  "name": "mva-bundling",
  "scripts": {
    "start": "tsc && webpack && concurrently 'npm run tsc:w'
    'npm run wp:w' 'npm run lite'",
    "lite": "lite-server",
    "postinstall": "npm install -S @types/node @types/core-js",
    "tsc": "tsc",
    "tsc:w": "tsc -w",
    "wp": "webpack",
    "wp:w": "webpack --watch"
  },
  "dependencies": {
    "@angular/common": "2.0.0",
    "@angular/compiler": "2.0.0",
    "@angular/core": "2.0.0",
    "@angular/platform-browser": "2.0.0",
    "@angular/platform-browser-dynamic": "2.0.0",
    "core-js": "^2.4.1",
    "reflect-metadata": "^0.1.3",
    "rxjs": "5.0.0-beta.12",
    "zone.js": "^0.6.23"
  },
  "devDependencies": {
    "concurrently": "^2.2.0",
    "lite-server": "^2.2.2",
    "typescript": "^2.0.2",
    "webpack": "^1.13.2"
  }
}
```

Whether or not `webpack` and `typescript` belong to `devDependencies` here is a matter of dispute and is largely subject to how you manage your local environment. If you've already installed them with the global flag, then you don't need to list it here as a dependency. This is because `npm` will search for globally installed packages and find them for you to run `npm` scripts. Furthermore, listing it here will install a duplicate `webpack` local to this project, which is obviously redundant.

For the purpose of this recipe, it is helpful to have it here. This is because you can ensure that a single `npm install` on the command line will fetch all the packages you need off the bat, and this will let you specify the version you want within the project.

Now, when you execute `npm start`, the following occurs:

- TypeScript does an initial compilation of `.ts` files into `.js` files.
- Webpack does an initial bundling of all the JS files into a single `bundle.js` in the `dist/` directory.
- Simultaneously, `lite-server` is started, the TypeScript compiler watcher is started, and the Webpack watcher is started. Upon a `.ts` file change, TypeScript will compile it into a `.js` file, and Webpack will pick up that file change and rebundle it into `bundle.js`. The `lite-server` will see that `bundle.js` is changed and reload the page, so you can see the changes being updated automatically.

 Without specifying the configurations more closely, the TypeScript, Webpack, and the `lite-server` file watch lists will use their default settings, which may be too broad and therefore would watch files they do not care about. Ideally, TypeScript would only watch `.ts` files (which does this with your `tsconfig.json`), Webpack would only watch `.html`, `.js`, and `.css` files, and `lite-server` would only watch the files it actually serves to the client.

See also

- *Incorporating shims and polyfills into Webpack* gives you a handy way of managing Angular 2 polyfill dependencies
- *HTML generation with html-webpack-plugin* shows you how you can configure an npm package to add compiled files to your HTML automatically

Incorporating shims and polyfills into Webpack

So far, this has been a much cleaner implementation, but you still have the two dangling shims inside the `index.html` file. You've pared down `index.html` such that it is now requesting only a handful of JS files instead of each module target individually, but you can go even further and bundle all the JS files into a single file.

The challenge in this is that browser shims aren't delivered via modules; in other words, there aren't any other files that will import these to use them. They just assume their use is available. Therefore, the standard Webpack bundling won't pick up these targets and include them in the bundled file.

 The code, links, and a live example of this are available at
`http://ngcookbook.herokuapp.com/7479/`.

Getting ready

You should complete the *Migrating the minimum viable application to Webpack bundling* recipe first, which will give you all the source files needed for this recipe.

How to do it...

There are a number of ways to go about doing this, including some that involve the addition of Webpack plugins, but there's an extremely simple way as well: just add the imports manually.

Create a new `polyfills.ts`:

```
[src/polyfills.ts]

import "reflect-metadata";
import "zone.js";
```

Import this module from `main.ts`:

```
[src/main.ts]

import './polyfills';
import {platformBrowserDynamic}
  from '@angular/platform-browser-dynamic';
import {AppModule} from './app/app.module';


platformBrowserDynamic().bootstrapModule(AppModule);
```

Finally, clean up `index.html`:

```
[index.html]

<html>
<head>
  <title>Angular 2 Minimum Viable Application</title>
<body>
  <app-root></app-root>
  <script src="dist/bundle.js"></script>
</body>
</html>
```

Now, Webpack should be able to resolve the shim imports, and all the needed files will be included inside `bundle.js`.

How it works...

The only reason that the polyfills are not discovered by Webpack is because they are not required anywhere in the application. Rather, anywhere they are used leads to the assumption that the exposed targets, such as `Zone`, have previously been made available. Therefore, it is easy for you to simply import them at the very top of your application, which has a well-defined point in the code. With this Webpack, you will be able to discover the existence of polyfills and incorporate them into the generated bundle.

See also

- *Migrating the minimum viable Angular 2 application to Webpack bundling* describes how to integrate Webpack into your Angular application build process
- *HTML generation with html-webpack-plugin* shows you how you can configure an npm package to add compiled files to your HTML automatically

HTML generation with html-webpack-plugin

Ideally, you would like to be able to have Webpack manage the bundled file and its injection into the template. By default, Webpack is unable to do this, as it is only concerned with the files related to scripting. Fortunately, Webpack offers an extremely popular plugin that allows you to expand the scope of Webpack's file concerns.

 The code, links, and a live example of this are available at
`http://ngcookbook.herokuapp.com/7185/`.

Getting ready

Install the plugin and add it to `devDependencies` of `package.json` with the following:

```
npm install html-webpack-plugin --save-dev
```

How to do it...

First, you'll need to incorporate the plugin into `package.json` if it isn't already:

```
[package.json]

{
  "name": "mva-bundling",
  "scripts": {
    "start": "tsc&&webpack&& concurrently 'npm run tsc:w'
    'npm run wp:w' 'npm run lite'",
    "lite": "lite-server",
    "postinstall": "npm install -S @types/node @types/core-js",
    "tsc": "tsc",
    "tsc:w": "tsc -w",
    "wp": "webpack",
    "wp:w": "webpack --watch"
  },
  "dependencies": {
    "@angular/common": "2.0.0",
    "@angular/compiler": "2.0.0",
    "@angular/core": "2.0.0",
    "@angular/platform-browser": "2.0.0",
    "@angular/platform-browser-dynamic": "2.0.0",
    "core-js": "^2.4.1",
```

```
      "reflect-metadata": "^0.1.3",
      "rxjs": "5.0.0-beta.12",
      "zone.js": "^0.6.23"
    },
    "devDependencies": {
      "concurrently": "^2.2.0",
      "html-webpack-plugin": "^2.22.0",
      "imports-loader": "^0.6.5",
      "lite-server": "^2.2.2",
      "typescript": "^2.0.2",
      "webpack": "^1.13.2"
    }
  }
```

Once this module is installed, define its operation inside the Webpack config:

```
[webpack.config.js]

var HtmlWebpackPlugin = require('html-webpack-plugin');

module.exports = {
  entry: "./src/main.js",
  output: {
    path: "./dist",
    filename: "bundle.js"
  },
  plugins: [new HtmlWebpackPlugin({
    template: './src/index.html'
  })]
};
```

This specifies the output HTML file that will serve the entire application. Since the plugin will automatically generate the HTML file for you, you'll need to modify the existing one that is designated as the template:

```
[src/index.html]

<html>
<head>
  <title>Angular 2 Minimum Viable Application</title>
</head>
<body>
  <app-root></app-root>
</body>
</html>
```

Finally, because `index.html` is now served out of the `dist/` directory, you'll need to configure the development server to serve files out of there. Since `lite-server` is just a wrapper for BrowserSync, you can specify `baseDir` inside a `bs-config.json` file, which you should create now:

```
[bs-config.json]

{
    "server": { "baseDir": "./dist" }
}
```

How it works...

Webpack is very much aware of the bundle that it is creating, and so it makes sense that you would be able to maintain a reference to this bundle (or bundles) and directly pipe those paths into an index.html file. The plugin will append the scripts at the end of the body to ensure the entire initial DOM is present.

See also

- *Migrating the minimum viable Angular 2 application to Webpack bundling* describes how to integrate Webpack into your Angular application build process
- *Incorporating shims and polyfills into Webpack* gives you a handy way of managing Angular 2 polyfill dependencies

Setting up an application with Angular CLI

In tandem with the Angular 2 framework, the Angular team also supports a build tool that can create, build, and run an Angular 2 application right out of the box. What's more, it includes a generator that can create style-guide-compliant files and directories for various application pieces from the command line.

The code, links, and a live example of this are available at
`http://ngcookbook.herokuapp.com/4068/`.

Getting ready

Angular's CLI is an `npm` module. You'll need to have Node.js installed on your system—v7.0.0 or later works as a suitable recent release that's compatible with the Angular CLI.

There is another option you have: manage your Node environments with `nvm`, the Node version manager. This gives you a transparent wrapper that can separately manage environments with the Node version as well as the installed `npm` packages in that environment. If you've ever dealt with messiness involving `sudo npm install -g`, you will be delighted by this tool.

Once Node is installed (and if you use `nvm`, you've selected which environment to use), install the Angular CLI:

```
npm install -g angular-cli
```

How to do it...

Angular CLI comes ready to generate a fully working Angular 2 application. To create an application named `PublisherApp`, invoke the following command:

```
ng new publisher
```

The Angular CLI will dutifully assemble all the files needed for a minimal Angular 2 TypeScript application, initialize a Git repository, and install all the required `npm` dependencies. The created file list should look as follows:

```
create README.md
createsrc/app/app.component.css
createsrc/app/app.component.html
createsrc/app/app.component.spec.ts
createsrc/app/app.component.ts
createsrc/app/app.module.ts
```

```
createsrc/app/index.ts
createsrc/app/shared/index.ts
createsrc/environments/environment.prod.ts
createsrc/environments/environment.ts
createsrc/favicon.ico
createsrc/index.html
createsrc/main.ts
createsrc/polyfills.ts
createsrc/styles.css
createsrc/test.ts
createsrc/tsconfig.json
createsrc/typings.d.ts
create angular-cli.json
create e2e/app.e2e-spec.ts
create e2e/app.po.ts
create e2e/tsconfig.json
create .gitignore
create karma.conf.js
createpackage.json
create protractor.conf.js
   create tslint.json
```

Use `cd publisher` to move into the application's directory, which will allow you to invoke all the project-specific Angular CLI commands.

Running the application locally

To run this application, start up the server:

```
ng serve
```

The default application page will be available on `localhost:4200`.

Testing the application

To run the application's unit tests, use this:

```
ng test
```

To run the application's end-to-end tests, use this:

```
ng e2e
```

How it works...

Let's roughly go through what each of these files offer to you:

Project configuration files

- `angular-cli.json` is the configuration file specifying how the Angular CLI should bundle and manage your application's files and directories.
- `package.json` is the npm package configuration file. Inside it, you'll find scripts and command-line targets that the Angular CLI commands will tie into.

TypeScript configuration files

- `tslint.json` specifies the configuration for the `tslint` npm package. The Angular CLI creates for you a lint command for `.ts` files with `npm run lint`.
- `src/tsconfig.json` is part of the TypeScript specification; it informs the compiler that this is the root of the TypeScript project. Its contents define how the compilation should occur, and its presence enables the `tsc` command to use this directory as the root compilation directory.
- `e2e/tsconfig.json` is the end-to-end TypeScript compiler configuration file.
- `src/typings.d.ts` is the specification file for the `typings` npm module. It allows you to describe how external modules should be wrapped and incorporated into the TypeScript compiler. This `typings.d.ts` file specifies the System namespace for SystemJS.

Test configuration files

- `karma.conf.js` is the configuration file for Karma, the test runner for the project
- `protractor.conf.js` is the configuration file for Protractor, the end-to-end test framework for the project
- `src/test.ts` describes to the Karma configuration how to start up the test runner and where to find the test files throughout the application

Core application files

- `src/index.html` is the root application file that is served to run the entire single-page application. Compiled JS and other static assets will be automatically added to this file by the build script.
- `src/main.ts` is the top-level TypeScript file that serves to bootstrap your application with its AppModule definition.
- `src/polyfills.ts` is just a file that keeps the long list of imported polyfill modules out of `main.ts`.
- `src/styles.css` is the global application style file.

Environment files

- `src/environments/environment.ts` is the default environment configuration file. Specifying different environments when building and testing your application will override these.
- `src/environments/environment.prod.ts` is the prod environment configuration, which can be selected from the command line with `--prod`.

AppComponent files

Every Angular 2 application has a top-level component, and Angular CLI calls this AppComponent.

- `src/app/app.component.ts` is the core TypeScript component class definition. This is where all of the logic that controls this component should go.
- `src/app/app.component.html` and `src/app/app.component.css` are the templating and styling files specific to AppComponent. Recall that styling specified in ComponentMetadata is encapsulated only to this component.
- `src/app/app.module.ts` is the NgModule definition for AppComponent.
- `src/app/index.ts` is the file that informs the TypeScript compiler which modules are available inside this directory. Any modules that are exported in this directory and used elsewhere in the application must be specified here.

AppComponent test files

- `src/app/app.component.spec.ts` are the unit tests for AppComponent
- `e2e/app.e2e-spec.ts` are the end-to-end tests for `AppComponent`
- `e2e/app.po.ts` is the page object definition for use in `AppComponent` end-to-end testing

There's more...

When looking at the entire project codebase, the bulk of the files break down into four categories:

- **Files that are sent to the browser**: This includes your uncompiled/unminified application files and also the compiled/minified files. When developing your application, you want to be able to test your application locally with uncompiled files. You also want to be able to ship your application to production with compiled and minified files, which optimizes browser performance. The uncompiled/unminified files are collected by the build scripts, to be combined into the compiled/minified files.
- **Files used for testing**: The test files themselves are usually sprinkled throughout your application and are not compiled. This category also includes configuration files and test scripts that control what actually happens when you run the tests and where the test runners can find the test files in your project directory.
- **Files that control your development environment**: Depending on your setup, your single-page application may run by itself (with no backend codebase), or it may be built alongside a substantial backend codebase that exposes APIs and other server-side behavior. Quickstart repositories or application generators (such as Angular CLI) usually provide you with a minimal HTTP server to get you off the ground and serve your static assets to the browser. How exactly you run your development environment will vary, but the files in this category manage how your application will work both locally and in production.

- **Files that compile your application**: The files you edit in your code editor of choice are not the ones that reach the browser in a production application. Build scripts are usually set up to combine all your files into the smallest and fewest files possible. Frequently, this will mean a single compiled JS and compiled CSS file delivered to the browser. These files will minify your codebase, compile TypeScript into vanilla JavaScript, select environment files and other context-specific files, and organize file includes and other files and module dependencies so that your application works when it's compiled. Usually, the files they create will be dumped into a dist directory, which will contain files that are served to the browser in production.

See also

- *Composing package.json for a minimum viable Angular 2 application* describes how all the pieces work for the core node project file
- *Configuring TypeScript for a minimum viable Angular 2 application* talks about how to configure compilation to support an Angular 2 project
- *Performing in-browser transpilation with SystemJS* demonstrates how SystemJS can be used to connect uncompiled static files together
- *Composing application files for a minimum viable Angular 2 application* walks you through how to create an extremely simple Angular 2 app from scratch
- *Incorporating shims and polyfills into Webpack* gives you a handy way of managing Angular 2 polyfill dependencies

9
Angular 2 Testing

This chapter will cover the following recipes:

- Creating a minimum viable unit test suite with Karma, Jasmine, and TypeScript
- Writing a minimum viable unit test suite for a simple component
- Writing a minimum viable end-to-end test suite for a simple application
- Unit testing a synchronous service
- Unit testing a component with a service dependency using stubs
- Unit testing a component with a service dependency using spies

Introduction

Writing tests is like brushing your teeth. You can get away with skipping it for a while, but it'll catch up with you eventually.

The world of testing is awash with conflicting ideologies, platitudes, and grandstanding. What's more, there is a dizzying array of tools available that allow you to write and run your tests in different ways, automate your tests, or analyze your test coverage or correctness. On top of that, each developer's utility and style of testing is unique; someone hacking away at a pre-seed startup will not have the same requirements as a developer that is part of a large team inside a Fortune 500 company.

The goal of this chapter is to walk you through the available testing utilities that the Angular 2 framework comes with out of the box, as well as some strategies for deploying these utilities. The recipes will focus on unit tests rather than E2E tests, as an overwhelming majority of robust test suites will be unit tests.

Creating a minimum viable unit test suite with Karma, Jasmine, and TypeScript

Before you jump into the intricacies of testing an Angular 2 application, it's important to first examine the supporting infrastructure that will make running these tests possible. The bulk of official Angular resources offer tests on top of Karma and Jasmine, and there's no reason to rock the boat on this one, as these are both fine testing tools. That said, it's a whole new world with TypeScript involved, and using them in tests will require some considerations.

This recipe will demonstrate how to put together a very simple unit test suite. It will use Karma and Jasmine as the test infrastructure, TypeScript and Webpack for compilation and module support, and PhantomJS as the test browser. For those unfamiliar with these tools, here's a bit about them:

- **Karma** is a unit test runner. You run tests through Karma on the command line. It has the ability to start up a test server that understands how to find test files and serve them to the test browser.
- **Jasmine** is a test framework. When you use keywords such as "it" and "describe," remember that they are part of Jasmine unit tests. It integrates with Karma and understands how to expose and run the tests you've written.
- **PhantomJS** is a headless webkit browser. (*Headless* means it runs as a process that does not have a visible user interface but still constructs a DOM and has a JS runtime.) Unit tests require a browser to run, as the JavaScript unit tests are designed to execute inside a browser runtime. Karma supports a large number of browser plugins to run the tests on, including standard browsers such as Chrome and Firefox. If you were to incorporate these browser plugins, Karma would start up an instance of the browser and run the tests inside it. For the purpose of creating a minimum viable unit test suite, you are fine doing the testing inside a headless browser, which will cleanly report its results to the command line. If you want to run your tests inside an actual browser, Karma will expose the server at a specified port, which you can access directly, for example, visiting `http://localhost:9876` in the desired test browser.

The code, links, and a live example related to this recipe are available at `http://ngcookbook.herokuapp.com/3998/`.

Getting ready

Start out with a `package.json` file:

```
[package.json]

{}
```

> This still needs to be a valid JSON file, as `npm` needs to be able to parse it and add to it.

How to do it...

Start off by creating the file that will be tested. You intend to use TypeScript, so go ahead and use its syntax here:

```
[src/article.ts]

export class Article {
  title:string =
    "Lab Mice Strike for Improved Working Conditions, Benefits"
}
```

Writing a unit test

With the Article class defined, you can now import it into a new test file, `article.spec.ts`, and use it.

> Jasmine test files, by convention, are suffixed with `.spec.ts`. Test files generated by the Angular CLI will exist alongside the file they test, but by no means is this mandatory. You can define your convention inside your Karma configuration later on.

Start off by importing the `Article` class and create an empty Jasmine test suite using `describe`:

```
[src/article.spec.ts]

import {Article} from './article';

describe('Article unit tests', () => {
```

```
});
```

describe defines a spec suite, which includes a string title called Article unit tests, and an anonymous function, which contains the suite. A spec suite can be nested inside another spec suite.

Inside a describe suite function, you can define beforeEach and afterEach, which are functions that execute before and after each unit test is defined inside the suite. Therefore, it is possible to define nested setup logic for unit tests using nested describe blocks.

Inside the spec suite function, write the unit test that is using it:

```
[src/article.spec.ts]

import {Article} from './article';

describe('Article unit tests', () => {
  it('Has correct title', () => {
    let a = new Article();
    expect(a.title)
      .toBe("Lab Mice Strike for Improved Working Conditions,
      Benefits");
  });
});
```

Note that both the code and the test are written in TypeScript.

Configuring Karma and Jasmine

First, install Karma, the Karma CLI, Jasmine, and the Karma Jasmine plugin:

```
npm install karma jasmine-core karma-jasmine --save-dev
npm install karma-cli -g
```

Alternately, if you want to save a few keystrokes, the following is equivalent:

```
npm i -D karma jasmine-core karma-jasmine
npm i karma-cli -g
```

Karma reads its configuration out of a karma.conf.js file, so create that now:

```
[karma.conf.js]

module.exports = function(config) {
```

```
    config.set({
    })
}
```

Karma needs to know how to find the test files and also how to use Jasmine:

```
[karma.conf.js]

module.exports = function(config) {
  config.set({
    frameworks: [
      'jasmine'
    ],
    files: [
      'src/*.spec.js'
    ],
    plugins : [
      'karma-jasmine',
    ]
  })
}
```

Configuring PhantomJS

PhantomJS allows you to direct tests entirely from the command line, but Karma needs to understand how to use PhantomJS. Install the PhantomJS plugin:

```
npm install karma-phantomjs-launcher --save-dev
```

Next, incorporate this plugin into the Karma config:

```
[karma.conf.js]

module.exports = function(config) {
  config.set({
    browsers: [
      'PhantomJS'
    ],
    frameworks: [
      'jasmine'
    ],
    files: [
      'src/*.spec.js'
    ],
    plugins : [
      'karma-jasmine',
      'karma-phantomjs-launcher'
```

```
      ]
    })
  }
```

Karma now knows it has to run the tests in PhantomJS.

Compiling files and tests with TypeScript

If you're paying attention closely, you'll note that the Karma config is referencing test files that do not exist. Since you're using TypeScript, you must create these files. Install TypeScript and the Jasmine type definitions:

```
npm install typescript @types/jasmine --save-dev
```

Add script definitions to your `package.json`:

```
[package.json]

{
  "scripts": {
    "tsc": "tsc",
    "tsc:w": "tsc -w"
  },
  "devDependencies": {
    "@types/jasmine": "^2.5.35",
    "jasmine-core": "^2.5.2",
    "karma": "^1.3.0",
    "karma-cli": "^1.0.1",
    "karma-jasmine": "^1.0.2",
    "karma-phantomjs-launcher": "^1.0.2",
    "typescript": "^2.0.3"
  }
}
```

Create a `tsconfig.json` file. Since you're fine with the compiled files residing in the same directory, a simple one will do:

```
[tsconfig.json]

{
  "compilerOptions": {
    "target": "es5",
    "module": "commonjs",
    "moduleResolution": "node"
  }
}
```

> You would probably not do it this way for a production application, but for a minimum viable setup, this will do in a pinch. A production application would most likely put compiled files into an entirely different directory, frequently named `dist/`.

Incorporating Webpack into Karma

Of course, you'll need a way of resolving module definitions for code and tests. Karma isn't capable of doing this on its own, so you'll need something to do this. Webpack is perfectly suitable for such a task, and Karma has a terrific plugin that allows you to preprocess your test files before they reach the browser.

Install Webpack and its Karma plugin:

```
npm install webpack karma-webpack --save-dev
```

Modify the Karma config to specify Webpack as the preprocessor. This allows your module definitions to be resolved properly:

```
[karma.conf.js]

module.exports = function(config) {
  config.set({
    browsers: [
      'PhantomJS'
    ],
    frameworks: [
      'jasmine'
    ],
    files: [
      'src/*.spec.js'
    ],
    plugins : [
      'karma-webpack',
      'karma-jasmine',
      'karma-phantomjs-launcher'
    ],
    preprocessors: {
      'src/*.spec.js': ['webpack']
    }
  })
}
```

Writing the test script

You can kick off the Karma server with the following:

```
karma start karma.conf.js
```

This will initialize the test server and run the tests, watching for changes and rerunning the tests. However, this sidesteps the fact that the TypeScript files require compilation in the files that Karma is watching. The TypeScript compiler also has a file watcher that will recompile on the fly. You would like both of these to recompile whenever you save changes to a source code file, so it makes sense to run them simultaneously. The concurrently package is suitable for this task.

 concurrently not only allows you to run multiple commands at once, but also to kill them all at once. Without it, a kill signal from the command line would only target whichever process was run most recently, ignoring the process that is running in the background.

Install concurrently with the following:

```
npm install concurrently --save-dev
```

Finally, build your test script to run Karma and the TypeScript compiler simultaneously:

```
[package.json]

{
  "scripts": {
    "test": "concurrently 'npm run tsc:w' 'karma start
    karma.conf.js'",
    "tsc": "tsc",
    "tsc:w": "tsc -w"
  },
  "devDependencies": {
    "@types/jasmine": "^2.5.35",
    "concurrently": "^3.1.0",
    "jasmine-core": "^2.5.2",
    "karma": "^1.3.0",
    "karma-cli": "^1.0.1",
    "karma-jasmine": "^1.0.2",
    "karma-phantomjs-launcher": "^1.0.2",
    "karma-webpack": "^1.8.0",
    "typescript": "^2.0.3",
    "webpack": "^1.13.2"
  }
}
```

With this, you should be able to run your tests:

```
npm test
```

If everything is done correctly, the Karma server should boot up and run the tests, outputting the following:

```
PhantomJS 2.1.1 (Linux 0.0.0): Executed 1 of 1 SUCCESS (0.038 secs / 0.001
secs)
```

How it works...

Karma and Jasmine work together to deliver test files to the test browser. TypeScript and Webpack are tasked with converting your TypeScript files into a JavaScript format that will be usable by the test browser.

There's more...

An interesting consideration of this setup is how exactly TypeScript is handled.

Both the code and test files are written in TypeScript, which allows you to use the ES6 module notation, as opposed to some mix-and-match strategy. However, this leaves you with some choices to make on how the test setup should work.

The tests need to be able to use different pieces of your application in a piecemeal fashion, as opposed to the standard application setup where all the modules get pulled together at once. This recipe had TypeScript independently compile the .ts files, and it then directed Karma to watch the resultant .js files. This is perhaps easier to comprehend by someone who is easing into tests, but it might not be the most efficient way to go about it. Karma also supports TypeScript plugins, which allow you to preprocess the files into TypeScript before handing them off to the Webpack preprocessor.

Karma supports the chaining of preprocess steps, which will be useful if you want to compile the TypeScript on the fly as part of preprocessing.

See also

- *Writing a minimum viable unit test suite for a simple component* shows you a basic example of unit testing Angular 2 components

- *Unit testing a synchronous service* demonstrates how an injection is mocked in unit tests
- *Unit testing a component with a service dependency using Stubs* shows how you can create a service mock to write unit tests and avoid direct dependencies
- *Unit testing a component with a service dependency using Spies* shows how you can keep track of service method invocations inside a unit test

Writing a minimum viable unit test suite for a simple component

Unit tests are the bread and butter of your application testing process. They exist as a companion to your source code, and most of the time, the bulk of your application tests will be unit tests. They are lightweight, run quickly, are easy to read and reason about, and can give context as to how the code should be used and how it might behave.

Setting up Karma, Jasmine, TypeScript, and Angular 2 along with all the connecting configurations between them is a bit of an imposing task; it was deemed to be out of the scope of this chapter. It's not a very interesting discussion to get all of them to work together, especially since there are already so many example projects that have put together their own setups for you. It's far more interesting to dive directly into the tests themselves and see how they can actually interact with Angular 2.

 The code, links, and a live example related to this recipe are available at `http://ngcookbook.herokuapp.com/3935/`.

Getting ready

This recipe will assume you are using a working Angular 2 testing environment. The one provided in the application generated by the Angular CLI is ideal. Tests can be run in this environment with the following command inside the project directory:

```
ng test
```

Begin with the following component:

```
[src/app/article/article.component.ts]
```

```
import {Component} from '@angular/core';

@Component({
  selector: 'app-article',
  template: `
    <h1>
      {{ title }}
    </h1>
  `
})
export class ArticleComponent {
  title: string = 'Captain Hook Sues Over Spork Snafu';
}
```

Your goal is to entirely flesh out `article.component.spec.ts` to test this class.

How to do it...

The simplest possible test you can think of is the one that will simply check that you are able to instantiate an instance of `ArticleComponent`. Begin with that test:

```
[src/app/article/article.component.spec.ts]

import {ArticleComponent} from './article.component';

describe('Component: Article', () => {
  it('should create an instance', () => {
    let component = new ArticleComponent();
    expect(component).toBeTruthy();
  });
});
```

Nothing tricky is going on here. Since `ArticleComponent` is just a plain old TypeScript class, nothing is preventing you from creating an instance and inspecting it in the memory.

However, for it to actually behave like an Angular 2 component, you'll need some other tools.

Using TestBed and async

When you try to puppet an Angular 2 environment for the component in a test, there are a number of considerations you'll need to account for. First, Angular 2 unit tests heavily rely upon `TestBed`, which can be thought of as your testing multitool.

The denomination of unit tests when dealing with a component involves ComponentFixture. TestBed.createComponent() will create a fixture wrapping an instance of the desired component.

 The need for fixtures is centered in how unit tests are supposed to work. An ArticleComponent does not make sense when instantiated as it was with the initial test you wrote. There is no DOM element to attach to, no running application, and so on. It doesn't make sense for the component unit tests to have an explicit dependency on these things. So, ComponentFixture is Angular's way of letting you test only the concerns of the component as it would normally exist, without worrying about all the messiness of its innate dependencies.

The TestBed fixture's asynchronous behavior mandates that the test logic is executed inside an async() wrapper.

 The async() wrapper simply runs the test inside its own zone. This allows the test runner to wait for all the asynchronous calls inside the test to complete them before ending the test.

Begin by importing TestBed and async from the Angular testing module and put together the skeleton for two more unit tests:

```
[src/app/article/article.component.spec.ts]

import {TestBed, async} from '@angular/core/testing';
import {ArticleComponent} from './article.component';

describe('Component: Article', () => {
  it('should create an instance', () => {
    let component = new ArticleComponent();
    expect(component).toBeTruthy();
  });

  it('should have correct title', async(() => {
  }));

  it('should render title in an h1 tag', async(() => {
  }));
});
```

Now that you have the skeletons for the two tests you'd like to write, it's time to use
`TestBed` to define the test module. Angular 2 components are paired with a module
definition, but when performing unit tests, you'll need to use the `TestBed` module's
definition for the component to work properly. This can be done with
`TestBed.configureTestModule()`, and you'll want to invoke this before each test.

Jasmine's `describe` allows you to group `beforeEach` and `afterEach` inside it, and it is
perfect for use here:

```
[src/app/article/article.component.spec.ts]

import {TestBed, async} from '@angular/core/testing';
import {ArticleComponent} from './article.component';

describe('Component: Article', () => {
  it('should create an instance', () => {
    let component = new ArticleComponent();
    expect(component).toBeTruthy();
  });

  describe('Async', () => {
    beforeEach( () => {
      TestBed.configureTestingModule({
        declarations: [
          ArticleComponent
        ],
      });
    });

    it('should have correct title', async(() => {
    }));

    it('should render title in an h1 tag', async(() => {
    }));
  });
});
```

Creating a ComponentFixture

`TestBed` gives you the ability to create a fixture, but you have yet to actually do it. You'll
need a fixture for both the `async` tests, so it makes sense to do this in `beforeEach` too:

```
[src/app/article/article.component.spec.ts]

import {TestBed, async} from '@angular/core/testing';
import {ArticleComponent} from './article.component';
```

```
describe('Component: Article', () => {
  let fixture;

  it('should create an instance', () => {
    let component = new ArticleComponent();
    expect(component).toBeTruthy();
  });

  describe('Async', () => {
    beforeEach( () => {
      TestBed.configureTestingModule({
        declarations: [
          ArticleComponent
        ],
      });

      fixture = TestBed.createComponent(ArticleComponent);
    }));

    afterEach(() => {
      fixture = undefined;
    });

    it('should have correct title', async(() => {
    }));

    it('should render title in an h1 tag', async(() => {
    }));
  });
});
```

 Here, fixture is assigned to undefined in the afterEach teardown. This is technically superfluous for the purpose of these tests, but it is good to get into the habit of performing a robust teardown of shared variables in unit tests. This is because one of the most frustrating things to debug in a test suite is test variable bleed. After all, these are just functions running in a sequence in a browser.

Now that the fixture is defined for each test, you can use its methods to inspect the instantiated component in different ways.

For the first test, you'd like to inspect the ArticleComponent object itself from within ComponentFixture. This is exposed with the componentInstance property:

```
[src/app/article/article.component.spec.ts]

import {TestBed, async} from '@angular/core/testing';
```

```
import {ArticleComponent} from './article.component';

describe('Component: Article', () => {
  let expectedTitle = 'Captain Hook Sues Over Spork Snafu';
  let fixture;

  it('should create an instance', () => {
    let component = new ArticleComponent();
    expect(component).toBeTruthy();
  });

  describe('Async', () => {
    beforeEach(async(() => {
      TestBed.configureTestingModule({
        declarations: [
          ArticleComponent
        ],
      });
      fixture = TestBed.createComponent(ArticleComponent);
    }));

    afterEach(() => {
      fixture = undefined;
    });

    it('should have correct title', async(() => {
      expect(fixture.componentInstance.title)
        .toEqual(expectedTitle);
    }));

    it('should render title in an h1 tag', async(() => {
    }));
  });
});
```

For the second test, you want access to the DOM that the fixture has attached the component instance to. The root element that the component is targeting is exposed with the nativeElement property:

```
[src/app/article/article.component.spec.ts]

import {TestBed, async} from '@angular/core/testing';
import {ArticleComponent} from './article.component';

describe('Component: Article', () => {
  let expectedTitle = 'Captain Hook Sues Over Spork Snafu';
  let fixture;
```

```
it('should create an instance', () => {
  let component = new ArticleComponent();
  expect(component).toBeTruthy();
});

describe('Async', () => {
  beforeEach(async(() => {
    TestBed.configureTestingModule({
      declarations: [
        ArticleComponent
      ],
    });
    fixture = TestBed.createComponent(ArticleComponent);
  }));

  afterEach(() => {
    fixture = undefined;
  });

  it('should have correct title', async(() => {
    expect(fixture.componentInstance.title)
      .toEqual(expectedTitle);
  }));

  it('should render title in an h1 tag', async(() => {
    expect(fixture.nativeElement.querySelector('h1')
      .textContent).toContain(expectedTitle);
  }));
});
});
```

If you run these tests, you will notice that the last test will fail. The test sees an empty string inside <h1></h1>. This is because you are binding a value in the template to a component member. Since the fixture controls the entire environment surrounding the component, it also controls the change detection strategy—which, here, is to not run until it is told to do so. You can trigger a round of change detection using the detectChanges() method:

```
[src/app/article/article.component.spec.ts]

import {TestBed, async} from '@angular/core/testing';
import {ArticleComponent} from './article.component';

describe('Component: Article', () => {
  let expectedTitle = 'Captain Hook Sues Over Spork Snafu';
  let fixture;

  it('should create an instance', () => {
```

[348]

```
      let component = new ArticleComponent();
      expect(component).toBeTruthy();
    });

    describe('Async', () => {
      beforeEach(async(() => {
        TestBed.configureTestingModule({
          declarations: [
            ArticleComponent
          ],
        });
        fixture = TestBed.createComponent(ArticleComponent);
      }));

      afterEach(() => {
        fixture = undefined;
      });

      it('should have correct title', async(() => {
          expect(fixture.componentInstance.title)
            .toEqual(expectedTitle);
      }));

      it('should render title in an h1 tag', async(() => {
        fixture.detectChanges();
        expect(fixture.nativeElement.querySelector('h1')
          .textContent).toContain(expectedTitle);
      }));
    });
  });
```

With this, you should see Karma run and pass all three tests.

How it works...

When it comes to testing components, fixture is your friend. It gives you the ability to inspect and manipulate the component in an environment that it will behave comfortably in. You are then able to manipulate the instances of input made to the component, as well as inspect their output and resultant behavior.

This is the core of unit testing: the "thing" you are testing—here, a component class—should be treated as a black box. You control what goes into the box, and your tests should measure and define what they expect to come out of the box. If the tests account for all the possible cases of input and output, then you have achieved 100 percent unit test coverage of that thing.

See also

- *Creating a minimum viable unit test suite with Karma, Jasmine, and TypeScript* gives you a gentle introduction to unit tests with TypeScript
- *Unit testing a synchronous service* demonstrates how an injection is mocked in unit tests
- *Unit testing a component with a service dependency using Stubs* shows how you can create a service mock to write unit tests and avoid direct dependencies
- *Unit testing a component with a service dependency using Spies* shows how you can keep track of service method invocations inside a unit test

Writing a minimum viable end-to-end test suite for a simple application

End-to-end testing (or **e2e** for short) is on the other end of the spectrum as far as unit testing is concerned. The entire application exists as a black box, and the only controls at your disposal—for these tests—are actions the user might take inside the browser, such as firing click events or navigating to a page. Similarly, the correctness of tests is only verified by inspecting the state of the browser and the DOM itself.

More explicitly, an end-to-end test will (in some form) start up an actual instance of your application (or a subset of it), navigate to it in an actual browser, do stuff to a page, and look to see what happens on the page. It's pretty much as close as you are going to get to having an actual person sit down and use your application.

In this recipe, you'll put together a very basic end-to-end test suite so that you might better understand the concepts involved.

The code, links, and a live example related to this recipe are available at `http://ngcookbook.herokuapp.com/8985/`.

Getting ready

You'll begin with the code files created in the minimum viable application recipe from
Chapter 8, *Application Organization and Management.* The most important files that you'll be
editing here are AppComponent and package.json:

```
[package.json]

{
  "scripts": {
    "start": "tsc && concurrently 'npm run tsc:w' 'npm run lite'",
    "lite": "lite-server",
    "postinstall": "npm install -s @types/node @types/core-js",
    "tsc": "tsc",
    "tsc:w": "tsc -w"
  },
  "dependencies": {
    "@angular/common": "2.1.0",
    "@angular/compiler": "2.1.0",
    "@angular/core": "2.1.0",
    "@angular/platform-browser": "2.1.0",
    "@angular/platform-browser-dynamic": "2.1.0",
    "core-js": "^2.4.1",
    "reflect-metadata": "^0.1.3",
    "rxjs": "5.0.0-beta.12",
    "systemjs": "0.19.27",
    "zone.js": "^0.6.23"
  },
  "devDependencies": {
    "concurrently": "^2.2.0",
    "lite-server": "^2.2.2",
    "typescript": "^2.0.2"
  }
}
[app/app.component.ts]

import {Component} from '@angular/core';
@Component({
  selector: 'app-root',
  template: '<h1>AppComponent template!</h1>'
})
export class AppComponent {}
```

How to do it...

The Angular team maintains the Protractor project, which by many accounts is the best way to go about performing end-to-end tests on your applications, at least initially. It comes with a large number of utilities out of the box to manipulate the browser when writing your tests, and explicit integrations with Angular 2, so it's a terrific place to start.

Getting Protractor up and running

Protractor relies on Selenium to automate the browser. The specifics of Selenium aren't especially important for the purpose of creating a minimum viable e2e test suite, but you will need to install a Java runtime:

```
sudo apt-get install openjdk-8-jre
```

I run Ubuntu, so the OpenJDK Java Runtime Environment V8 is suitable for my purposes. Your development setup may differ. Runtimes for different operating systems can be found on Oracle's website.

Protractor itself can be installed from npm, but it should be global. You'll be using it with Jasmine, so install it and its TypeScript typings as well:

```
npm install jasmine-core @types/jasmine --save-dev
npm install protractor -g
```

You may need to fiddle with this configuration. Sometimes, it may work if you install protractor locally rather than globally. Errors involving webdriver-manager are part of the protractor package, so they will most likely be involved where your protractor package installation is as well.

It should come as no surprise that protractor is configured with a file, so create it now:

```
[protractor.conf.js]

exports.config = {
  specs: [
    './e2e/**/*.e2e-spec.ts'
  ],
  capabilities: {
    'browserName': 'chrome'
  },
  baseUrl: 'http://localhost:3000/',
```

```
    framework: 'jasmine',
  }
```

None of these settings should surprise you:

- The e2e test files are going to live in an `e2e/` directory and will be suffixed with `.e2e-spec.ts`
- Protractor is going to spin up a Chrome instance that it will puppeteer with Selenium
- The server you're going to spin up will exist at `localhost:3000`, and all the URLs inside the Protractor tests will be relative to this
- The Protractor tests will be written with the Jasmine syntax

For simplicity, the server you are starting up for the end-to-end tests will be the same lite-server you've been using all along. When it starts up, lite-server will open up a browser window of its own, which will prove to be a bit annoying here. Since it is a thin wrapper for BrowserSync, you can configure it to not do this by simply directing it not to do so in a config file that is only used when running e2e tests.

Create this file now inside the test directory:

```
[e2e/bs-config.json]

{
  "open": false
}
```

 The lite-server wrapper won't find this automatically, but you'll direct it to the file in a moment.

Making Protractor compatible with Jasmine and TypeScript

First, create a `tsconfig.json` file inside the test directory:

```
[e2e/tsconfig.json]

{
  "compilerOptions": {
    "target": "es5",
    "module": "commonjs",
```

```
        "moduleResolution": "node"
    }
}
```

Next, create the actual e2e test file skeleton:

```
[e2e/app.e2e-spec.ts]

describe('App E2E Test Suite', () => {
  it('should have the correct h1 text', () => {
  });
});
```

This uses the standard Jasmine syntax to declare a spec suite and an empty test within it.

Before fleshing out the test, you need to ensure that Protractor can actually use this file. Install the ts-node plugin so that Protractor can perform the compilation and use these files in e2e tests:

```
npm install ts-node --save-dev
```

Next, instruct Protractor to use this to compile the test source files into a usable format. This can be done in its config file:

```
[protractor.conf.js]

exports.config = {
  specs: [
    './e2e/**/*.e2e-spec.ts'
  ],
  capabilities: {
    'browserName': 'chrome'
  },
  baseUrl: 'http://localhost:3000/',
  framework: 'jasmine',
  beforeLaunch: function() {
    require('ts-node').register({
      project: 'e2e'
    });
  }
}
```

With all this, you're left with a working but empty end-to-end test.

Building a page object

An excellent convention that I highly recommend using is the page object.

The idea behind this is that all of the logic surrounding the interaction with the page can be extracted into its own page object class, and the actual test behavior can use this abstracted page object inside the class. This allows the tests to be written independently of the DOM structure or routing definitions, which makes for superior test maintenance. What's more, it makes your tests totally independent of Protractor, which makes it easier should you want to change your end-to-end test runner.

For this simple end-to-end test, you'll want to specify how to arrive at this page and how to inspect it to get what you want. Define the page object as follows with two member methods:

```
[e2e/app.po.ts]

import {browser, element, by} from 'protractor';

export class AppPage {
  navigate() {
    browser.get('/');
  }

  getHeaderText() {
    return element(by.css('app-root h1')).getText();
  }
}
```

`navigate()` instructs Selenium to the root path (which, as you may recall, is based on localhost:3000), and `getHeaderText()` inspects a DOM element for its text contents.

Note that `browser`, `element`, and `by` are all utilities imported from the protractor module. More on this later in the recipe.

Writing the e2e test

With all of the infrastructure in place, you can now easily write your end-to-end test. You'll want to instantiate a new page object for each test:

```
[e2e/app.e2e-spec.ts]
```

```
import {AppPage} from './app.po';

describe('App E2E Test Suite', () => {
  let page:AppPage;

  beforeEach(() => {
    page = new AppPage();
  });

  it('should have the correct h1 text', () => {
    page.navigate();

    expect(page.getHeaderText())
      .toEqual('AppComponent template!');
  });
});
```

Scripting the e2e tests

Finally, you'll want to give yourself the ability to easily run the end-to-end test suite.
Selenium is often being updated, so it behoves you to explicitly update it before you run the
tests:

```
[package.json]

{
  "scripts": {
    "pree2e": "webdriver-manager update && tsc",
    "e2e": "concurrently 'npm run lite -- -c=e2e/bs-config.json'
    'protractor protractor.conf.js'",
    "start": "tsc && concurrently 'npm run tsc:w' 'npm run lite'",
    "lite": "lite-server",
    "postinstall": "npm install -s @types/node @types/core-js",
    "tsc": "tsc",
    "tsc:w": "tsc -w"
  },
  "dependencies": {
    ...
  },
  "devDependencies": {
    ...
  }
}
```

Finally, Angular 2 needs to integrate with Protractor and be able to tell it when the page is ready to be interacted with. This requires one more addition to the Protractor configuration:

```
[protractor.conf.js]

exports.config = {
  specs: [
    './e2e/**/*.e2e-spec.ts'
  ],
  capabilities: {
    'browserName': 'chrome'
  },
  baseUrl: 'http://localhost:3000/',
  framework: 'jasmine',
  useAllAngular2AppRoots: true,
  beforeLaunch: function() {
    require('ts-node').register({
      project: 'e2e'
    });
  }
}
```

That's all! You should now be able to run the end-to-end test suite by invoking it with the corresponding npm script:

```
npm run e2e
```

This will start up a lite-server instance (without starting up its default browser), and protractor will run the tests and exit.

How it works...

At the top of the `app.po.ts` page object file, you imported three targets from Protractor: `browser`, `element`, and `by`. Here's a bit about these targets:

- `browser` is a protractor global object that allows you to perform browser-level actions, such as visiting URLs, waiting for events to occur, and taking screenshots.
- `element` is a global function that takes a `Locator` and returns an `ElementFinder`. `ElementFinder` is the point of contact to interact with the matching DOM element, if it exists.
- `by` is a global object that exposes several `Locator` factories. Here, the `by.css()` locator factory performs an analogue of `document.querySelector()`.

The entire Protractor API can be found at
`http://www.protractortest.org/#/api`.

The reason for writing the tests this way may feel strange to you. After all, it's a real browser running a real application, so it might make sense to reach for DOM methods and the like.

The reason for using the Protractor API instead is simple: the test code you are writing is not being executed inside the browser runtime. Instead, Protractor is handing off these instructions to Selenium, which in turn will execute them inside the browser and return the results. Thus, the test code you write can only indirectly interface with the browser and the DOM.

There's more...

The purpose of this recipe was to assemble a very simple end-to-end test suite so that you can get a feel of what goes on behind the scenes in some form. While the tests themselves will appear more or less as they do here, regardless of the test infrastructure they are running on, the infrastructure itself is far from being optimal; a number of changes and additions could be made to make it more robust.

When running unit tests, it is often useful for the unit tests to detect the changes in files and run them again immediately. A large part of this is because unit tests should be very lightweight. Any dependencies on the rest of the application are mocked or abstracted away so that a minimal amount of code can be run to prepare your unit test environment. Thus, there is little cost to running a suite of unit tests in a sequence.

End-to-end tests, on the other hand, behave in the opposite way. They do indeed require the entire application to be constructed and run, which can be computationally expensive. Page navigations, resetting the entire application, initializing and clearing authentication, and other operations that might commonly be performed in an end-to-end test can take a long time. Therefore, it doesn't make as much sense here to run the end-to-end tests with a file watcher observing for changes made to the tests.

See also

- *Creating a minimum viable unit test suite with Karma, Jasmine, and TypeScript* gives you a gentle introduction to unit tests with TypeScript

Unit testing a synchronous service

Angular 2 service types are essentially classes designated for injectability. They are easy to test since you have a great deal of control over how and where they are provided, and consequently, how many instances you'll be able to create. Therefore, tests for services will exist largely as they would for any normal TypeScript class.

It'll be better if you are familiar with the content of the first few recipes of this chapter before you proceed further.

> The code, links, and a live example related to this recipe are available at
> `http://ngcookbook.herokuapp.com/3107.`

Getting ready

Suppose you want to build a "magic eight ball" service. Begin with the following code, with added comments for clarity:

```
[src/app/magic-eight-ball.service.ts]

import {Injectable} from '@angular/core';

@Injectable()
export class MagicEightBallService {
  private values:Array<string>;
  private lastIndex:number;

  constructor() {
    // Initialize the values array
    // Must have at least two entries
    this.values = [
      'Ask again later',
      'Outlook good',
      'Most likely',
      'Don't count on it'
    ];

    // Initialize with any valid index
    this.lastIndex = this.getIndex();
  }

  private getIndex():number {
```

```
    // Return a random index for this.values
    return Math.floor(Math.random() * this.values.length);
  }

  reveal():string {
    // Generate a new index
    let newIdx = this.getIndex();

    // Check if the index was the same one used last time
    if (newIdx === this.lastIndex) {
      // If so, shift up one (wrapping around) in the array
      // This is still random behavior
      newIdx = (++newIdx) % this.values.length;
    }
    // Save the index that you are now using
    this.lastIndex = newIdx;

    // Access the string and return it
    return this.values[newIdx];
  }
}
```

There are several things to note about how this service behaves:

- This service has several private members but only one public member method
- The service is randomly selected from an array
- The service shouldn't return the same value twice in a row

The way your unit tests are written should account for these as well as completely test the behavior of this service.

How to do it...

Begin by creating the framework of your test file:

```
[src/app/magic-eight-ball.service.spec.ts]

import {TestBed} from '@angular/core/testing';
import {MagicEightBallService} from
  './magic-eight-ball.service';

describe('Service: MagicEightBall', () => {
  beforeEach(() => {
    TestBed.configureTestingModule({
      providers: [
```

```
            MagicEightBallService
        ]
      });
    });
  });
```

So far, none of this should surprise you. `MagicEightBallService` is an injectable; it needs to be provided inside a module declaration, which is done here. However, to actually use it inside a unit test, you need to perform a formal injection since this is what would be required to access it from inside a component. This can be accomplished with `inject`:

```
[src/app/magic-eight-ball.service.spec.ts]

import {TestBed, inject} from '@angular/core/testing';
import {MagicEightBallService} from
  './magic-eight-ball.service';

describe('Service: MagicEightBall', () => {
  beforeEach(() => {
    TestBed.configureTestingModule({
      providers: [
        MagicEightBallService
      ]
    });
  });

  it('should be able to be injected', inject([MagicEightBallService],
    (magicEightBallService: MagicEightBallService) => {
      expect(magicEightBallService).toBeTruthy();
    })
  );
});
```

Off to a good start, but this doesn't actually test anything about what the service is doing. Next, write a test that ensures that a string of non-zero length is being returned:

```
[src/app/magic-eight-ball.service.spec.ts]

import {TestBed, inject} from '@angular/core/testing';
import {MagicEightBallService} from
  './magic-eight-ball.service';

describe('Service: MagicEightBall', () => {
  beforeEach(() => {
    TestBed.configureTestingModule({
      providers: [
        MagicEightBallService
      ]
```

```
    });
  });

  it('should be able to be injected', inject([MagicEightBallService],
    (magicEightBallService: MagicEightBallService) => {
      expect(magicEightBallService).toBeTruthy();
    })
  );

  it('should return a string with nonzero length',
  inject([MagicEightBallService],
    (magicEightBallService: MagicEightBallService) => {
      let result = magicEightBallService.reveal();

      expect(result).toEqual(jasmine.any(String));
      expect(result.length).toBeGreaterThan(0);
    })
  );
});
```

Finally, you should write a test to ensure that the two values returned are not the same. Since this method is random, you can run it until you are blue in the face and still not be totally sure. However, checking this 50 times in a row is a fine way to be fairly certain:

```
[src/app/magic-eight-ball.service.spec.ts]

import {TestBed, inject} from '@angular/core/testing';
import {MagicEightBallService} from
  './magic-eight-ball.service';

describe('Service: MagicEightBall', () => {
  beforeEach(() => {
    TestBed.configureTestingModule({
      providers: [
        MagicEightBallService
      ]
    });
  });

  it('should be able to be injected', inject([MagicEightBallService],
    (magicEightBallService: MagicEightBallService) => {
      expect(magicEightBallService).toBeTruthy();
    })
  );

  it('should return a string with nonzero length',
  inject([MagicEightBallService],
    (magicEightBallService: MagicEightBallService) => {
```

```
      let result = magicEightBallService.reveal();

      expect(result).toEqual(jasmine.any(String));
      expect(result.length).toBeGreaterThan(0);
    })
  );

  it('should not return the same value twice in a row',
  inject([MagicEightBallService],
    (magicEightBallService: MagicEightBallService) => {
      let last;
      for(let i = 0; i < 50; ++i) {
        let next = magicEightBallService.reveal();
        expect(next).not.toEqual(last);
        last = next;
      }
    })
  );
});
```

Terrific! All these tests have passed; you've done a good job building some incremental and descriptive code coverage for your service.

How it works...

The `inject` test function performs dependency injection for you each time it is invoked, using the array of injectable classes passed as the first argument. The arrow function that is passed as its second argument will behave in essentially the same way as a component constructor, where you are able to use the `magicEightBallService` parameter as an instance of the service.

One important difference from how it is injected compared to a component constructor is that inside a component constructor, you would be able to use `this.magicEightBallService` right away. With respect to injection into unit tests, it does not automatically attach to `this`.

There's more...

Important considerations for unit testing are what tests should be written and how they should proceed. Respecting the boundaries of public and private members is essential. Since these tests are written in a way that only utilizes the public members of the service, the author is free to go about changing, extending, or refactoring the internals of the service without worrying about breaking or needing to update the tests. A well-designed class will be fully testable from its public interface.

> This notion brings up an interesting philosophical point regarding unit testing. You should be able to describe the behavior of a well-formed service as a function of its public members. Similarly, a well-formed service should then be relatively easy to write unit tests, given that the former statement is true.
>
> If it is then the case that you find your unit tests are difficult to write—for example, you are needing to reach into a private member of the service to test it properly—then consider the notion that your service might not be as well designed as it could be.
>
> In short, if it's hard to test, then you might have written a class in a weird way.

Testing without injection

An observant developer will note here that the service you are testing doesn't have any meaningful dependence on injection. Injecting it into various places in the application surely provides it with a consistent way, but the service definition is wholly unaware of this fact. After all, instantiation is instantiation, and this service doesn't appear to be more than an injectable class. Therefore, it is certainly possible to not bother injecting the service at all and merely instantiating it using the `new` keyword:

```
[src/app/magic-eight-ball.service.spec.ts]

import {MagicEightBallService} from
  './magic-eight-ball.service';

describe('Service: MagicEightBall', () => {
  let magicEightBallService;

  beforeEach(() => {
    magicEightBallService = new MagicEightBallService();
```

```
    });

    it('should be able to be injected', () => {
      expect(magicEightBallService).toBeTruthy();
    });

    it('should return a string with nonzero length', () => {
      let result = magicEightBallService.reveal();

      expect(result).toEqual(jasmine.any(String));
      expect(result.length).toBeGreaterThan(0);
    });

    it('should not return the same value twice in a row', () => {
      let last;
      for(let i = 0; i < 50; ++i) {
        let next = magicEightBallService.reveal();
        expect(next).not.toEqual(last);
        last = next;
      }
    });
  });
```

Of course, this requires that you keep track of whether the service cares about whether or not it has been injected anywhere.

See also

- *Unit testing a component with a service dependency using stubs* shows how you can create a service mock to write unit tests and avoid direct dependencies
- *Unit testing a component with a service dependency using spies* shows how you can keep track of service method invocations inside a unit test

Unit testing a component with a service dependency using stubs

Standalone component testing is easy, but you will rarely need to write meaningful tests for a component that exists in isolation. More often than not, the component will have one or many dependencies, and writing good unit tests is the difference between delight and despair.

The code, links, and a live example related to this recipe are available at
`http://ngcookbook.herokuapp.com/6651/`.

Getting ready

Suppose you already have the service from the *Unit testing a synchronous service* recipe. In addition, you have a component, which makes use of this service:

```
[src/app/magic-eight-ball/magic-eight-ball.component.ts]

import {Component} from '@angular/core';
import {MagicEightBallService} from
  '../magic-eight-ball.service';

@Component({
  selector: 'app-magic-eight-ball',
  template: `
    <button (click)="update()">Click me!</button>
    <h1>{{ result }}</h1>
  `
})
export class MagicEightBallComponent {
  result: string = '';

  constructor(private magicEightBallService_: MagicEightBallService) {}

  update() {
    this.result = this.magicEightBallService_.reveal();
  }
}
```

Your objective is to write a suite of unit tests for this component without setting an explicit dependency on the service.

How to do it...

Begin with a skeleton of your test file:

```
[src/app/magic-eight-ball/magic-eight-ball.component.spec.ts]

import {TestBed, async} from '@angular/core/testing';
import {MagicEightBallComponent} from
```

```
'./magic-eight-ball.component';
import {MagicEightBallService} from
  '../magic-eight-ball.service';

describe('Component: MagicEightBall', () => {
  beforeEach(async(() => {
  }));

  afterEach(() => {
  });

  it('should begin with no text', async(() => {
  }));

  it('should show text after click', async(() => {
  }));
});
```

You'll first want to configure the test module so that it properly provides these imported targets in the test:

```
[src/app/magic-eight-ball/magic-eight-ball.component.spec.ts]

import {TestBed, async} from '@angular/core/testing';
import {MagicEightBallComponent} from
  './magic-eight-ball.component';
import {MagicEightBallService} from
  '../magic-eight-ball.service';

describe('Component: MagicEightBall', () => {
  let fixture;

  beforeEach(async(() => {
    TestBed.configureTestingModule({
      declarations: [
        MagicEightBallComponent
      ],
      providers: [
        MagicEightBallService
      ]
    });
    fixture = TestBed.createComponent(MagicEightBallComponent);
  }));

  afterEach(() => {
    fixture = undefined;
  });
```

```
  it('should begin with no text', async(() => {
  }));

  it('should show text after click', async(() => {
  }));
});
```

Stubbing a service dependency

Injecting the actual service works just fine, but this isn't what you want to do. You don't want to actually inject an instance of `MagicEightBallService` into the component, as that would set a dependency on the service and make the unit test more complicated than it needs to be. However, `MagicEightBallComponent` needs to import *something* that resembles a `MagicEightBallService`. An excellent solution here is to create a service stub and inject it in its place:

[src/app/magic-eight-ball/magic-eight-ball.component.spec.ts]

```
import {TestBed, async} from '@angular/core/testing';
import {MagicEightBallComponent} from
  './magic-eight-ball.component';
import {MagicEightBallService} from
  '../magic-eight-ball.service';

describe('Component: MagicEightBall', () => {
  let fixture;
  let magicEightBallResponse = 'Answer unclear';
  let magicEightBallServiceStub = {
    reveal: () => magicEightBallResponse
  };

  beforeEach(async(() => {
    TestBed.configureTestingModule({
      declarations: [
        MagicEightBallComponent
      ],
      providers: [
        {
          provide: MagicEightBallService,
          useValue: magicEightBallServiceStub
        }
      ]
    });
    fixture = TestBed.createComponent(MagicEightBallComponent);
  }));
```

```
    afterEach(() => {
      fixture = undefined;
    });

    it('should begin with no text', async(() => {
    }));

    it('should show text after click', async(() => {
    }));
  });
```

A component can't tell the difference between the actual service and its mock, so it will behave normally in the test conditions you've set up.

Next, you should write the preclick test by checking that the fixture's `nativeElement` contains no text:

```
[src/app/magic-eight-ball/magic-eight-ball.component.spec.ts]

import {TestBed, async} from '@angular/core/testing';
import {MagicEightBallComponent} from
  './magic-eight-ball.component';
import {MagicEightBallService} from
  '../magic-eight-ball.service';

describe('Component: MagicEightBall', () => {
  let fixture;
  let getHeaderEl = () =>
    fixture.nativeElement.querySelector('h1');
  let magicEightBallResponse = 'Answer unclear';
  let magicEightBallServiceStub = {
    reveal: () => magicEightBallResponse
  };

  beforeEach(async(() => {
    TestBed.configureTestingModule({
      declarations: [
        MagicEightBallComponent
      ],
      providers: [
        {
          provide: MagicEightBallService,
          useValue: magicEightBallServiceStub
        }
      ]
    });
    fixture = TestBed.createComponent(MagicEightBallComponent);
  }));
```

```
afterEach(() => {
  fixture = undefined;
});

it('should begin with no text', async(() => {
  fixture.detectChanges();
  expect(getHeaderEl().textContent).toEqual('');
}));

it('should show text after click', async(() => {
}));
});
```

Triggering events inside the component fixture

For the second test, you should trigger a click on the button, instruct the fixture to perform change detection, and then inspect the DOM to see that the text was properly inserted. Since you have defined the text that the stub will return, you can just compare it directly with that:

```
[src/app/magic-eight-ball/magic-eight-ball.component.spec.ts]

import {TestBed, async} from '@angular/core/testing';
import {MagicEightBallComponent} from
  './magic-eight-ball.component';
import {MagicEightBallService} from
  '../magic-eight-ball.service';
import {By} from '@angular/platform-browser';

describe('Component: MagicEightBall', () => {
  let fixture;
  let getHeaderEl = () =>
    fixture.nativeElement.querySelector('h1');
  let magicEightBallResponse = 'Answer unclear';
  let magicEightBallServiceStub = {
    reveal: () => magicEightBallResponse
  };

  ...

  it('should begin with no text', async(() => {
    expect(getHeaderEl().textContent).toEqual('');
  }));
it('should show text after click', async(() => {
  fixture.debugElement.query(By.css('button'))
    .triggerEventHandler('click', null);
```

```
    fixture.detectChanges();
    expect(getHeaderEl().textContent)
      .toEqual(magicEightBallResponse);
  }));
});
```

You'll note that this needs to import and use the `By.css` predicate, which is required to perform `DebugElement` inspections.

How it works…

As demonstrated in the dependency injection chapter, providing a stub to the component is no different than providing a regular value to the core application.

The stub here is a single function that returns a static value. There is no concept of randomly selecting from the service's array of strings, and there doesn't need to be. The unit tests for the service itself ensure that it is behaving properly. Instead, the only value provided by the service here is the information it passes back to the component for interpolation back into the template.

See also

- *Writing a minimum viable unit test suite for a simple component* shows you a basic example of unit testing Angular 2 components
- *Unit testing a synchronous service* demonstrates how injection is mocked in unit tests
- *Unit testing a component with a service dependency using spies* shows how you can keep track of service method invocations inside a unit test

Unit testing a component with a service dependency using spies

The ability to stub out services is useful, but it can be limiting in a number of ways. It can also be tedious, as the stubs you create must remain up to date with the public interface of the service. Another excellent tool at your disposal when writing unit tests is the spy.

A spy allows you to select a function or method. It also helps you collect information about if and how it was invoked as well as how it will behave once it is invoked. It is similar in concept to a stub but allows you to have a much more robust unit test.

 The code, links, and a live example related to this recipe are available at `http://ngcookbook.herokuapp.com/3444/`.

Getting ready

Begin with the component tests you wrote in the last recipe:

```
[src/app/magic-eight-ball/magic-eight-ball.component.spec.ts]

import {TestBed, async} from '@angular/core/testing';
import {MagicEightBallComponent} from
  './magic-eight-ball.component';
import {MagicEightBallService} from
  '../magic-eight-ball.service';
import {By} from '@angular/platform-browser';

describe('Component: MagicEightBall', () => {
  let fixture;
  let getHeaderEl = () => fixture.nativeElement.querySelector('h1');
  let magicEightBallResponse = 'Answer unclear';
  let magicEightBallServiceStub = {
    reveal: () => magicEightBallResponse
  };

  beforeEach(async(() => {
    TestBed.configureTestingModule({
      declarations: [
        MagicEightBallComponent
      ],
      providers: [
        {
          provide: MagicEightBallService,
          useValue: magicEightBallServiceStub
        }
      ]
    });
    fixture = TestBed.createComponent(MagicEightBallComponent);
  }));
```

```
    afterEach(() => {
      fixture = undefined;
    });

    it('should begin with no text', async(() => {
      fixture.detectChanges();
      expect(getHeaderEl().textContent).toEqual('');
    }));

    it('should show text after click', async(() => {
      fixture.debugElement.query(By.css('button'))
        .triggerEventHandler('click', null);
      fixture.detectChanges();
      expect(getHeaderEl().textContent)
        .toEqual(magicEightBallResponse);
    }));
  });
```

How to do it...

Instead of using a stub, configure the test module to provide the actual service:

[src/app/magic-eight-ball/magic-eight-ball.component.spec.ts]

```
import {TestBed, async} from '@angular/core/testing';
import {MagicEightBallComponent} from
  './magic-eight-ball.component';
import {MagicEightBallService} from
  '../magic-eight-ball.service';
import {By} from '@angular/platform-browser';

describe('Component: MagicEightBall', () => {
  let fixture;
  let getHeaderEl = () => fixture.nativeElement.querySelector('h1');
  let magicEightBallResponse = 'Answer unclear';

  beforeEach(async(() => {
    TestBed.configureTestingModule({
      declarations: [
        MagicEightBallComponent
      ],
      providers: [
        MagicEightBallService
      ]
    });
    fixture = TestBed.createComponent(MagicEightBallComponent);
```

```
    })));

    afterEach(() => {
      fixture = undefined;
    });

    it('should begin with no text', async(() => {
      fixture.detectChanges();
      expect(getHeaderEl().textContent).toEqual('');
    }));

    it('should show text after click', async(() => {
      fixture.debugElement.query(By.css('button'))
        .triggerEventHandler('click', null);
      fixture.detectChanges();
      expect(getHeaderEl().textContent)
        .toEqual(magicEightBallResponse);
    }));
  });
```

Setting a spy on the injected service

Your goal is to use a method spy to intercept calls to `reveal()` on the service. The problem here, however, is that the service is being injected into the component; therefore, you don't have a direct ability to get a reference to the service instance and set a spy on it. Fortunately, the component fixture provides this for you:

[src/app/magic-eight-ball/magic-eight-ball.component.spec.ts]

```
import {TestBed, async} from '@angular/core/testing';
import {MagicEightBallComponent} from
  './magic-eight-ball.component';
import {MagicEightBallService} from
  '../magic-eight-ball.service';
import {By} from '@angular/platform-browser';

describe('Component: MagicEightBall', () => {
  let fixture;
  let getHeaderEl = () => fixture.nativeElement.querySelector('h1');
  let magicEightBallResponse = 'Answer unclear';
  let magicEightBallService;

  beforeEach(async(() => {
    TestBed.configureTestingModule({
      declarations: [
        MagicEightBallComponent
```

```
    ],
    providers: [
      MagicEightBallService
    ]
  });
  fixture = TestBed.createComponent(MagicEightBallComponent);
  magicEightBallService = fixture.debugElement.injector
    .get(MagicEightBallService);
}));

afterEach(() => {
  fixture = undefined;
  magicEightBallService = undefined;
});

...
});
```

Next, set a spy on the service instance using `spyOn()`. Configure the spy to intercept the method call and return the static value instead:

```
[src/app/magic-eight-ball/magic-eight-ball.component.spec.ts]

import {TestBed, async} from '@angular/core/testing';
import {MagicEightBallComponent} from
  './magic-eight-ball.component';
import {MagicEightBallService} from
  '../magic-eight-ball.service';
import {By} from '@angular/platform-browser';

describe('Component: MagicEightBall', () => {
  let fixture;
  let getHeaderEl = () => fixture.nativeElement.querySelector('h1');
  let magicEightBallResponse = 'Answer unclear';
  let magicEightBallService;
  let revealSpy;

  beforeEach(async(() => {
    TestBed.configureTestingModule({
      declarations: [
        MagicEightBallComponent
      ],
      providers: [
        MagicEightBallService
      ]
    });
    fixture = TestBed.createComponent(MagicEightBallComponent);
    magicEightBallService = fixture.debugElement.injector
```

[375]

```
      .get(MagicEightBallService);
    revealSpy = spyOn(magicEightBallService, 'reveal')
      .and.returnValue(magicEightBallResponse);
  }));

  afterEach(() => {
    fixture = undefined;
    magicEightBallService = undefined;
    revealSpy = undefined;
  });
  ...
});
```

With this spy, you are now capable of seeing how the rest of the application interacts with this captured method. Add a new test, and check that the method is called once and returns the proper value after a click (this also pulls the clicking action into its own test helper):

```
[src/app/magic-eight-ball/magic-eight-ball.component.spec.ts]

import {TestBed, async} from '@angular/core/testing';
import {MagicEightBallComponent} from
  './magic-eight-ball.component';
import {MagicEightBallService} from
  '../magic-eight-ball.service';
import {By} from '@angular/platform-browser';

describe('Component: MagicEightBall', () => {
  let fixture;
  let getHeaderEl = () => fixture.nativeElement.querySelector('h1');
  let magicEightBallResponse = 'Answer unclear';
  let magicEightBallService;
  let revealSpy;

  let clickButton = () => {
    fixture.debugElement.query(By.css('button'))
      .triggerEventHandler('click', null);
  };

  beforeEach(async(() => {
    TestBed.configureTestingModule({
      declarations: [
        MagicEightBallComponent
      ],
      providers: [
        MagicEightBallService
      ]
    });
    fixture = TestBed.createComponent(MagicEightBallComponent);
```

```
    magicEightBallService = fixture.debugElement.injector
      .get(MagicEightBallService);
    revealSpy = spyOn(magicEightBallService, 'reveal')
      .and.returnValue(magicEightBallResponse);
}));

afterEach(() => {
  fixture = undefined;
  magicEightBallService = undefined;
  revealSpy = undefined;
});

it('should begin with no text', async(() => {
  fixture.detectChanges();
  expect(getHeaderEl().textContent).toEqual('');
}));

it('should call reveal after a click', async(() => {
  clickButton();
  expect(revealSpy.calls.count()).toBe(1);
  expect(revealSpy.calls.mostRecent().returnValue)
    .toBe(magicEightBallResponse);
}));

it('should show text after click', async(() => {
  clickButton();
  fixture.detectChanges();
  expect(getHeaderEl().textContent)
    .toEqual(magicEightBallResponse);
}));
});
```

 Note that `detectChanges()` is only required to resolve the data binding, not to execute event handlers.

How it works...

Jasmine spies act as method interceptors and are capable of inspecting everything about the given method invocation. It can track if and when a method was called, what arguments it was called with, how many times it was called, how it should behave, and so on. This is extremely useful when trying to remove dependencies from component unit tests, as you can mock out the public interface of the service using spies.

There's more...

Spies are not beholden to replace the method outright. Here, it is useful to be able to prevent the execution from reaching the internals of the service, but it is not difficult to imagine cases where you would only want to passively observe the invocation of a certain method and allow the execution to continue normally.

For such a purpose, instead of using `.and.returnValue()`, Jasmine allows you to use `.and.callThrough()`, which will allow the execution to proceed uninterrupted.

See also

- *Writing a minimum viable unit test suite for a simple component* shows you a basic example of unit testing Angular 2 components
- *Unit testing a synchronous service* demonstrates how injection is mocked in unit tests
- *Unit testing a component with a service dependency using stubs* shows how you can create a service mock to write unit tests and avoid direct dependencies

10
Performance and Advanced Concepts

This chapter will cover the following recipes:

- Understanding and properly utilizing enableProdMode with pure and impure pipes
- Working with zones outside Angular
- Listening for NgZone events
- Execution outside the Angular zone
- Configuring components to use explicit change detection with OnPush
- Configuring ViewEncapsulation for maximum efficiency
- Configuring the Angular 2 Renderer Service to use web workers
- Configuring applications to use ahead-of-time compilation
- Configuring an application to use lazy loading

Introduction

Angular 2 was a total rebuild for a number of reasons, but one of the biggest ones was certainly efficiency. The framework that emerged from the ashes is a sleek and elegant one, but not without its complexities.

This chapter serves to explore some of the new features that it builds upon and how to most effectively employ them to streamline your application.

Understanding and properly utilizing enableProdMode with pure and impure pipes

Angular 2's change detection process is an elegant but fickle beast that is challenging to understand at first. While it offers huge efficiency gains over the 1.x framework, the gains can come at a cost. The development mode of Angular is activated by default, which will alert you when your code is in danger of behaving in a way that defeats the change detection efficiency gains. In this recipe, you'll implement a feature that violates Angular's change detection schema, correct it, and safely use enableProdMode.

 The code, links, and a live example related to this recipe are available at
`http://ngcookbook.herokuapp.com/0623/`.

Getting ready

Begin with a simple component:

```
[src/app/app.component.ts]

import {Component} from '@angular/core';

@Component({
  selector: 'app-root',
  template: `
    <input #t>
    <button (click)="update(t.value)">Save</button>
    <h1>{{ title }}</h1>
  `
})
export class AppComponent {
  title:string = '';

  update(newTitle:string) {
    this.title = newTitle;
  }
}
```

When the button in this component is clicked, it grabs the value of the input and interpolates it to the header tag. As is, this implementation is perfectly suitable.

How to do it...

To demonstrate the relevance of `enableProdMode`, you'll need to introduce a behavior that `enableProdMode` would mask. More specifically, this means a piece of your application will behave differently when two sequential passes of change detection are run.

 There are a significant number of ways to implement this, but for the purpose of this recipe, you'll implement a nonsensical pipe that changes every time it's used.

Generating a consistency error

Create a nonsensical pipe, namely `AddRandomPipe`:

```
[src/app/add-random.pipe.ts]

import {Pipe, PipeTransform} from '@angular/core';

@Pipe({
  name: 'addRandomPipe'
})
export class AddRandomPipe implements PipeTransform {
  transform(value:string):string {
    return value + Math.random();
  }
}
```

Next, take this pipe and introduce it to your component:

```
[src/app/app.component.ts]

import {Component} from '@angular/core';
import {AddRandomPipe} from './add-random.pipe';

@Component({
  selector: 'app-root',
  template: `
    <input #t>
    <button (click)="update(t.value)">Save</button>
    <h1>{{ title | addRandomPipe }}</h1>
  `
})
export class AppComponent {
  title:string = '';
```

```
    update(newTitle:string) {
      this.title = newTitle;
    }
  }
```

This won't create an error yet, though.

 Angular will indeed run the change detection process twice, so it might seem mysterious that it doesn't create an error. Even though the pipe will generate a new output every time its transform method is invoked, Angular is smart enough to recognize that the input of the interpolation aren't changing, and therefore, reevaluating the pipe is unnecessary. This is called a "pure" pipe, which is the Angular default.

In order to get Angular to evaluate the pipe during each change detection cycle, specify the pipe as "impure":

```
[src/app/add-random.pipe.ts]

import {Pipe, PipeTransform} from '@angular/core';

@Pipe({
  name: 'addRandomPipe',
  pure: false
})
export class AddRandomPipe implements PipeTransform {
  transform(value:string):string {
    return value + Math.random();
  }
}
```

Now the fun begins. When you run the application, you should see something similar to the following error message:

```
EXCEPTION: Error in ./AppComponent class AppComponent - inline template:3:8
caused by: Expression has changed after it was checked. Previous value:
'0.0495151713435904'. Current value: '0.9266277919907477'.
```

Introducing change detection compliance

The error is being thrown as soon as the application starts up, before you're even given a chance to press the button. This means that Angular is detecting the binding mismatch as the component is being instantiated and rendered for the first time.

You've created a pipe that intentionally changes each time, so your goal is to instruct Angular to not bother checking the pipe output twice against itself upon component instantiation.

At this point, you've managed to get Angular to throw a consistency error, which it does because it's running change detection checks twice and getting different results. Switching on enableProdMode at this point would stop the error since Angular would then only run change detection once and not bother to check for consistency. This is because it trusts you to have verified compliance before using enableProdMode. Turning on enableProdMode to mask consistency error messages is a bit like coming home to find your house is on fire and then deciding to go on a vacation.

Angular allows you to control this by specifying the change detection strategy for the component. The default is to always perform a change detection check, but this can be overridden with the OnPush configuration:

```
[src/app/app.component.ts]

import {Component, ChangeDetectionStrategy }
  from '@angular/core';
import {AddRandomPipe} from './add-random.pipe';

@Component({
  selector: 'app-root',
  template: `
    <input #t>
    <button (click)="update(t.value)">Save</button>
    <h1>{{ title | addRandomPipe }}</h1>
  `,
  changeDetection: ChangeDetectionStrategy.OnPush
})
export class AppComponent {
  title:string = '';

  update(newTitle:string) {
    this.title = newTitle;
  }
}
```

Now when the component instance is initialized, you should no longer see the consistency error.

Switching on enableProdMode

Since your application is now compliant with Angular's change detection mechanism, you're free to use `enableProdMode`. This lets your application run change detection once each time. This is because it assumes the application will arrive in a stable state.

In your application's bootstrapping file, invoke `enableProdMode` before you start bootstrapping:

```
[src/main.ts]

import {platformBrowserDynamic}
  from '@angular/platform-browser-dynamic';
import {enableProdMode} from '@angular/core';
import {AppModule} from './app/';

enableProdMode();

platformBrowserDynamic().bootstrapModule(AppModule);
```

How it works...

`enableProdMode` will configure your application in a number of ways, including silencing error and informational error messages, among others; however, none of these ways is as visible as the suppression of the secondary change detection process.

There's more...

There are other ways to mitigate this consistency problem. For example, suppose you want to generate a pipe that will append a random number to the input. It doesn't necessarily need to be a different random number every single time; rather, you can have one for each unique input within a certain period of time. Such a situation could allow you to have a pipe that utilizes some sort of caching strategy. If the pipe caches results for a period of time longer than change detection takes to complete (which is not very long), then altering the change detection strategy of the component is not necessary. This is because multiple pipe invocations will yield an identical response. For example, refer to the following code:

```
[src/app/add-random.pipe.ts]

import {Pipe, PipeTransform} from '@angular/core';

@Pipe({
  name: 'addRandomPipe',
```

```
    pure: false
  })
  export class AddRandomPipe implements PipeTransform {
    cache:Object = {};

    transform(input:string):string {
      let value = this.cache[input];
      if (!value || value.expire < Date.now()) {
        value = {
          text: input + Math.random(),
          // Expires in one second
          expire: Date.now() + 1000
        }
        this.cache[input] = value;
      }
      return value.text;
    }
  }
```

With this, you can safely strike `changeDetection: ChangeDetectionStrategy.OnPush` from `ComponentMetadata` of your `AppComponent` and you will not see any consistency errors.

See also

- *Configuring the Angular 2 renderer service to use web workers* guides you through the process of setting up your application to render on a web worker
- *Configuring applications to use ahead-of-time compilation* guides you through how to compile an application during the build

Working with zones outside Angular

Working with zones entirely inside of the Angular framework conceals what they are really doing behind the scenes. It would be a disservice to you, the reader, to just gloss over the underlying mechanism. In this recipe, you'll take the vanilla `zone.js` implementation outside of Angular and modify it a bit in order to see how Angular can make use of it.

There will be no Angular used in this recipe, only zone.js inside a simple HTML file. Furthermore, this recipe will be written in plain ES5 JavaScript for simplicity.

The code, links, and a live example related to this recipe are available at `http://ngcookbook.herokuapp.com/0591/`.

Getting ready

Begin with the following simple HTML file:

```
[index.html]

<button id="button">Click me</button>
<button id="add">Add listener</button>
<button id="remove">Remove listener</button>

<script>
var button = document.getElementById('button');
var add = document.getElementById('add');
var remove = document.getElementById('remove');

var clickCallback = function() {
  console.log('click!');
};

setInterval(function() {
  console.log('set interval!');
}, 1000);
add.addEventListener('click', function() {
  button.addEventListener('click', clickCallback);
});
remove.addEventListener('click', function() {
  button.removeEventListener('click', clickCallback);
});
</script>
```

Each of these callbacks has log statements inside them so you can see when they are invoked:

- `setInterval` calls its associated listener every second
- Clicking on **Click me** calls its listener if it is attached
- Clicking on **Add listener** attaches a click listener to the button
- Clicking on **Remove listener** removes the click listener

There's nothing special going on here, because all of these are default browser APIs. The magic of zones, as you will see, is that the zone behavior can be introduced around this without modifying any code.

How to do it...

First, add the `zone.js` script to the top of the file:

```
[index.html]

<script
src="https://cdnjs.cloudflare.com/ajax/libs/zone.js/0.6.26/zone.js">
</script>

<button id="button">Click me</button>
<button id="add">Add listener</button>
<button id="remove">Remove listener</button>
...
```

There's no special setup needed for `zone.js`, but it needs to be added before you set listeners or do anything that could have asynchronous implications. Angular needs this dependency to be added before it is initialized.

Adding this script introduces `Zone` to the global namespace. `zone.js` has already created a global zone for you. This can be accessed with the following:

```
Zone.current
```

Forking a zone

The global zone isn't doing anything interesting yet. To customize a zone, you'll need to create your own by forking the one we have and running relevant code inside it. Do this as follows:

```
[index.html]

<script
  src="https://cdnjs.cloudflare.com/ajax/libs/zone.js/0.6.26/zone.js">
</script>

<button id="button">Click me</button>
<button id="add">Add listener</button>
```

```
<button id="remove">Remove listener</button>

<script>
var button = document.getElementById('button');
var add = document.getElementById('add');
var remove = document.getElementById('remove');

Zone.current.fork({}).run(function() {
  var clickCallback = function() {
    console.log('click!');
  };

  setInterval(function() {
    console.log('set interval!');
  }, 1000);
  add.addEventListener('click', function() {
   button.addEventListener('click', clickCallback);
  });
  remove.addEventListener('click', function() {
   button.removeEventListener('click', clickCallback);
  });
});
</script>
```

Behaviorally, this doesn't change anything from the perspective of the console. `fork()` takes an empty `ZoneSpec` object literal, which you will modify next.

Overriding zone events with ZoneSpec

When a piece of code is run in a zone, you are able to attach behaviors at important points in the asynchronous behavior flow. Here, you'll override four zone events:

- scheduleTask
- invokeTask
- hasTask
- cancelTask

You'll begin with `scheduleTask`. Define an override method inside `ZoneSpec`. Overrides use the event names prefixed with `on`:

```
[index.html]

<script
  src="https://cdnjs.cloudflare.com/ajax/libs/zone.js/0.6.26/zone.js">
</script>
```

```
<button id="button">Click me</button>
<button id="add">Add listener</button>
<button id="remove">Remove listener</button>

<script>
var button = document.getElementById('button');
var add = document.getElementById('add');
var remove = document.getElementById('remove');

Zone.current.fork({
  onScheduleTask: function(zoneDelegate, zone, targetZone, task) {
    console.log('schedule');
    zoneDelegate
      .scheduleTask(targetZone, task);
  }
}).run(function() {
  var clickCallback = function() {
    console.log('click!');
  };

  setInterval(function() {
    console.log('set interval!');
  }, 1000);
  add.addEventListener('click', function() {
   button.addEventListener('click', clickCallback);
  });
  remove.addEventListener('click', function() {
   button.removeEventListener('click', clickCallback);
  });
});
</script>
```

With this addition, you should see that the zone recognizes that three tasks are being scheduled. This should make sense, as you are declaring three instances that can generate asynchronous actions: `setInterval`, `addEventListener`, and `removeEventListener`. If you click on **Add listener**, you'll see it schedule the fourth task as well.

 `zoneDelegate.scheduleTask()` is required because you are actually overwriting what the zone is using for that handler. If you don't perform this action, the scheduler handler will exit before actually scheduling the task.

The opposite of scheduling a task is canceling it, so override that event handler next:

```
[index.html]

Zone.current.fork({
```

```
    onScheduleTask: function(zoneDelegate, zone, targetZone, task) {
      console.log('schedule');
      zoneDelegate
        .scheduleTask(targetZone, task);
    },
    onCancelTask: function(zoneDelegate, zone, targetZone, task) {
      console.log('cancel');
      zoneDelegate
        .cancelTask(targetZone, task);
    }
  }).run(function() {
    ...
  });
```

A cancel event occurs when a scheduled task is destroyed, in this example, when `removeEventListener()` is invoked. If you click on **Add listener** and then **Remove listener**, you'll see a cancel event occur.

The scheduling of tasks is visible during the startup, but each time a button is clicked or a `setInterval` handler is executed, you don't see anything being logged. This is because scheduling a task, which occurs during registration, is distinct from invoking a task, which is when the asynchronous event actually occurs.

To demonstrate this, add an `invokeTask` override:

```
[index.html]

Zone.current.fork({
  onScheduleTask: function(zoneDelegate, zone, targetZone, task) {
    console.log('schedule');
    zoneDelegate
      .scheduleTask(targetZone, task);
  },
  onCancelTask: function(zoneDelegate, zone, targetZone, task) {
    console.log('cancel');
    zoneDelegate
      .cancelTask(targetZone, task);
  },
  onInvokeTask: function(zoneDelegate, zone, targetZone, task,
                         applyThis, applyArgs) {
    console.log('invoke');
    zoneDelegate
      .invokeTask(targetZone, task, applyThis, applyArgs);
  }
}).run(function() {
  ...
});
```

With this addition, you should now be able to see a console log each time a task is invoked—for a button click or a `setInterval` callback.

So far, you've been able to see when the zone has tasks scheduled and invoked, but now, do the reverse of this to detect when all the tasks have been completed. This can be accomplished with `hasTask`, which can also be overridden:

```
[index.html]

Zone.current.fork({
  onScheduleTask: function(zoneDelegate, zone, targetZone, task) {
    console.log('schedule');
    zoneDelegate
      .scheduleTask(targetZone, task);
  },
  onCancelTask: function(zoneDelegate, zone, targetZone, task) {
    console.log('cancel');
    zoneDelegate
      .cancelTask(targetZone, task);
  },
  onInvokeTask: function(zoneDelegate, zone, targetZone, task,
                         applyThis, applyArgs) {
    console.log('invoke');
    zoneDelegate
      .invokeTask(targetZone, task, applyThis, applyArgs);
  },
  onHasTask: function(zoneDelegate, zone, targetZone, isEmpty) {
    console.log('has');
    zoneDelegate.hasTask(targetZone, isEmpty);
  }
}).run(function() {
  ...
});
```

The `isEmpty` parameter of `onHasTask` has three properties: `eventTask`, `macroTask`, and `microTask`. These three properties map to Booleans describing whether the associated queues have any tasks inside them.

With these four callbacks, you have successfully intercepted four important points in the component life cycle:

- When a task "generator" is scheduled, which may generate tasks from browser or timer events
- When a task "generator" is canceled
- When a task is actually invoked

- How to determine whether any tasks are scheduled and of what type

How it works...

The concept that forms the core of zones is the interception of asynchronous tasks. More directly, you want the ability to know when asynchronous tasks are being created, how many there are, and when they're done.

`zone.js` accomplishes this by shimming all the relevant browser methods that are responsible for setting up asynchronous tasks. In fact, all the methods used in this method—`setInterval`, `addEventListener`, and `removeEventListener`—are all shimmed so that the zone they are run inside is aware of any asynchronous tasks they might add to the queue.

There's more...

To begin to relate this to Angular, you'll need to take a step back to examine the zone ecosystem.

Understanding zone.run()

You'll notice in this example that invoke is printed for each asynchronous action, even for those that were registered inside another asynchronous action. This is the power of zones. Anything done inside the `zone.run()` block will cascade within the same zone. This way, the zone can keep track of an unbroken segment of asynchronous behavior without an ocean of boilerplate code.

Microtasks and macrotasks

This actually has nothing to do with `zone.js` at all but rather with how the browser event loop works. All the events generated by you in this example—clicks, timer events, and so on—are macrotasks. That is, the browser respects their handlers as a synchronous, blocking segment of code. The code that executes around these tasks—the `zone.js` callbacks, for example—are microtasks. They are distinct from macrotasks but are still synchronously executed as part of the entire "turn" for that macrotask.

A macrotask may generate more microtasks for itself within its own turn.

Once the microtask and macrotask queues are empty, the zone can be considered to be stable, since there is no asynchronous behavior to be anticipated. For Angular, this sounds like a great time to update the UI.

In fact, this is exactly what Angular is doing behind the scenes. Angular views the browser through the task-centric goggles of zone.js and uses this clever tool to decide when to go about rendering.

See also

- *Listening for NgZone events* gives a basic understanding of how Angular is using zones
- *Execution outside the Angular zone* shows you how to perform long-running operations without incurring a zone overhead
- *Configuring components to use explicit change detection with OnPush* describes how to manually control Angular's change detection process

Listening for NgZone events

With the introduction of Angular 2 comes the concept of zones. Before you begin this recipe, I strongly recommended you to begin by working through the *Working with zones outside Angular* recipe.

zone.js

`zone.js` is a library that Angular 2 directly depends upon. It allows Angular to be built upon a zone that allows the framework to intimately manage its execution context.

More plainly, this means that Angular can tell when asynchronous things are happening that it might care about. If this sounds a bit like how `$scope.apply()` was relevant in Angular 1.x, you are thinking in the right way.

NgZone

Angular 2's integration with zones takes the form of the `NgZone` service, which acts as a sort of wrapper for the actual Angular zones. This service exposes a useful API that you can tap into.

 The code, links, and a live example related to this recipe are available at `http://ngcookbook.herokuapp.com/8676/`.

Getting ready

All that is needed for this recipe is a component into which the `NgZone` service can be injected:

```
[src/app/app.component.ts]

import {Component} from '@angular/core';

@Component({
  selector: 'app-root',
  template: ``
})
export class AppComponent {
  constructor() {
  }
}
```

How to do it...

Begin by injecting the `NgZone` service into your component, which is made available inside the core Angular module:

```
[src/app/app.component.ts]

import {Component, NgZone} from '@angular/core';

@Component({
  selector: 'app-root',
  template: ``
})
export class AppComponent {
```

```
constructor(private zone:NgZone) {
}
}
```

The `NgZone` service exposes a number of `EventEmitters` that you can attach to. Since zones are capable of tracking asynchronous activity within it, the `NgZone` service exposes two `EventEmitters` that understand when an asynchronous activity becomes enqueued and dequeued as microtasks.

The `onUnstable EventEmitter` lets you know when one or more microtasks are enqueued; `onStable` is fired when the the microtask queue is empty and Angular does not plan to enqueue any more.

Add handlers to each:

```
[src/app/app.component.ts]

import {Component, NgZone} from '@angular/core';

@Component({
  selector: 'app-root',
  template: ``
})
export class AppComponent {
  constructor(private zone:NgZone) {
    zone.onStable.subscribe(() => console.log('stable'));
    zone.onUnstable.subscribe(() => console.log('unstable'));
  }
}
```

Terrific! However, the log output of this is quite boring. At application startup, you'll see that the application is reported as stable, but nothing further.

Demonstrating the zone life cycle

If you understand how Angular uses zones, the lack of logging shouldn't surprise you. There's nothing to generate asynchronous tasks in this zone. Go ahead and add some by creating a button with a handler that sets a timeout log statement:

```
[src/app/app.component.ts]

import {Component, NgZone} from '@angular/core';

@Component({
  selector: 'app-root',
```

```
  template: `<button (click)="foo()">foo</button>`
})
export class AppComponent {
  constructor(private zone:NgZone) {
    zone.onStable.subscribe(() => console.log('stable'));
    zone.onUnstable.subscribe(() => console.log('unstable'));
  }

  foo() {
    setTimeout(() => console.log('timeout handler'), 1000);
  }
}
```

Now with each click, you should see an unstable-stable pair, followed by an unstable-timeout handler-stable set one second later. This means you've successfully tied into Angular's zone emitters.

How it works...

In order to obviate the necessity of a `$scope.apply()` construct, Angular needs the ability to intelligently decide when it should check to see whether the state of the application has changed.

In an asynchronous setting, such as a browser environment, this seems like a messy task at first. Something like timed events and input events are, by their very nature, difficult to keep track of. For example, refer to the following code:

```
element.addEventListener('click', _ => {
  // do some stuff
  setInterval(_ => {
    // do some stuff
  }, 1000);
});
```

This code is capable of changing the model in two different places, both of which are asynchronous. Code such as this is written all the time and in so many different places; it's difficult to imagine a way of keeping track of such code without sprinkling something like `$scope.$apply()` all over the place.

The utility of zone.js

The big idea of zones is to give you the ability to grasp how and when the browser is performing asynchronous actions that you care about.

NgZone is wrapping the underlying zone API for you instead of exposing EventEmitters to the various parts of the life cycle, but this shouldn't confuse you one bit. For this example, the log output is demonstrating the following:

1. The application initializes and examines the application zone. There are no tasks scheduled, so Angular emits a stable event.
2. You click on the button.
3. This generates a click event, which in turn generates a task inside the zone to execute the click handler. Angular sees this and emits an unstable event.
4. The click handler is executed, scheduling a task in 1 second.
5. The click handler is completed, and the application once again has no pending tasks. Angular emits a stable event.
6. One second elapses and the browser timer adds the setTimeout handler to the task queue. Since this is shimmed by the zone, Angular sees this occur and emits an unstable event.
7. The setTimeout handler is executed.
8. The setTimeout handler is completed, and the application once again has no pending tasks. Angular emits a stable event.

See also

- *Working with zones outside Angular* is an excellent introduction to how zones work in the browser
- *Execution outside the Angular zone* shows you how to perform long-running operations without incurring a zone overhead
- *Configuring components to use explicit change detection with OnPush* describes how to manually control Angular's change detection process

Execution outside the Angular zone

The utility of zone.js is terrific, since it works automatically, but a seasoned software engineer knows this often comes at a price. This is especially true when the concept of data binding comes into play.

In this recipe, you'll learn how to execute outside the Angular zone and what benefits this affords you.

The code, links, and a live example related to this recipe are available at `http://ngcookbook.herokuapp.com/3362/`.

How to do it...

To compare execution in different contexts, create two buttons that run the same code in different zone contexts. The buttons should count to 100 with `setTimeout` increments. Use the performance global to measure the time it takes:

```
[src/app/app.component.ts]

import {Component, NgZone} from '@angular/core';

@Component({
  selector: 'app-root',
  template: `
    <button (click)="runInsideAngularZone()">
      Run inside Angular zone
    </button>
    <button (click)="runOutsideAngularZone()">
      Run outside Angular zone
    </button>
  `
})
export class AppComponent {
  progress: number = 0;
  startTime: number = 0;

  constructor(private zone: NgZone) {}

  runInsideAngularZone() {
    this.start();
    this.step(() => this.finish('Inside Angular zone'));
  }

  runOutsideAngularZone() {
    this.start();
    this.step(() => this.finish('Outside Angular zone'));
  }

  start() {
    this.progress = 0;
    this.startTime = performance.now();
```

```
    }

    finish(location:string) {
      this.zone.run(() => {
        console.log(location);
        console.log('Took ' +
          (performance.now() - this.startTime) + 'ms');
      });
    }

    step(doneCallback: () => void) {
      if (++this.progress < 100) {
        setTimeout(() => {
          this.step(doneCallback);
        }, 10);
      } else {
        doneCallback();
      }
    }
  }
}
```

At this point, the two buttons will behave identically, as both of them are being executed inside the Angular zone.

In order to execute outside the Angular zone, you'll need to use the runOutsideAngular() method exposed by NgZone:

```
runInsideAngularZone() {
  this.start();
  this.step(() => this.finish('Inside Angular zone'));
}

runOutsideAngularZone() {
  this.start();
  this.zone.runOutsideAngular(() => {
    this.step(() => this.finish('Outside Angular zone'));
  });
}
```

At this point, you can run both of them again side by side and verify that they still take (roughly) the same amount of time to execute. This should not surprise you, as they are still performing the same task. The inclusion of zone.js means that the browser APIs are shimmed outside Angular, so even running this outside the Angular zone means it is still running inside a zone.

In order to see a performance difference, you'll need to introduce some binding inside the template:

```
[src/app/app.component.ts]

import {Component, NgZone} from '@angular/core';

@Component({
  selector: 'app-root',
  template: `
    <h3>Progress: {{progress}}%</h3>
    <button (click)="runInsideAngularZone()">
      Run inside Angular zone
    </button>
    <button (click)="runOutsideAngularZone()">
      Run outside Angular zone
    </button>
  `
})
export class AppComponent {
  ...
}
```

Now you should begin to see a substantive difference between the runtimes of each button. This shows that when the overhead of bindings is causing the application to slow down, `runOutsideAngular()` has the potential to yield surprisingly substantive performance optimizations.

How it works...

When you examine the `NgZone` source, you'll find that the "outer" zone is merely the topmost browser zone. Angular forks this zone upon initialization and builds upon it to yield the nice `NgZone` service wrapper.

However, because zones do not discriminate in the realm of asynchronous callbacks and data binding, each invocation of the `setTimeout` handler inside the Angular zone is recognized as an event that has implications on the template rendering process. In every invocation, Angular sees an update to the bound data following an asynchronous task, and proceeds to rerender the view. When this is done 100 times, it adds up to several hundred extra milliseconds of execution.

When this is run outside the Angular zone, Angular is no longer aware of the `setTimeout` tasks that are being executed and so does not require a rerender. Upon the very final iteration though, invoke `NgZone.run()`; this will cause the execution to rejoin the Angular zone. Angular sees the task and the modified data and updates the bindings accordingly; this time though, this is done only once.

There's more…

In this recipe, the `finish()` method invokes the `run()` method for both the Angular zone and the non-Angular zone. When the zone that this is invoked upon is already the contextual zone in which the task is being executed, using `run()` becomes redundant and is effectively a no-op.

See also

- *Working with zones outside Angular* is an excellent introduction to how zones work in the browser
- *Listening for NgZone events* gives a basic understanding of how Angular is using zones
- *Configuring components to use explicit change detection with OnPush* describes how to manually control Angular's change detection process

Configuring components to use explicit change detection with OnPush

The convention of Angular's data flow, in which data flows downward through the component tree and events float upwards, engenders some interesting possibilities. One of these involves controlling when Angular should perform change detection at a given node in the component tree.

 The code, links, and a live example related to this recipe are available at `http://ngcookbook.herokuapp.com/4909/`.

Getting ready

Begin with the following simple application:

```
[app/root.component.ts]

import {Component} from '@angular/core';
import {Subject} from 'rxjs/Subject';
```

```
import {Observable} from 'rxjs/Observable';

@Component({
  selector: 'root',
  template: `
    <button (click)="shareSubject.next($event)">Share!</button>
    <article [shares]="shareEmitter"></article>
  `
})
export class RootComponent  {
  shareSubject:Subject<Event> = new Subject();
  shareEmitter:Observable<Event> =
    this.shareSubject.asObservable();
}
[app/article.component.ts]

import {Component, Input, ngOnInit} from '@angular/core';
import {Observable} from 'rxjs/Observable';

@Component({
  selector: 'article',
  template: `
    <h1>{{title}}</h1>
    <p>Shares: {{count}}</p>
  `
})
export class ArticleComponent implements OnInit {
  @Input() shares:Observable<Event>;
  count:number = 0;
  title:string =
    'Insurance Fraud Grows In Wake of Apple Pie Hubbub';
  ngOnInit() {
    this.shares.subscribe((e:Event) => ++this.count);
  }
}
```

This very simple application is just using an observable to pass share events down, from a parent component to a child component. The child component keeps track of the click event count and interpolates this count to the page.

Your objective is to modify this setup so that the child component only detects a change when an event is emitted from the observable.

How to do it…

Out of the box, Angular already has a very robust way of detecting change: zones. Whenever there is an event inside a zone, Angular recognizes that this event has the potential to modify the application in a meaningful way. It then performs change detection from the top of the component tree down to the bottom, checking whether anything needs to be updated in the changed model. Since data only flows downward, this is already an extremely efficient way of handling it.

However, you might like to exert some control in this situation since you may be able to hand-optimize when change detection should occur inside a component. Most likely you will very easily be able to tell when a component may or may not change, based on what is happening around it.

Configuring the ChangeDetectionStrategy

Angular offers you the option of changing how the change detection scheme works. If you would prefer that Angular refrain from listening to zone events to kick off a round of change detection, you can instead configure a component to only perform change detection when an input is changed. This can be done by configuring the component to use the `OnPush` strategy instead of the default.

Surely, this will occur less often than the firehose of browser events. If the component will only change when an input is changed, then this will save Angular the trouble of doing an iteration of change detection on that component.

Modify `ArticleComponent` to instead use `OnPush`:

```
[app/article.component.ts]

import {Component, Input, ngOnInit, ChangeDetectionStrategy}
  from '@angular/core';
import {Observable} from 'rxjs/Observable';

@Component({
  selector: 'article',
  template: `
    <h1>{{title}}</h1>
    <p>Shares: {{count}}</p>
  `,
  changeDetection: ChangeDetectionStrategy.OnPush
})
export class ArticleComponent implements OnInit {
  @Input() shares:Observable<Event>;
```

```
  count:number = 0;
  title:string =
    'Insurance Fraud Grows In Wake of Apple Pie Hubbub';
  ngOnInit() {
    this.shares.subscribe((e:Event) => ++this.count);
  }
}
```

This successfully changes the strategy, but there is one significant problem now: the count will no longer be updated. This happens, of course, because the input to this component is not being changed.

The count only updated before because Angular was seeing click events on the button, which caused change detection on `ArticleComponent`. Now, Angular has been instructed to ignore these click events, even though the count inside the child component is still being updated from the observable handlers.

Requesting explicit change detection

You are able to inject a reference to the component's change detector. With this, it exposes a method that allows you to force a round of change detection whenever you like. Since the model is being updated inside an observable handler, this seems like a fine place to trigger the change detection process:

```
[app/article.component.ts]

import {Component, Input, ngOnInit, ChangeDetectionStrategy,
        ChangeDetectorRef} from '@angular/core';
import {Observable} from 'rxjs/Observable';

@Component({
  selector: 'article',
  template: `
    <h1>{{title}}</h1>
    <p>Shares: {{count}}</p>
  `,
  changeDetection: ChangeDetectionStrategy.OnPush
})
export class ArticleComponent implements OnInit {
  @Input() shares:Observable<Event>;
  count:number = 0;
  title:string =
    'Insurance Fraud Grows In Wake of Apple Pie Hubbub';
  constructor(private changeDetectorRef_: ChangeDetectorRef) {}
  ngOnInit() {
    this.shares.subscribe((e:Event) => {
```

```
        ++this.count;
        this.changeDetectorRef_.markForCheck();
      });
    }
  }
```

Now you will see the count getting updated once again.

How it works...

Using OnPush essentially converts a component to operate like a black box. If the input doesn't change, then Angular assumes that the state inside the component will remain constant, and therefore there is no need to proceed further with regard to detecting a change.

Since change detection always flows from top to bottom in the component tree, the request for change detection uses markForCheck(), marks the component's change detector to run only when Angular reaches that component inside the tree.

There's more...

This is a useful pattern if you're looking to squeeze additional performance from your application, but in some cases, doing this can develop into an anti-pattern. The need to explicitly define when Angular should perform change detection can become tedious as your component code grows in size. There can potentially be bugs that arise from missing one place where markForCheck() should have been invoked but was not. Angular's change detection strategy is already quite performant and robust, so use this configuration wisely.

See also

- *Working with zones outside Angular* is an excellent introduction to how zones work in the browser
- *Listening for NgZone events* gives a basic understanding of how Angular is using zones
- *Execution outside the Angular zone* shows you how to perform long-running operations without incurring a zone overhead

- *Configuring ViewEncapsulation for maximum efficiency* shows how you can configure components to utilize the shadow DOM

Configuring ViewEncapsulation for maximum efficiency

Although it may sound clichéd, Angular 2 was built for the browsers of tomorrow. You can point to why this is the case in a large number of ways, but there is one way where this is extremely true: component encapsulation.

The ideal component model for Angular 2 is the one in which components are entirely sandboxed, save for the few pieces that are externally visible and modifiable. In this respect, it does a bang-up job, but even the most modern browsers limit its ability to strive for such efficacy. This is especially true in the realm of CSS styling.

Several features of Angular's component styling are especially important:

- You are able to write styles that are guaranteed to be only applicable to a component
- You can explicitly specify styles that should be inherited downward through the component tree
- You can specify an encapsulation strategy on a piecewise basis

There are a number of interesting ways to accomplish an efficient component styling schema.

 The code, links, and a live example related to this recipe are available at `ht tp://ngcookbook.herokuapp.com/1463/`.

Getting ready

Begin with a simple application component:

```
[src/app/app.component.ts]

import {Component} from '@angular/core';

@Component({
```

```
    selector: 'app-root',
    template: `
      <h1>
        {{title}}
      </h1>
    `,
    styles: [`
      h1 {
        color: red;
      }
    `]
})
export class AppComponent {
  title = 'app works!';
}
```

How to do it...

Angular will default to not using ShadowDOM for components, as the majority of browsers do not support it to a satisfactory level. The next best thing, which it will default to, is to emulate this styling encapsulation by nesting your selectors. The preceding component is effectively the equivalent of the following:

```
[src/app/app.component.ts]

import {Component, ViewEncapsulation} from '@angular/core';

@Component({
  selector: 'app-root',
  template: `
    <h1>
      {{title}}
    </h1>
  `,
  styles: [`
    h1 {
      color: red;
    }
  `],
  encapsulation: ViewEncapsulation.Emulated
})
export class AppComponent {
  title = 'app works!';
}
```

Emulated styling encapsulation

How exactly does Angular perform this emulation? Look at the rendered application to find out. Your component will appear something like the following:

```
<app-root _nghost-mqf-1="">
  <h1 _ngcontent-mqf-1="">
    app works!
  </h1>
</app-root>
```

In the head of the document:

```
<style>
  h1[_ngcontent-mqf-1] {
    color: red;
  }
</style>
```

The picture should be a bit clearer now. Angular is assigning this component class (not an instance) a unique ID, and the styles defined for the global document will only be applicable to tags that have the matching attribute.

No styling encapsulation

If this encapsulation isn't necessary, you are free to use `encapsulation: ViewEncapsulation.None`. Angular will happily skip the unique ID assignment step for you, giving you a vanilla:

```
<app-root>
  <h1>
    app works!
  </h1>
</app-root>
```

In the head of the document:

```
<style>
  h1 {
    color: red;
  }
</style>
```

Native styling encapsulation

The best, most futuristic, and least supported method of going about this is to use ShadowDOM instances to go along with each component instance. This can be accomplished using `encapsulation: ViewEncapsulation.Native`. Now, your component will render:

```
<app-root>
  #shadow-root
    <style>
      h1 {
        color: red;
      }
    </style>
    <h1>
      app works!
    </h1>
</app-root>
```

How it works...

Angular is smart enough to recognize where it needs to put your styles and how to modify them to make them work for your component configuration:

- For `None` and `Emulated`, styles go into the document head
- For `Native`, styles go inline with the rendered component
- For `None` and `Native`, no style modifications are needed
- For `Emulated`, styles are restricted by attribute selectors

There's more...

An important consideration of `ViewEncapsulation` choices is CSS performance. It is well known and entirely intuitive that CSS styling is more efficient when it has to traverse a smaller part of the DOM and has to match using a simpler selector.

Emulating component encapsulation adds an attribute selector to each and every style that is defined for that component. At scale, it isn't hard to see how this can degrade performance. ShadowDOM elegantly solves this problem by offering unmodified styles inside a restricted piece of DOM. Its styles cannot escape but can be applied downward to other components. Furthermore, ShadowDOM components can be nested and strategically applied.

See also

- *Understanding and properly utilizing enableProdMode with pure and impure pipes* describes how to take the training wheels off your application
- *Configuring components to use explicit change detection with OnPush* describes how to manually control Angular's change detection process

Configuring the Angular 2 Renderer to use web workers

One of the most compelling introductions in the new rendition of the Angular framework is the total abstraction of the rendering execution. This stems from one of the core ideas of Angular: you should be able to seamlessly substitute out any behavior module and replace it with another. This, of course, means that Angular cannot have any dependency bleed outside of the modules.

One place that Angular puts emphasis on being configurable is the location where code execution takes place. This is manifested in a number of ways, and this recipe will focus on Angular's ability to perform rendering execution at a location other than inside the main browser's JavaScript runtime.

 The code, links, and a live example related to this recipe are available at `http://ngcookbook.herokuapp.com/1859/`.

Getting ready

Begin with some simple application elements that do not yet form a full application:

```
[index.html]

<!DOCTYPE html>
<html>
  <head>
    <script src="zone.js "></script>
    <script src="reflect-metadata.js"></script>
    <script src="system.src.js"></script>
    <script src="system-config.js"></script>
  </head>
```

```
    <body>
      <article></article>
      <script>
        System.import('system-config.js')
          .then(function() {
            System.import('main.ts');
          });
      </script>
    </body>
</html>
[app/article.component.ts]

import {Component} from '@angular/core';

@Component({
  selector: 'article',
  template: `
    <h2>{{title}}</h2>
  `
})
export class ArticleComponent {
  title:string =
    'Survey Indicates Plastic Funnel Best Way to Drink Rare Wine';
}
```

Note that this recipe uses SystemJS to handle modules and TypeScript transpilation, but this is merely to keep the demonstration simple. A properly compiled application can use regular JavaScript to accomplish the same feat, with no dependency on SystemJS.

This recipe will start off by assuming you have a basic knowledge of what web workers are and how they work. There is a discussion of their properties later in this recipe.

How to do it...

The SystemJS startup configuration kicks off the application from `main.ts`, so you'll begin there. Instead of bootstrapping the application in this file as you normally would, you'll use an imported Angular helper to initialize the web worker instance:

```
[main.ts]

import {bootstrapWorkerUi} from "@angular/platform-webworker";

bootstrapWorkerUi(window.location.href + "loader.js");
```

Concern yourself with the precise details of what this is doing later, but the high-level idea is that this is creating a web worker instance that is integrated with the Angular Renderer.

 Recall that initializing a web worker requires a path to its startup JS file, and a relative path inside this file might not always work; therefore, you're using the window location to provide an absolute URL. The necessity of this may differ based on your development setup.

Since this file references a web worker initialization file called `loader.js`, write it next. Workers cannot be given a TypeScript file:

```
[loader.js]

importScripts(
   "system.js",
   "zone.js",
   "reflect-metadata.js",
   "./system-config.js");

System.import("./web-worker-main.ts");
```

This file first imports the same files that are listed inside the `<head>` tag of `index.html`. This should make sense since the web worker will need to perform some of the duties of Angular but without direct access to anything that exists inside the main JavaScript runtime. For example, since this web worker will be rendering a component, it needs to be able to understand the `@Component({})` notation, which cannot be done without the reflect-metadata extension.

Just like the main application, the web worker also has an initialization file. This takes the form of `web-worker-main.ts`:

```
[web-worker-main.ts]

import {AppModule} from './app/app.module';
import {platformWorkerAppDynamic}
   from '@angular/platform-webworker-dynamic';

platformWorkerAppDynamic().bootstrapModule(AppModule);
```

Compared to a normal `main.ts` file, this file should look delightfully familiar. Angular provides you with a totally separate platform module, but one that affords you an identical API, which you are using here to bootstrap the application from the yet-to-be-defined `AppModule`. Define this next:

```
[app/app.module.ts]
```

```
import {NgModule} from '@angular/core';
import {WorkerAppModule} from '@angular/platform-webworker';
import {AppModule} from './app.module';
import {ArticleComponent} from './article.component';

@NgModule({
  imports: [
    WorkerAppModule
  ],
  bootstrap: [
    ArticleComponent
  ],
  declarations: [
    ArticleComponent
  ]
})
export class AppModule {}
```

Similar to how you would normally use `BrowserModule` within a conventional top-level app module, Angular provides a web-worker-flavored `WorkerAppModule` that handles all the necessary integration.

How it works...

Make no mistake about what is happening here: your application is now running on two separate JavaScript threads.

Web workers are basically just really dumb JavaScript execution buckets. When initialized, they are given an initial piece of JavaScript to run, which in this example took the form of `loader.js/`. They have no understanding of what is going on in the main browser runtime. They can't interact with the DOM, and you are only able to communicate with them via PostMessages. Angular builds an elegant abstraction on top of PostMessages to create a bus interface, and it is this interface that is used to join the two runtimes together.

If you look into the PostMessage specification, you will notice that all of the data passed as the message must be serialized into a string. How then can this rendering configuration possibly work with the DOM in the main browser, handling events and displaying the HTML and the web worker performing the rendering on a DOM it cannot touch?

The answer is simple: Angular serializes everything. When the initial rendering occurs, or an event in the browser occurs, Angular grabs everything it needs to know about the current state, wraps it up into a serialized string, and ships it off to the web worker renderer on the proper channel. The web worker renderer understands what's being passed to it. Although it cannot access the main DOM, it is certainly able to construct HTML elements, understand how the serialized events passed to it will affect them, and perform the rendering.

When the time comes to tell the browser what to actually render, it will in turn serialize the rendered component and send it back to the main browser runtime, which will unpack the string and insert it into the DOM.

To the Angular framework, because it is abstracted from all the browser dependencies that might get in the way of this, everything seems normal. Events come in, they're handled, and a renderer service tells it what to put into the DOM. Everything that happens in between is unimportant to the Angular framework, which doesn't care that everything happened in a totally separate JavaScript runtime.

 Note that the elements you begin with have nothing unusual about them to allow web worker compatibility. This underscores the elegance of Angular's web worker abstraction.

There's more...

As web workers are more fully supported and utilized, patterns such as these will most likely become more and more common, and it is extremely prescient of the Angular team to support this behavior. There are, however, some considerations.

Optimizing for performance gains

One of the primary benefits of using web workers is that you now have access to an execution context that is not blocked by anything running on the browser execution context. For performance drags, such as reflow and blocking of event loop handlers, the web worker will continue with the execution without a care for what is happening elsewhere.

Therefore, getting a performance benefit becomes a problem of optimization. Communication between the two JavaScript threads requires serialization and transmission of events, which is obviously not as fast as handling them in the same thread. However, in an especially complicated application, rendering can quickly become one of the most expensive things your application will do. Therefore, you may need to experiment and make a judgment call for your application, as not all applications will see performance gains from using web workers—only those where rendering becomes prohibitively expensive.

Compatibility considerations

Web workers have extremely good support, but there is still a very significant number of browsers that do not support them. If your application needs to work universally, web workers are not recommended; since they will not gracefully degrade, your application will merely fail.

See also

- *Configuring the Angular 2 renderer service to use web workers* guides you through the setting up of your application to render on a web worker
- *Configuring applications to use ahead-of-time compilation* guides you through how to compile an application during the build
- *Configuring an application to use lazy loading* shows how you can delay serving chunks of application code until needed

Configuring applications to use ahead-of-time compilation

Angular 2 introduces the concept of **ahead-of-time** compilation (**AOT**). This is an alternate configuration in which you can run your applications to move some processing time from inside the browser (referred to as just-in-time compilation or JIT) to when you compile your application on the server.

 The code, links, and a live example related to this recipe are available at `http://ngcookbook.herokuapp.com/9253/`.

Getting ready

AOT compilation is application-agnostic, so you should be able to add this to any existing Angular 2 application with minimal modification.

For the purposes of this example, suppose you have an existing `AppModule` inside `app/app.module.ts`. You needn't concern yourself with its content since it is irrelevant for the purpose of AOT.

How to do it...

Using AOT means you will compile and bootstrap your application differently. Depending on how it is configured, you will probably want to use sibling files with "aot" added to the name. Bear in mind that this is only for organizational purposes; Angular is not concerned with what you name your files.

Installing AOT dependencies

Angular requires a new compilation tool `ngc`, which is included in the `@angular/compiler-cli` package. It will also make use of `platformBrowser` to bootstrap, which is provided inside the `@angular/platform-browser` package. Install both of these and save the dependency to `package.json`:

```
npm install @angular/compiler-cli @angular/platform-server --save
```

Configuring ngc

`ngc` will essentially perform a superset of duties of the tsc compilation tool you are accustomed to using. It is wise to provide it with a separate config file, which can be named `tsconfig-aot.json` (but you are not beholden to this name).

The file should appear identical to your existing `tsconfig.json` file but with the following important modifications:

```
[tsconfig-aot.json]

{
  "compilerOptions": {
    (lots of settings here already, only change 'module')
    "module": "es2015",
  },
```

```
"files": [
  "app/app.module.ts",
  "main.ts"
],
"angularCompilerOptions": {
  "genDir": "aot",
  "skipMetadataEmit" : true
}}
```

Aligning component definitions with AOT requirements

AOT compilation requires your application to be organized in a few specific ways. Nothing should break an existing application, but they're important to do and take note of. If you've been following Angular best practices, they should be a breeze.

First, component definitions must have a `moduleId` specified. You will find that components generated with the Angular CLI already have this included. If not, the `moduleId` should always be `module.id`, as shown here:

```
@Component({
  moduleId: module.id,
  (lots of other stuff)
})
```

Since the module is undefined when compiling in AOT, you can provide a dummy value in the root template:

```
<script>window.module = 'aot';</script>
```

 AOT doesn't need the module ID, but it allows you to have a compilation without errors. Note that these steps involving `moduleId` may be changed or eliminated entirely in future versions of Angular, as they only exist to allow you to have compatibility between both JIT and AOT compilations.

Next, you'll need to change the path of the templates, both CSS and HTML, to be relative to the component definition file, not application-root-relative. If you are using the convention given by the Angular CLI or the style guide, you are probably already doing this.

Compiling with ngc

`ngc` isn't available directly on the command line; you'll need to run the binary file directly. Additionally, since in this example it's not using the `tsconfig.json` naming convention, you'll need to point the binary to the location of the alternate config file. Run the following command from the root of your application to execute the compilation:

```
node_modules/.bin/ngc -p tsconfig-aot.json
```

This command will output a collection of `NgFactory` files with `.ngfactory.ts` inside the aot directory, as you specified earlier in the `angularCompilerOptions` section of `tsconfig-aot.json`.

The compilation is done, but your application doesn't yet know how to use these `NgFactory` instances.

Bootstrapping with AOT

Your application will now start off with `AppModuleNgFactory` instead of `AppModule`. Bootstrap it using `platformBrowser`:

```
[main.ts]

import {platformBrowser} from '@angular/platform-browser';
import {AppModuleNgFactory} from 'aot/app/app.module.ngfactory';

platformBrowser().bootstrapModuleFactory(AppModuleNgFactory);
```

With this, you'll be able to run your application normally but this time using precompiled files.

How it works...

Compiling in Angular is a complex subject, but there are several main points relevant to switching an application to an AOT build process:

- The Angular compiler lives inside the `@angular/compiler` module, which is quite large. Using AOT means this module no longer needs to be delivered to the browser, which yields substantial bandwidth savings.

- The Angular compilation process involves taking the template strings inside your components, which exist as defined by `template` or `templateUrl`, and converting them into `NgFactory` instances. These instances specify how Angular understands how you defined the template. The conversion to `Factory` instances happens both in JIT and AOT compilation; switching to AOT simply means you are doing this processing on the server instead of the client and serving `NgFactory` definitions directly instead of uncompiled template strings.
- AOT will obviously slow down your build time since more computation is required each time the code base needs updating. Since you can trust that Angular will be able to correctly interpret `NgFactory` definitions that the AOT compilation generates, it is best to do JIT compilation when developing the application and AOT compilation when building and deploying production applications.

There's more...

AOT is cool, but it might not be for everybody. It will very likely reduce the load time and initialization time of your Angular application, but your build process is considerably more involved now. What's more, if you want to use JIT in development but AOT in production, you now have to maintain two versions of three different files: `index.html`, `main.ts`, and `tsconfig.json`. Perhaps this additional build complexity overhead is worth it, but it should certainly be a judgment call based on your development situation.

Going further with Tree Shaking

Angular also supports a separate step of optimization called Tree Shaking. This uses a separate npm library called `rollup`. Essentially, this library reads in your entire application (as JS files), figures out what modules are not being used, and cuts them out of the compiled codebase and therefore of the payload that is delivered to the browser. This is analogous to shaking a tree to make the dead branches fall out, hence "tree shaking."

 The es2015 module configuration specified earlier in `tsconfig-aot.json` was for supporting the rollup library, as it is a requirement for compatibility.

If your application code base is well-maintained, you will most likely see limited benefits of tree shaking since unused imports and the like will be caught when coding. What's more, one could make the argument that tree shaking might be an anti-pattern since it subtly encourages a liberal use of module inclusion by the developer with the knowledge that tree shaking will do the dirty working of cutting out any unused modules. This may then lead to a cluttered code base.

Using tree shaking can be a useful tool when it comes to Angular 2 applications, but its usefulness is in many ways evaporated by keeping a code base tidy.

See also

- *Understanding and properly utilizing enableProdMode with pure and impure pipes* describes how to take the training wheels off your application
- *Configuring the Angular 2 renderer service to use web workers* guides you through the process of setting up your application to render on a web worker
- *Configuring an application to use lazy loading* shows how you can delay serving chunks of application code until needed

Configuring an application to use lazy loading

Lazy loaded applications are those that defer the retrieval of relevant resources until they are actually necessary. Once applications begin to scale, this can yield meaningful gains in performance, and Angular 2 supports lazy loading right out of the box.

 The code, links, and a live example related to this recipe are available at `http://ngcookbook.herokuapp.com/0279/`.

Getting ready

Suppose you begin with the following simple application:

`[app/root.component.ts]`

```
import {Component} from '@angular/core';

@Component({
  selector: 'root',
  template: `
    <h1>Root component</h1>
    <router-outlet></router-outlet>
  `
})
export class RootComponent {}
[app/link.component.ts]

import {Component} from '@angular/core';

@Component({
  selector: 'app-link',
  template: `
    <a routerLink="/article">article</a>
  `
})
export class LinkComponent {}
[app/article.component.ts]

import {Component} from '@angular/core';

@Component({
  selector: 'article',
  template: `
    <h1>{{title}}</h1>
  `
})
export class ArticleComponent {
  title:string =
    'Baboon's Stock Picks Crush Top-Performing Hedge Fund';
}
[app/app.module.ts]

import {NgModule} from '@angular/core';
import {BrowserModule} from '@angular/platform-browser';
import {RouterModule, Routes} from '@angular/router';
import {RootComponent} from './root.component';
import {ArticleComponent} from './article.component';
import {LinkComponent} from './link.component';

const appRoutes:Routes = [
  {
    path: 'article',
    component: ArticleComponent
```

[421]

```
    },
    {
      path: '**',
      component: LinkComponent
    }
];

@NgModule({
  imports: [
    BrowserModule,
    RouterModule.forRoot(appRoutes)
  ],
  declarations: [
    ArticleComponent,
    LinkComponent,
    RootComponent
  ],
  bootstrap: [
    RootComponent
  ]
})
export class AppModule {}
```

This application has only two routes: the default route, which displays a link to the article page, and the article route, which display ArticleComponent. Your objective is to defer the loading of the resources required by the article route until it is actually visited.

How to do it...

Lazy loading means the initial application module that is loaded cannot have any dependencies on the module that you wish to lazily load since none of that code will be present before the new URL is visited. First, move the ArticleComponent reference to its own module:

```
[app/article.module.ts]

import {NgModule} from '@angular/core';
import {ArticleComponent} from './article.component';

@NgModule({
  declarations: [
    ArticleComponent
  ],
  exports: [
    ArticleComponent
  ]
```

```
})
export class ArticleModule {}
```

Removing all dependencies means moving the relevant route definitions to this module as well:

```
[app/article.module.ts]

import {NgModule} from '@angular/core';
import {ArticleComponent} from './article.component';
import {Routes, RouterModule} from '@angular/router';

const articleRoutes:Routes = [
  {
    path: '',
    component: ArticleComponent
  }
];

@NgModule({
  imports: [
    RouterModule.forChild(articleRoutes)
  ],
  declarations: [
    ArticleComponent
  ],
  exports: [
    ArticleComponent
  ]
})
export class ArticleModule {}
```

Next, remove all these module references from AppModule. In addition, modify the route definition, so that instead of specifying a component to render, it simply references a path to the lazily loaded module, as well as the name of the module using a special # syntax:

```
[app/app.module.ts]

import {NgModule} from '@angular/core';
import {BrowserModule} from '@angular/platform-browser';
import {RouterModule, Routes} from '@angular/router';
import {RootComponent} from './root.component';
import {LinkComponent} from './link.component';

const appRoutes:Routes = [
  {
    path: 'article',
    loadChildren: './app/article.module#ArticleModule'
```

```
  },
  {
    path: '**',
    component: LinkComponent
  }
];

@NgModule({
  imports: [
    BrowserModule,
    RouterModule.forRoot(appRoutes)
  ],
  declarations: [
    LinkComponent,
    RootComponent
  ],
  bootstrap: [
    RootComponent
  ]
})
export class AppModule {}
```

This is all that's required to set up lazy loading. Your application should behave identically to when you began this recipe.

How it works...

To verify that it is in fact performing a lazy load, start the application and keep an eye on the Network tab of your browser's developer console.

When you click on the article `routerLink`, you should see `article.module.ts` and `article.component.ts` requests go out before the rendering occurs. This means Angular is only fetching the required files once you actually visit the route. The `loadChildren` route property tells Angular that when it visits this route, if it hasn't loaded the module already, it should use the relative path you may have provided to fetch the module. Once the module file is retrieved, Angular is able to parse it and know which other files it needs to request to load all the module's dependencies.

There's more...

You'll note that this introduces a bit of additional latency to your application since Angular waits to load the resources right when it actually needs them. What's more, in this example, it has to actually perform *two* additional round trips to the server when it visits the article

URL: one to request the module file and one to request the module's dependencies.

In a production environment, this latency might be unacceptable. A workaround might be to compile the lazily loaded payload into a single file that can be fetched with one request. Depending on how your application is built, your mileage may vary.

Accounting for shared modules

The lazily loaded module is totally separated from your main application module, and this includes injectables. If a service is provided to the top-level application module, you will find that it will create two separate instances of that service for each place it is provided—certainly unexpected behavior, given that an application loaded normally will only create one instance if it is only provided once.

The solution is to piggyback on the `forRoot` method that Angular uses to simultaneously provide and configure services. More relevant to this recipe, it allows you to technically provide a service at multiple locations; however, Angular will know how to ignore duplicates of this, provided it is done inside `forRoot()`.

First, define the `AuthService` that you wish to create only a single instance of:

```
[app/auth.service.ts]

import {Injectable} from '@angular/core';

@Injectable()
export class AuthService {
  constructor() {
    console.log('instantiated AuthService');
  }
}
```

This includes a log statement so you can see that only one instantiation occurs.

Next, create an `NgModule` wrapper specially for this service:

```
[app/auth.module.ts]

import {NgModule, ModuleWithProviders} from "@angular/core";
import {AuthService} from "./auth.service";

@NgModule({})
export class AuthModule {
  static forRoot():ModuleWithProviders {
    return {
      ngModule: AuthModule,
      providers: [
```

```
            AuthService
        ]
    };
  }
}
```

Since this utilizes the `forRoot()` strategy as detailed in the preceding code, you're free to import this module both inside the application module as well as the lazily loaded module:

[app/app.module.ts]

```
import {NgModule} from '@angular/core';
import {BrowserModule} from '@angular/platform-browser';
import {RouterModule, Routes} from '@angular/router';
import {RootComponent} from './root.component';
import {LinkComponent} from './link.component';
import {AuthModule} from './auth.module';

const appRoutes:Routes = [
  {
    path: 'article',
    loadChildren: './app/article.module#ArticleModule'
  },
  {
    path: '**',
    component: LinkComponent
  }
];

@NgModule({
  imports: [
    BrowserModule,
    RouterModule.forRoot(appRoutes),
    AuthModule.forRoot()
  ],
  declarations: [
    LinkComponent,
    RootComponent
  ],
  bootstrap: [
    RootComponent
  ]
})
export class AppModule {}
```

You'll add it to the lazily loaded module too, but don't invoke `forRoot()`. This method is reserved for only the root application module:

```
[app/article.module.ts]

import {NgModule} from '@angular/core';
import {ArticleComponent} from './article.component';
import {Routes, RouterModule} from '@angular/router';
import {AuthModule} from './auth.module';

const articleRoutes:Routes = [
  {
    path: '',
    component: ArticleComponent
  }
];

@NgModule({
  imports: [
    RouterModule.forChild(articleRoutes),
    AuthModule
  ],
  declarations: [
    ArticleComponent
  ],
  exports: [
    ArticleComponent
  ]
})
export class ArticleModule {}
```

Finally, inject the service into `RootComponent` and `ArticleComponent` and use log statements to see that it does indeed reach both the components:

```
[app/root.component.ts]

import {Component} from '@angular/core';
import {AuthService} from './auth.service';

@Component({
  selector: 'root',
  template: `
    <h1>Root component</h1>
    <router-outlet></router-outlet>
  `
})
export class RootComponent {
  constructor(private authService_:AuthService) {
```

```
      console.log(authService_);
   }
}
[app/article.component.ts]

import {Component} from '@angular/core';
import {AuthService} from './auth.service';

@Component({
  selector: 'article',
  template: `
    <h1>{{title}}</h1>
  `
})
export class ArticleComponent {
  title:string =
     'Baboon's Stock Picks Crush Top-Performing Hedge Fund';

  constructor(private authService_:AuthService) {
    console.log(authService_);
  }
}
```

You should see a single service instantiation and successful injection into both the components.

See also

- *Configuring the Angular 2 renderer service to use web workers* guides you through the process of setting up your application to render on a web worker
- *Configuring applications to use ahead-of-time compilation* guides you through how to compile an application during the build

Index

B

BehaviorSubjects
  used, for creating Observable authentication
    service 184

C

change detection
  ChangeDetectionStrategy, configuring 403
  requesting 404
  used, for components configuring with OnPush
    401
child component
  members, passing from parent component 44,
    45
  parent component, referencing from 85, 86
child routes
  nested views, implementing 236
component
  building, decorators used 38, 41, 43
  directives, application migrating to 13, 17
  implementing, in AngularJS 1.5 18
  lifecycle hooks, utilizing 82, 84
  minimum viable unit test suite, writing for 342
  service, injecting 266
  styling, decorators used 38, 41, 43
controllerAs encapsulation
  used, for componentizing directives 8, 10, 13
controls
  building, with FormGroup 109
custom asynchronous validator
  creating, with Promises 138
  execution 142
  using, with Promises 138
custom events
  capturing, EventEmitter used 56
  emitting 59
  event data, capturing 58
  generating, EventEmitter used 56
  listening for 60
custom validator
  attributes, refactoring 134
  creating 131
  using 131

D

decorator metadata 41
decorators
  about 40
  class definition, writing 39
  Component Class Decorator, writing 40
  used, for building component 38, 41, 43
  used, for styling component 38, 41, 43
directed acyclic graph (DAG) 162
directives
  componentizing, controllerAs encapsulation used
    8, 10, 13
  DOM elements, behavior attaching 62
DOM elements
  behavior, attaching with directives 62
  events, attaching with HostListeners 65
downgradeComponent
  Angular 2 components, downgrading to Angular 1
    directives 29
downgradeInjectable
  Angular 2 providers, downgrading to Angular 1
    services 33, 35, 36

E

elements
  referencing, with template variables 74
enableProdMode
  about 380
  change detection compliance 382
  consistency error, generating 381
  switching on 384
  utilizing, with impure pipes 380
  utilizing, with pure pipes 380
end-to-end (e2e) testing 350
EventEmitter
  used, for capturing custom events 56
  used, for generating custom events 56

F

field validation
  implementing, with FormControl 104
  tagless controls 108
  validators 107
FormArray

S

service dependency
  component, unit testing with spies 371
  component, unit testing with stubs 365
  events, triggering inside component fixture 370
  stubbing 368
service injection
  aliasing, with useClass 277
  aliasing, with useExisting 277
  directive providers, refactoring 285
  dual services 278
  unified component 279
  with NgModule 270
service instance
  creating, controlling 270
  injecting, into components 275
  instantiation 276
  root module, splitting 273
service
  adding, as value with OpaqueTokens 287
  adding, as value with useValue 287
  injecting, into component 266
shims
  incorporating, into Webpack 322
spies
  setting, on injected service 374
  used, for unit testing with service dependency 371
stateful route behavior
  building, with RouterLinkActive 232, 235
stubs
  used, for unit testing with service dependency 365
Subjects
  used, for implementing Publish-Subscribe model 179
synchronous service
  unit testing 359
SystemJS
  using, for in-browser transpilation 309

T

template variables
  elements, referencing 74
Tree Shaking 419

two-way data binding
  implementing, with ngModel 100, 102
TypeScript
  compilation 306
  configuring, for minimum viable Angular 2
    application 303
  declaration files 304
  file, compilation 308
  minimum viable unit test suite, creating with 334
  source maps, generating 307
  tsconfig.json 304

U

unit testing
  synchronous service 359
  with service dependency, spies used 371
  with service dependency, stubs used 365
  without injection 364
UpgradeModule
  Angular 1 and Angular 2, connecting to 24, 27, 28
useClass
  service injection, aliasing with 277
useExisting
  service injection, aliasing with 277
useFactory
  provider-configured service, building 292
useValue
  service, adding as value 287

V

ViewChild
  parent-child awareness, configuring with 88
  reference, configuring 88
ViewChildren
  about 92
  changes, following with Observables 200
  changes, following with QueryLists 200
ViewEncapsulation
  configuring, for maximum efficiency 406
  native styling 409
  styling, avoiding 408
  styling, emulation 408